# HAMMERS HEAVEN AND HELL

Kirk Blows is a freelance journalist who has been reporting on West Ham United since the mid-1990s. He is formerly the editor of *Hammers News* – the club's official monthly magazine – and has previously written or co-authored four West Ham related books, including *Terminator: The Authorised Biography of Julian Dicks*, *Fortune's Always Hiding*, *The Essential History of West Ham United* and *Claret and Blue Blood*. He continues to attend every game on behalf of the *East London Advertiser*, the *Barking & Dagenham Post* and *The London Paper*, producing match coverage and a weekly opinion column. In what seems a former life, he edited a number of rock magazines, including *Metal Hammer* among others.

# ACKNOWLEDGEMENTS

To Karen and Alex.

Many thanks to:
   Alan Curbishley, Mervyn Day, Peter Grant, Eggert Magnússon, Alan Pardew.

   Patricia Laker, Karen, Jessica and Lewis Blows, David, Jennifer, John and Helen Laker.

   Justin and Yulia Allen, Brad Ashton, Rob Bailey, Steve Blowers, Laura Burkin, Gary Burman, Brita Burns, Jo Davies, Trevor Davies, David Edwards, Dave Evans, Tom Harvey, Ben Kosky, Gerry Levey, John Matthews, Tess McDermott, Sally Miller, Miranda Nagalingham, Rob Newell, Andy Potts, David Powter, Rob Pritchard, Khris Raistrick, John Raven, Joe Sach, Mark Segal, Ben Sharratt, Rob Shepherd, John Smith.

# CONTENTS

Preface      9

1  'The biggest game in West Ham's history'      11

2  'This team isn't bad, you know'      25

3  'We were so hungry to prove ourselves'      49

4  'The first trophy is always the hardest to win'      69

5  'It was guaranteed ... there were no get-out clauses'      93

6  'If you gave them the ball, they rarely gave it back'      107

7  'Certain things were not as I thought'      117

8  'There were reasons why I had to do it'      137

9  'Let's not get away from it: I haven't delivered results'      163

10  'These kinds of things happen at every football club'      189

11  'We've had a bit of luck, but I'm not complaining'      199

12  'I'm sorry, but I have no control over Tévez'      211

13  'The finish was spectacular and deserves a place in history'      225

14  'We will not be drawn into this form of public mudslinging'      243

# PREFACE

WEST HAM United have established many trademarks during their history, and stability has traditionally remained one of them. From the Cearns family's century-long association at board level and the club's famous loyalty to managers through to the commitment of their many long-serving players and the team's reputation for producing football with flair, the Hammers' solid foundations have rarely been shaken by too much turbulence over the years.

That's not to say that they haven't experienced fluctuating fortunes and periods of delight and despair. In a bid to play with style and guile, their results remain notoriously difficult to predict. But with continuity a key part of the club's philosophy, the journey was more of an undulating adventure than a frenetic assault on the senses.

That was until 2005 when West Ham reached the play-off final as they looked to secure promotion to the Premiership. It was the start of a spectacular sequence of events that would take supporters on a two-year roller-coaster ride that would leave them exhausted with emotion. The club appeared to be on the verge of achieving major success. But the elation would be followed by anxiety. The hope would turn to horror. The dreams would disintegrate and die.

In the middle of it all, the club would undergo a traumatic transformation as power changed hands both in the boardroom and in the dressing-room. And when it appeared that normality was returning under a new regime, a discreetly placed ticking timebomb would explode to reverberate not just down the corridors of Upton Park but throughout football itself. The controversial climax would cause chaos and conflict, dissent and discord, resentment and rancour.

The story would embrace a contrasting cast of characters from Britain, Iceland, Russia, Iran, Israel and Argentina – among many other places – and escape the confines of sport to infiltrate the worlds of business, politics and law. Money would be a common denominator and fuel the ambitions of those in pursuit of gratification and glory with West Ham the vehicle to try and realise those goals.

The winds of change had been sweeping through football for many years, but few people envisaged that the Hammers would eventually get caught in the eye of a storm that would develop into a tornado. When the debris and dust finally settled, the landscape would never quite be the same again.

# 1

## 'THE BIGGEST GAME IN WEST HAM'S HISTORY'

ALAN PARDEW was entitled to appear rather pleased with himself as he briskly negotiated the complex network of corridors and stairs within the deepest quarters of the Millennium Stadium. Less than half an hour earlier, his West Ham United team had secured promotion to the Premiership with a 1–0 play-off final success against Preston North End. And there was no disguising the manager's delight when he finally sat down to reflect on the significance of the achievement – not just for the club and its long-suffering supporters but also his personal future. 'It got very close to the board of directors having to make a decision about me,' he admitted in a moment of understatement while, as the champagne was circulating in the dressing-room, first-team coach Peter Grant savoured the importance of the moment. 'We knew what the consequences of defeat would be,' he said. 'West Ham *needed* promotion – and there were a multitude of reasons why.'

Indeed there were. The Hammers had been relegated to the Nationwide First Division in 2003 – or mismanaged into it, according to many supporters – although the root causes for the club's demise can be traced back to the 2000–01 campaign when star defender Rio Ferdinand was sold to Leeds United for £18 million and manager Harry Redknapp was sacked.

Reserve-team coach Glenn Roeder – ill-equipped to deal with the problems of Premiership management given his unsuccessful stints in charge of Gillingham and Watford in the lower divisions – proved a disastrous successor when he failed to prevent a squad containing such talents as Paolo Di Canio, Frédéric Kanouté, Joe Cole, Jermain Defoe, Michael Carrick, Glen Johnson, David James and Trevor Sinclair from dropping out of the top flight in his second season at the helm.

With a wage bill of £30 million – estimated as being the sixth highest in the country – and debts of around £44 million, West Ham's survival as a club would have been in serious jeopardy had it not been for the number of quality players it could sell. Some £18.6 million was raised through the sales of Cole, Johnson, Kanouté and Sinclair, while the wage bill was reduced by another £10 million with the release of a further dozen members of the first-team squad.

The club had initially pledged to hold on to many of its better players, knowing how important it was to secure promotion at the first attempt, but chairman Terence Brown was eventually forced to admit that he had no choice but to play a cloak-and-dagger game. 'If I had explained to the whole football world that we were running out of cash and needed to raise £20 million in the transfer market, my former colleagues in the Premier League would have smelled blood in the water, and the financial consequences do not bear thinking about,' he said. 'Those who say we should have kept the whole squad together need to understand that by November we would have run out of cash and any cheques would have bounced.'

Roeder eventually paid the price for relegation when he was sacked just four games into the 2003–04 season – a decision put on hold while he recovered from surgery on a brain tumour – and Pardew was subsequently installed as West Ham's tenth permanent boss following a protracted departure from Reading.

As a former Crystal Palace, Charlton and Barnet midfielder, Pardew had no previous links with the Hammers – considered a prerequisite to run the club by some supporters – but had impressed as a coach by lifting the Royals into Division One and then fourth place as they chased a second successive promotion. 'He knows this division and what it is like to try and get results at places like Gillingham,' said director and caretaker boss Trevor Brooking following a 2–0 defeat at, yes, Gillingham, having firmly ruled himself out of the running.

Pardew immediately set about imposing his managerial philosophies, which were heavily dependent on sports science, intensive training routines, a strong sense of discipline and a super-positive mentality. 'Luck is what happens when preparation meets opportunity' appeared alongside other messages of inspiration and hope around the Chadwell Heath training ground, prompting a mixed – and sometimes cynical – response from the playing staff at first. Even the editor of the club magazine was hauled over the coals for allowing former Hammers striker Tony Cottee to express his doubts about the team's promotion credentials. 'Let's be up, up, up!' Pardew told a room full of journalists after one match, dismayed by what he felt was a negative line of questioning.

Yet the new manager was forced to wait eight long games for his first victory, and automatic promotion always looked beyond his side as he fought hard to instil his progressive ideas while overcoming an element of resistance and a host of other difficulties. 'There were issues at the club I wasn't happy with, and I was putting out fires for a long time,' he said. A top-six play-off place was the least expected of the Hammers, but that was never going to be easy as Pardew attempted to reshape a squad that had been ripped apart and then hastily thrown back together with a variety of bargain-basement buys, free transfers and loan signings.

Key recruits were secured in the shape of striker Marlon Harewood and midfielders Hayden Mullins and Nigel Reo-Coker, while Grant was brought in to replace Paul Goddard as first-team coach, with Pardew insisting that 'the chemistry needed to change'. But the fact that 36 different players would eventually appear for West Ham during the 2003–04 campaign – 24 of them for the very first time – says everything about the turmoil and turbulence at the club. Chairman Brown had insisted that no more players would be sold for financial reasons, but, with a play-off place the best the Hammers could realistically hope for, his tune had changed by the time the Premiership transfer window opened in January. England goalkeeper James and defender Ian Pearce, both on large salaries, were sold to Manchester City and Fulham respectively, but it was the sacrifice of hotshot striker Defoe that raised the biggest questions about West Ham's ambition.

The youngster, who had provoked fan fury by submitting a transfer request less than 24 hours after the club's relegation (and was famously dubbed 'a rat' by Hammers legend Julian Dicks), had made it clear he had no intention of extending his contract, which had just 18 months left to run. And with the striker having undermined the team's recent efforts with displays of petulance that earned him three dismissals, West Ham agreed to sell him to Tottenham for a fee of £7 million, with Bobby Zamora making the opposite journey in part exchange. 'We felt it was in the best interests of West Ham to maximise the potential transfer income,' explained Brown, while Pardew insisted there was 'a business logic' to the move. That 'business logic' was questioned by many fans and journalists who considered it dangerous to jeopardise the club's play-off chances – and the estimated £30 million jackpot that promotion would bring – for the sake of maximising Defoe's 'potential transfer income'.

The 22 year old had bagged 15 goals in 22 games, so there was huge pressure on former Brighton hero Zamora – who Pardew insisted was vital to the deal being authorised – delivering the goods as his replacement. That feeling intensified when it was announced that none of the Defoe fee would be invested in new faces, with Pardew admitting, 'We can't afford to spend it. The money is needed in case we don't get promoted.' While Brown insisted there was no 'financial crisis', the natural conclusion was that there might indeed be one if the club was condemned to a second year outside the Premiership.

Zamora scored on his debut and twice in his first three games – but his less-than-convincing tally of five goals in twenty West Ham outings that term left many observers wondering what might have been had Defoe been forced to see out the season at Upton Park. The Hammers did indeed reach the play-offs, claiming fourth place to book a two-legged semi-final place against Ipswich after a dramatic final league game at promotion hopefuls Wigan. Had Brian Deane's header not salvaged a 1–1 draw in injury time, West Ham would have finished fifth and been forced to return to the JJB Stadium six days later. Instead, Wigan's loss of a crucial point in the dying seconds saw Crystal Palace sneak above them into sixth place and rearrange the play-off fixtures entirely.

Psychology had always been a major part of Pardew's weaponry, but West Ham supporters enjoyed their first real benefits of it following the first-leg defeat at Ipswich. The Portman Road crowd had helped inspire their side to a 1–0 victory, but Pardew responded by warning the Suffolk outfit that a 'hostile reception' awaited them at Upton Park a few days later. 'The place will be jumping,' he insisted. The ploy worked to perfection – not only did the Ipswich players probably feel a sense of intimidation but Hammers fans raised the roof to produce the atmosphere demanded of them. And in a match played at a frenzied and frenetic pace, second-half goals by Matthew Etherington and Christian Dailly proved enough to send West Ham into the final, where, inevitably, they found themselves facing Pardew's former club Palace – managed by ex-Hammers striker Iain Dowie.

With plenty of good fortune helping to fuel the momentum of the Eagles as they charged up the table in the final months of the campaign, there was a strong suspicion among West Ham fans that fate was very much against their side ahead of the game at Cardiff's Millennium Stadium on 29 May. Or maybe there was just a fear of failure, knowing that Premiership football was more imperative for the Hammers than for Palace, who had spent six years outside the top flight. Either way, there was a sense of foreboding among much of the West Ham support – and their fears were fully justified as their team failed to impose themselves on the occasion. Neil Shipperley's 62nd-minute goal decided a lacklustre affair in Palace's favour, and West Ham's apparent lack of hunger was reflected in the fact that referee Graham Poll admitted he had denied them a late penalty – after Michael Carrick was tripped by Mikele Leigertwood – because none of the players had bothered to call for it.

Back in the West Ham dressing-room, Pardew immediately went to work on his despondent players. 'Remember this feeling and how low you will feel for the rest of the summer, because we never want to go through this again,' he told them. Outside the stadium, as the disconsolate West Ham faithful trudged their way back to the railway station, there was disbelief about the manager's decision to withdraw Zamora, Harewood and David Connolly – who had scored 45 goals between them that term – when the team was trying to muster a recovery. Pardew claimed the substitutions appeared 'valid at the time', but nothing on the pitch justified a strategy that only served to diminish some of the confidence supporters had in him. The manager had lost a Division Two play-off final with Reading in 2001, and some fans wondered if West Ham had appointed a 'nearly man'.

As he began to reflect on the disappointment, Pardew admitted that 'tough decisions' would have to be made. 'I need to cut the wage bill while trying to make us stronger,' he warned, indicating another huge cull of players despite the promise of a second year's parachute payment of £6 million from the Premier League. In reality, the personnel changes were all very much of Pardew's choosing – with the exception of midfielder Carrick's inevitable departure.

The England Under-21 player admitted it had been 'disheartening' to see fellow youngsters such as Cole, Johnson and Defoe leave the club – following home-grown Hammers Ferdinand and Frank Lampard before them – but a groin injury the previous summer had prevented him from joining the exodus. And although he acknowledged that Pardew 'doesn't let anyone have an off-day – he's on us all the time', Carrick was publicly uncomplaining of his plight, and his improved displays in the second half of the season saw him named as the only West Ham player in the Professional Footballers' Association's Team of the Year and the runner-up to winger Etherington in the Hammer of the Year poll.

With just a year remaining on his contract, Carrick refused to sign a new deal, so the club had two options: exploit what remained of his transfer value or persuade him to play for another season in the hope he could inspire the team to automatic promotion. Recent history, in the case of Defoe, proved that West Ham never gambled in such situations, and losing the classy Carrick for nothing under the Bosman ruling could not be entertained. Many people were still surprised when the club publicly announced that the midfielder was available, and the fact he was sold to London rivals Tottenham for a mere £2.75 million – hardly a true reflection of his quality – left some questioning the wisdom of West Ham's actions. Supporters were left shaking their heads in disbelief two years later when Carrick moved on to Manchester United for an astonishing £18.6 million fee, with it being reported that the Hammers were counting the cost of failing to negotiate a sell-on clause that would have earned them a percentage of Tottenham's huge profit on the player.

Pardew revealed his personal gambling instincts, however, when he sold 27-year-old striker Connolly to Leicester City just a week after signing Teddy Sheringham on a free transfer. The 38-year-old former England international may have been far more suited to the playmaking forward's role that had seen Connolly's predatory skills compromised during the final part of the 2003–04 season, but the fear was that West Ham could live to regret strengthening the Foxes, who were seen as likely promotion rivals. Pardew was unconcerned, however, insisting that the two deals were necessary to 'progress the team'.

Other recruits included Sergei Rebrov, Carl Fletcher, Chris Powell, Luke Chadwick, Malky Mackay and Calum Davenport – the latter cleverly snatched on loan from Tottenham just ten days after he secured a £3 million move from Coventry, much to the discontent of his former club. Pardew was full of optimism shortly into the newly named Coca-Cola Championship campaign, insisting, 'We've definitely got a squad that's capable of winning this league, and I'm a lot more comfortable than I've been for some time.'

That comfort would soon turn into extreme discomfort as West Ham's strong start – sixteen points from eight games that took them to within a point of table-toppers Stoke City – began to wilt as autumn turned into winter. The next dozen league outings produced just four wins as the team's efforts were undermined by a lack of midfield creativity and a number of injury problems. And as Christmas approached, it became obvious that a play-off place was again a more realistic goal than automatic promotion.

Chairman Brown hardly improved the mood of the frustrated Upton Park support by hailing the club's financial results for the 12-month period ending May 2004 – which revealed pre-tax profits of £11.8 million (following the previous year's deficit of £5.3 million) – as 'little short of extraordinary' and 'a remarkable achievement'. While the directors were merrily slapping themselves on the back for having turned around the club's financial fortunes, the fans were painfully aware that this had mainly been accomplished through the sale of the club's best young players – a safety net few other relegated outfits could fall back on.

Brown spoke of sharing the fans' 'disappointment and frustration' over events on the field during the previous two years but insisted those feelings had to be channelled positively by giving manager Pardew and the team total support. Privately, however, it's believed that he began to consider the possibilities open to him, and reports emerged over the Christmas period that a tentative approach had been made to Gordon Strachan. The former Coventry boss had been out of work since leaving Southampton the previous season but did not rule out a move to Upton Park if the manager's position became available.

The pressure on Pardew intensified in January when his side failed to build on an impressive 2–0 win at top-of-the-table Ipswich on New Year's Day by suffering three successive defeats. West Ham's managing director Paul Aldridge did little to dispel the speculation about Pardew's position by refusing to give the manager a vote of confidence. 'We have never put a timescale on our backing for him. We are in the results business,' he stated.

Pardew's instructions had been to secure promotion within two seasons, but that didn't necessarily mean he would survive the entire period if results went badly wrong. Former player and caretaker boss Brooking, who had severed his official ties with the West Ham hierarchy the previous season to become the FA's director of football development, was forced to deny he'd been asked about returning to the club as manager. 'This story is unfair to West Ham United, Alan Pardew and myself,' he said, while a club statement declared, 'We continue to fully support the work of Alan and his coaching staff.'

The manager appeared to have turned the corner with three league wins on the spin in February, but another trio of defeats – by Leeds, Preston and former club Reading – dropped his side out of the play-off places and left him fighting to save his job. The last of those outings, at the Madejski Stadium, had seen the home support gleefully sing 'you're getting sacked in the morning' at their former boss as the Royals – who had gone 11 games without a win – cruised to an easy 3–1 victory. Pardew couldn't deny he was failing to get the best out of his players, while Reading goalkeeper Marcus Hahnemann offered a clue as to why that might be by revealing, 'Not many people liked Pardew when he was here. There were guys who didn't see eye to eye with him.'

Pardew later admitted that he'd 'made a wrong call' by naming midfielder Mullins as an emergency centre-half with the lack of height in defence being ruthlessly exposed by Reading striker Dave Kitson, who claimed a hat-trick. But the manager went on the attack after the 1–1 home draw with Crewe, storming, 'It wasn't me who got us relegated. I've taken over, but this club has to be rebuilt from the bottom upwards, and the team is still playing for me.'

Away from the spotlight, assistant Grant had recognised how difficult it was for the players – most of whom were in their early 20s – to perform at their best in a high-pressure environment, particularly in the tense atmosphere at Upton Park. 'Most of the young guys who had come to the club had never played under that weight of expectation, where they had to win games and play in a certain style as well,' he said. 'Some of the players couldn't handle that in the Championship.'

Striker Harewood allowed the stress to get the better of him when he failed to convert a late penalty in a 2–2 home draw with ten-man Leicester, which saw Pardew playing dumb when asked about his job being offered to the still-available Strachan. 'I'm a little naive in that I don't know what you're talking about,' he responded when the Scot's name was mentioned, before adding, 'We had a board meeting yesterday, and I didn't ask for any assurances about my position.'

Strachan eventually decided to accept the more lucrative opportunity to succeed Martin O'Neill as manager of Celtic, but it continued to be reported that Pardew was just one game away from the sack while West Ham remained out of the play-off places. The reality was that it served no purpose to dispose of the 43 year old's services while promotion remained a possibility – however slim the chances – because there was little time for any replacement to make a difference.

Few people realised that the turning point had already come – in the 87th minute of the defeat at Reading, to be precise – when Elliott Ward made his first league appearance for West Ham as a substitute for the malfunctioning Mullins in defence. Reunited with his former youth- and reserve-team colleague Anton Ferdinand, Ward helped form the solid defensive platform that saw the Hammers enjoy a run of thirteen games with just one defeat – taking them all the way to the Premiership.

A 2–1 win at Watford on the final day of the league season saw West Ham seal (some would say steal) sixth place – thanks largely to Reading losing their final three games to drop out of the play-offs – before Zamora stepped into the limelight to hog the headlines and the glory at the season's climax. With Ipswich once again the play-off semi-final opponents, Zamora added to Harewood's opener in the first leg at Upton Park only for the East Anglians to hit back through Tommy Miller's controversial free-kick – recorded as an own-goal by goalkeeper Jimmy Walker – and Shefki Kuqi to pull level at 2–2. The pendulum had swung firmly in Town's favour, but Zamora had other ideas, producing a fine second-leg double for West Ham to record a 4–2 aggregate victory and earn Pardew the plaudits for a successful tactical strategy that saw striker Harewood deployed on the right flank.

Yet the manager knew that victory against Preston in the final in Cardiff was essential if he wanted to remain at West Ham. He simply could not afford to lose at the Millennium Stadium for a second year running, especially with the vital Premiership parachute payments set to expire. His chairman refused to confirm that Pardew's job was on the line, however, claiming it would be 'unlikely' the axe would fall if the club missed out on promotion. 'We can see what Alan has done in difficult circumstances,' Brown said. Failure against Preston would see those circumstances become even more difficult, with it being estimated that the wage bill would need to be reduced by up to 50 per cent. 'I'm very aware of the financial implications of this game,' admitted Pardew.

The clash against Preston on 30 May was dubbed the 'biggest domestic game ever' because of the £30 million jackpot awaiting the winners. But there was a more upbeat mood among the West Ham support than there had been twelve months earlier, with it being anticipated that lessons had been learned from the defeat against Crystal Palace – although just five of the previous year's line-up were to start the game. Pardew booked his players into a different hotel this time around to avoid any negative reminders of the past, and, although Preston had won both the league encounters between the two sides as they improved throughout the season, it was West Ham who rose to the occasion in Cardiff.

'This time we realised it was our chance. We knew it wasn't going to come again,' said Zamora following his second-half winner. The Hammers had enjoyed the better of the game, with Harewood, Etherington, Tomáš Řepka and Zamora all going close. But it was Zamora who had the final say when he swept home Etherington's cross in the 57th minute, although West Ham had to endure some nervous moments late on when a nerve-racking seven minutes of injury time was added because of goalkeeper Walker being stretchered off with a serious knee injury. On another occasion, referee Mike Riley could well have applied the letter of the law and sent Walker off for carrying the ball out of the penalty area as he lost his balance. But it was West Ham's day.

'That was the biggest game in West Ham's history,' admitted Pardew. 'If we'd not won that game, we could have been trapped in the Championship for years. So there was huge pressure on us to succeed. Yes, there was a period when I started to have doubts about whether we were going to make it. But we got promotion within the timescale discussed and achieved an end to the cycle of misery.'

Not that the game could really be enjoyed – not until the final whistle, that is. 'It was very tense and there was a lot of nervousness, because we knew we were so close to getting promotion,' reflected coach Grant, who knew exactly what was at stake. 'Alan and myself probably wouldn't have been at West Ham much longer if we'd been beaten. We'd also have lost our major playing assets – the likes of Zamora, Harewood and Reo-Coker – while there would have been such a dull feeling around the place, having missed out on promotion two years running. But we eventually got to the Premiership and our worries diminished. We knew we were at the start of something we could really build on.'

# 2

## 'THIS TEAM ISN'T BAD, YOU KNOW'

IF ALAN Pardew was looking for any assurances about the security of his position or West Ham's prospects on their return to the Premiership, the bookmakers were the wrong people to consult. Flushed by the euphoria of promotion, chairman Terence Brown was adamant his manager's position had never been in jeopardy. 'Alan has been fantastic. He had two jobs: first to sort out the financial position – our debts are now down to less than £30 million – and then to create a team that could go up,' he said. 'He has a lot of guts, and I'm a big admirer. Alan will be working with a budget of £20 million in salaries and transfers.'

Yet the odds-makers were unconvinced, naming Pardew as 7–1 joint favourite (along with Portsmouth's Alain Perrin and Fulham's Chris Coleman) to become the first Premiership boss to be fired during the 2005–06 season, while West Ham were listed as 8–15 favourites for relegation. Pardew was bullish, however, genuinely believing the club would reacclimatise to the top-flight environment he considered their natural habitat. 'Some promoted managers say their aim is just to stay up, but we'll certainly target a mid-table finish as a position that is realistic,' he declared.

Certainly, the club's supporters felt that survival was far

more achievable than escaping from the Championship would have been the following year had West Ham faltered in their promotion efforts. But while the chairman had stated his intentions to invest heavily in the playing squad, it remained to be seen how much would actually be spent – and the final figure would surely determine what chances the team had of being competitive. As the financial and playing gulf between the Premiership and the Football League continued to widen, newly promoted clubs – especially those that had been out of the top division for many years or had never been there at all – were often faced with a major dilemma. Did they pay the huge transfer fees and wages necessary to attract top players, knowing the club could potentially be crippled if the gamble failed and they were relegated? Or did they take a cautious approach, ensuring the long-term financial stability of the club if, as likely, they quickly dropped back to the Football League?

In West Ham's case, the club believed the painful decisions of the previous two years had put them on a sound enough financial footing to invest healthily without endangering their future. 'Wages have been heavily trimmed over the last two years, and that now gives me room to strengthen what I think is a decent squad,' said Pardew, who knew that the last of the really high earners – midfielders Don Hutchison and Steve Lomas among them – were leaving the club. 'I'm going to have to bring in at least three or four quality players, and I know the areas we need to strengthen as we attack the Premiership.'

The manager certainly took a methodical approach to strengthening his team, starting at the back and gradually working his way forward. With goalkeeper Jimmy Walker set for at least a six-month absence as a result of the cruciate-ligament damage he sustained in the play-off final against Preston, Pardew moved quickly to secure the services of Northern Ireland international Roy Carroll, who had just been released by Manchester United after failing to agree terms on a new contract. Carroll may have been the subject of ridicule for allowing a Pedro Mendes lob to squirm over his shoulder and the goal line – a 'goal' somehow overlooked by the errant officials – during a match against Tottenham earlier in the year, but with 34 outings for the Red Devils that term, including an FA Cup final appearance and several in the Champions League, there was no doubting the 27 year old's top-quality experience. And back-up came in the popular figure of Shaka Hislop, who had played one hundred and thirty games for West Ham during a four-year period before spending a successful three-year tenure with Portsmouth, who now considered the thirty-six year old to be surplus to requirements.

The first transfer fees for new players were not agreed until early July, with it eventually being announced that West Ham had signed central defenders Danny Gabbidon and James Collins from Cardiff City and left-back Paul Konchesky from Charlton Athletic – all on the same day. West Ham managing director Paul Aldridge was keen to keep the fees undisclosed, but the selling clubs had different ideas, with Charlton openly declaring that they would receive an initial £1.5 million rising to £2 million for the 24-year-old Konchesky, subject to appearances. Cardiff owner Sam Hammam, meanwhile, referred to a 'confidentiality agreement' with the Hammers but revealed that '£2.5 million of the funds received' for Gabbidon and Collins would be 'set aside' to safeguard the Welsh club's immediate future before claiming that new manager Dave Jones could have the balance of £600,000 to spend on new players.

Cardiff had been in dire financial straits. Just a few months earlier, it had been revealed that the Championship club had sought help from the PFA to pay their players' wages, having failed to fulfil its £750,000 monthly bill at the beginning of March as a result of a near £30 million debt. West Ham boss

Pardew was quick to try and exploit the situation, making a £350,000 bid for Collins that was dismissed as 'derisory' by the Welsh outfit. It wasn't the first time that Pardew had descended like a vulture over the bones of a financially distressed outfit, having swooped on the club formerly known as Wimbledon to sign Nigel Reo-Coker, Jobi McAnuff and Adam Nowland during a one-week period in January 2004 for a total fee that was estimated to be £700,000 at the most.

There was no reason why West Ham shouldn't have fed off the more vulnerable clubs, having been in a similar situation themselves following relegation in 2003 when Chelsea closed in on Joe Cole and Glen Johnson. As chairman Brown admitted at that time, all a club can do when under pressure to sell players is fight to receive their true market value. Cardiff owner Hammam came close to doing so when eventually allowing Collins and Gabbidon – both Wales internationals – to head to Upton Park in a deal he appeared to value at £3.1 million. Gabbidon, who was 25, was considered by many to be Cardiff's crown jewel, but the fact that Pardew initially pursued the 21-year-old Collins said much about his belief in the latter's potential. The manager was well aware of the 'situation Cardiff was in' and was determined to secure the services of the two defenders. 'They were Cardiff's two best players – one an established international there were no doubts about [Gabbidon] and the other with fantastic technique and a real willingness to win,' he said, delighted that some solid building blocks had been put in place for his team.

All three new defenders were in their early 20s, and this reflected Pardew's intention to build an exciting young side that would have not just hunger and desire in the short term but the potential to mature and develop over the coming years. Just a fortnight after those purchases, West Ham confirmed the capture of midfielder Yossi Benayoun from Racing Santander for a fee of £2.5 million. The 25-year-old Israel international had been told 'not to hesitate' about moving to Upton Park by former Hammers favourite, international teammate and friend Eyal Berkovic, who knew the stylish playmaker would be ideally suited to the club's traditions of playing attacking football with entertainment a priority.

Benayoun had been pursued by a number of clubs, including Bolton Wanderers, whose manager Sam Allardyce slammed the Israeli for snubbing his outfit for the Hammers. 'If Benayoun didn't want to come to a great club like ours, then he went to West Ham for more money,' complained Allardyce. 'I think it was very stupid and a big mistake.'

The player was amazed by the attack but quickly put the Bolton manager in his place. 'Allardyce is talking nonsense,' he said. 'I didn't go to West Ham for the money. I went there because they play good football and I know I can do well.'

Pardew was delighted with the acquisition, recognising Benayoun as a clever player who could unlock defences and provide the ammunition for his strike force. Veteran Teddy Sheringham had proved an astute signing by Pardew the previous summer, going on to score 20 Championship goals and fully vindicate the manager's sacrifice of David Connolly (whose 17 goals in 2004–05 posed little threat to West Ham as Leicester finished a lowly 15th in the table). And the thirty-nine year old was rewarded with a new one-year contract and the opportunity to enjoy one last hurrah in the Premiership, which he'd said goodbye to when he'd left Portsmouth a year earlier.

Sheringham was one of a number of players who signed new deals to extend their stays at West Ham in the summer of 2005, with defender Christian Dailly, young centre-half Elliott Ward, winger Shaun Newton, teenage midfielder Mark Noble, defender Tomáš Řepka and injured goalkeeper Walker also doing so. But as his manager was only too aware, the former England international was at an age at which he would need to be carefully paced throughout the season, although his experience would prove invaluable in helping fellow strikers Marlon Harewood and Bobby Zamora continue their development as they found their feet in the Premiership. The former had scored 16 goals in his first full season at Upton Park following his move from Nottingham Forest, while the latter had also got into double figures during the promotion campaign, saving his most important strikes for the vital play-off games. But Pardew knew he needed top quality up front if West Ham were to score enough goals to avoid a relegation battle, and he soon concentrated his efforts on recruiting a new forward.

It was former West Ham manager Harry Redknapp, then in charge of Southampton, who confirmed his relegated club had rejected an offer of £6 million for Peter Crouch – the 6 ft 7 in. striker who had rediscovered his best form on the south coast following a disappointing big-money move from Portsmouth to Aston Villa in 2002. The news came as a relief to some Hammers supporters, who looked upon Crouch as a gangly figure who might struggle to fit into their team's pattern of play and ultimately prove a costly mistake. And West Ham could not afford to make mistakes if they were going to invest that type of money on a striker whose success or failure would surely determine the club's fate at the end of the season.

Redknapp also revealed that it was Crouch's desire to sign for recently crowned European champions Liverpool, who had initially made a smaller offer than West Ham but would eventually secure their target for what appeared an inflated figure of £7 million. 'Let's not kid ourselves,' shrugged Redknapp. 'Peter wants to go and play for Liverpool, where he can play in the Champions League and get eight times the pay.' Whether he was making a comparison with the player's current salary or his potential earnings at West Ham was unclear, but the Londoners were always in the reckoning. Indeed, first-team coach Peter

Grant believed Crouch would certainly have moved to Upton Park had the Reds not been on his tail. 'We were talking to Peter, but it was tough competing with Liverpool,' he admitted. 'Peter told us that if it hadn't been Liverpool chasing him he was going to come to West Ham.'

West Ham supporters could at least be reassured that the club was prepared to spend heavily and break its transfer record of £5.5 million in the quest to be competitive in the Premiership. And it soon became clear that Crouch had not been manager Pardew's only major target, with Benni McCarthy, Milan Baroš, Emmanuel Adebayor, Joseph-Désiré Job and Frédéric Kanouté all being the subject of firm enquiries.

Unwanted Liverpool striker Baroš was dismissive of West Ham's interest, however, preferring the claret and blue of Aston Villa instead. And although a fee was agreed with Middlesbrough for Job, the Cameroon international struggled to negotiate personal terms amid doubts about his fitness. Former West Ham striker Kanouté, who had been sold to Tottenham in the aftermath of relegation two years earlier, also appeared on Pardew's list when it was discovered that he was available – only for the manager to admit that the Hammers support had diluted his interest. 'There has been a negative feeling among our fan base that suggests it might not be right to bring him back, and I'd be foolish to ignore that,' he surprisingly admitted, just a week before the Mali international sealed a £4.4 million move to Spanish outfit Seville.

Pardew was certainly keen on 21-year-old Togo forward Adebayor, who was not the most prolific striker – having scored seventeen goals in a two-year period with Monaco following a £2 million move from Metz – but had shown promise and was being closely monitored by Arsenal manager Arsène Wenger. Monaco had initially been reluctant to discuss a sale with West Ham but eventually agreed a fee of £6 million in early August and granted the player permission to negotiate personal terms. Pardew and managing director Paul Aldridge flew to France and duly agreed a contract with Adebayor, only for Monaco to announce the next day that they had changed their minds and wanted to keep the player after all. In public, Pardew was philosophical, claiming that Monaco had 'every right' to have a change of heart and suggesting that 'fate' had intervened. Adebayor remained in France until completing a £7 million move to Arsenal just five months later.

Pardew spoke of pursuing 'other targets', but as the new season approached he conceded it was unlikely that a big-money striker would be signed before the action commenced. The club had admitted an interest in Porto forward McCarthy back in July, but although the South Africa international was eager to move to England (with Blackburn also linked), his club had rather different views. By the final week of August, with the season having started, West Ham submitted an offer of £4.5 million for the twenty-seven year old who had top scored in his two seasons with Porto and won the Champions League in 2004. The Portuguese club rejected the bid, despite McCarthy and his agent, Rob Moore, offering to forfeit their commissions in a desperate bid to push the deal through. At the time, it was reported the player had an $11 million – approximately £6 million – release clause in his contract, but this turned out to be incorrect as West Ham learned to their cost.

Just a few days before the transfer deadline on 31 August, an increased offer of around £5.5 million saw senior officials at Porto finally relent and allow McCarthy to speak to the Hammers. The breakthrough had seemingly been made, and the affable striker discussed terms with Aldridge and chewed the football fat with Pardew. Everything went well, only for Porto to perform a sudden U-turn and claim that president Jorge Nuno Pinto da Costa wanted McCarthy to stay. In a final effort, West

Ham raised their offer to a figure of £6.1 million, but when that was rejected with just two hours of the transfer window remaining it became clear that business with Porto was not going to be completed.

Pardew and his assistant Grant were bitterly frustrated to see all their efforts come to nothing, while McCarthy was also distressed to see his Premiership dreams disappear in smoke. 'Benni was crying,' admitted Grant. 'He was so disappointed that the deal wasn't happening. It was so close.' McCarthy, who was soon fined for an apparent breach of club discipline, did eventually make his escape from Porto when he joined Blackburn for a fee of just £2.5 million in the summer of 2006.

As they were when the Adebayor signing broke down, West Ham were keen to let their supporters know how close they had been to smashing their transfer record, only to be let down by the erratic behaviour of the clubs they had been dealing with. The Hammers had been accused of a lack of ambition at times in the past, and chairman Brown wanted it to be known that the lack of a big signing in attack had not been for the want of trying. Some back-up had been recruited in the form of French forwards David Bellion and Jérémie Aliadière – on loan from Manchester United and Arsenal respectively – as well as Czech youngster Petr Mikolanda. But their opportunities were always going to be limited with Harewood, Zamora and Sheringham having to shoulder the bulk of the goal-scoring responsibilities as the season got underway.

Many supporters feared that the failure to land McCarthy would prove catastrophic for West Ham. It seemed that the best they could hope for was the team limping through until the following January when the next transfer window opened. By that time, of course, the damage might already have been done, and it would then prove even harder to sign a quality striker if the team was struggling at the foot of the table.

The preparations for Premiership football had otherwise gone well, however, with the team completing a run of eight pre-season friendly games – which included trips to Sweden and Germany – without defeat. But there was a sense of apprehension in the air when West Ham took to the field against Blackburn in their opening league game at Upton Park. The starting line-up showed six changes to the one that had appeared in the play-off final three months earlier, with Carroll, Konchesky, Gabbidon and Benayoun making their competitive debuts. Indeed, the lack of familiarity among the players may have contributed to a somewhat nervy first 45 minutes that saw Andy Todd take advantage of sloppy play to put the visitors ahead.

In the West Ham dressing-room at half-time, an unhappy Pardew went to work on his players. 'Come on, this is not what this season is going to be about,' he told his team, which had been overrun in the early stages of the game. He then proceeded to 'rattle a few cages' before sending his players out for the second period. The transformation was immediate and spectacular. Sheringham stroked home an equaliser as the fans were still returning to their seats, Reo-Coker smashed in from 20 yards to put West Ham ahead just past the hour mark and Matthew Etherington tapped in the third with ten minutes remaining. Blackburn's miserable day was completed when striker Paul Dickov was dismissed for a lunge at Konchesky. 'That victory virtually set the scene for the rest of the season,' admitted Pardew. 'The first win in the Premier League is absolutely enormous for any promoted team, and to get it on the first day was a huge bonus.'

Assistant Grant was in no doubt about the importance of the victory against Blackburn, recognising a different mood within the West Ham support. 'The big fillip at the start of the season was going 1–0 down in our first game but coming back to win 3–1,' he reflected. 'For the first time in at least 18 months we had the full backing of Upton Park, because we weren't expected to win the Premiership, whereas there had been huge expectations of us the year before. So even when we had bad performances, the crowd stayed with us.'

The confidence from the thrilling opening-day triumph was evident in the following match at Newcastle, although hopes of a second win were heavily undermined when Konchesky was harshly sent off just ten minutes into the second half. The red card was later rescinded, but it said much about the growing spirit in the West Ham camp that they returned to London disappointed to have been deprived of victory. The unbeaten start was brought to an end in the next outing at Upton Park, however, with a typically efficient Bolton side claiming a 2–1 success. The key feature of the match was the number of good chances squandered by Harewood, who Pardew admitted 'did not have the best of games'.

Press criticism of the striker was fierce, while many supporters feared Harewood was simply not clinical enough – despite his record of 36 goals in 92 West Ham outings at that point – and that his habit of wasting chances could cost the team dear in the Premiership. Harewood needed full concentration to be at his best, and, sensing his levels were dropping, Pardew called the striker into his office for a few quiet words. 'I didn't want to make a big deal of it. I just told him that with Zamora itching to play it was important to take his chances,' he said.

Indeed, it was no formality that Harewood would line up against Aston Villa when the Hammers returned to action more than a fortnight later following an international break. Pardew had pondered the idea of handing Zamora his first start alongside Sheringham for the televised visit of Villa to Upton Park. But having seen McCarthy slip out of his grasp as the transfer window closed, the manager could not afford to see one of his key strikers suffer a prolonged confidence crisis, and he decided to pledge his faith in Harewood – for one more game.

That belief was rewarded beyond Pardew's wildest dreams, as Harewood helped destroy Villa with a sensational hat-trick in a 4–0 success that truly signalled West Ham's return to the Premiership. The striker had been hurt by criticism following the Bolton game, and when he opened his account for the season with his first goal of the night he somewhat arrogantly put his index finger to his lips as a sign of having silenced his detractors. While somewhat unnecessary, it was quickly forgotten as an instinctive close-range flick and a fierce far-post strike put West Ham 3–0 ahead before Benayoun twisted and turned his way past the visiting defence to score his first goal for the club late on.

'That hat-trick sealed Marlon's belief and was a key turning point for him,' reflected Pardew. It had been eight long years since a West Ham player had scored three times in a Premiership game at Upton Park, so Harewood's feat represented a major landmark as the team proved it was worth its place in the top-flight. The momentum was continued at Fulham the following weekend when Harewood struck twice in a 2–1 win, although the second goal was attributed to home goalkeeper Tony Warner after the ball rebounded off him having struck the post. Cottagers boss Coleman described the exciting London derby as 'the best I've seen for entertainment' as West Ham's free-flowing football started to win friends as well as points.

The tally of ten goals in the first five games was bettered only by table-toppers and defending champions Chelsea, the 4–0 demolition of Villa was the Premiership season's joint biggest victory at that point and Harewood had been the first top-flight player to claim a hat-trick. Pardew had promised ahead of the season that his side would 'attack every game', and he was delighted with the 'nice little buzz' that had developed within his squad. 'We respect everyone but don't fear them and are having a real go at teams,' he said. 'We're a good team to watch.'

Grant was surprised at the way some of his players acclimatised so easily to Premiership football having stuttered to win promotion. 'The pressure of expectation had diminished, but it gave the players confidence to produce performances that were above what I personally thought they were capable of,' he reflected. 'Teams also allowed us to play in certain respects and let us have a go at them while also trying to have a go at us.' Such a view adds weight to the theory that West Ham's traditional style of attacking football was more conducive to success in the Premiership than in the Football League, where the team sometimes struggled to impose themselves in games in which direct play, solid organisation and physical strength were often the dominant features.

The key element for Pardew was the enthusiasm of his side – and it was no accident. 'One of the things we consciously did was buy young players,' he said. 'We came into the division with an exuberance, and that can take you a long way.' Not only was the West Ham team predominately made up of young players – the average age of the outfield players that won at Fulham was just 24, with only Řepka in his 30s – but the majority were British. This was very much a rarity, with the Premiership having been engulfed by a foreign invasion as a result of the increased television revenue from Sky and the effects of the Bosman ruling. Czech defender Řepka and Israeli midfielder Benayoun were the only 'foreigners' in Pardew's regular line-up as Reo-Coker, Anton Ferdinand, Konchesky, Etherington, Hayden Mullins, Harewood, Zamora and Sheringham flew the flag for England.

Reo-Coker and Ferdinand, aged 20 and 21 respectively and members of the England Under-21 squad, were the youngest players in the West Ham team and both proved important components of the team as the first half of the season wore on. Ferdinand's early days at the club were blighted as he suffered unfair comparisons with older brother Rio, who left West Ham to join big-spending Leeds in 2000 before Manchester United invested £30 million for the England international's signature. Rio had often been described as a 'Rolls-Royce of a player' by former manager Redknapp, but, although they shared certain similar characteristics, Anton initially appeared to lack his brother's immaculate quality as he progressed through the club's ranks. Youth academy chief Tony Carr, who had overseen the development of young stars such as Cole, Frank Lampard and Michael Carrick among others, had always insisted that comparisons with Rio were unfair. 'You have to isolate your memory of Rio's achievements and remember that this is an individual in his own right,' he said. 'Everybody has got to be a bit more patient, because Anton is developing at a different rate.'

Suspicions that Carr was simply being diplomatic were ultimately banished as Ferdinand went on to prove his Premiership credentials. With Anton quickly forming a close understanding with new signing Gabbidon, the strength of the centre-half partnership was reflected in the fact that the team conceded no more than two goals in any one game at the start of the 2005–06 season until the latter was carried off with injury at Blackburn in early December. Indeed, Gabbidon's own impressive displays at the start of his first top-flight campaign played a part in the defender winning the 2005 Welsh Footballer of the Year award.

Ferdinand's form towards the end of the promotion-winning season had been rewarded in the shape of a new contract, agreed shortly after reports appeared that Liverpool had expressed an interest in the defender. Just six months later, he would be handed a new four-and-a-half year deal midway through the 2005–06 campaign as West Ham looked to secure the long-term futures of all those young players who had played a key role in the promising return to the Premiership.

Draws against Arsenal and Sunderland made it just one defeat in the opening seven games, and central midfielders Reo-Coker and Mullins were both awarded new five-year contracts in the first week of October. Reo-Coker had skippered Wimbledon as a teenager and became West Ham's youngest ever captain early in the promotion season, as well as leading out England's Under-21s. Journalists were certainly impressed by his first Upton Park press conference appearance following his arrival in January 2004, when he spoke with great intelligence and maturity about the challenges that lay ahead. It was obvious Reo-Coker was going places, and, even at that point, it seemed highly feasible that he could one day go on to become full England captain. 'I've always wanted to see how far I can go in this game, how far I can reach,' he said. He might have struggled to consistently impose himself on games during the previous season, but his partnership with Mullins in the second half of 2005 was an important part of West Ham's success.

Mullins had been Pardew's first purchase when making a £1 million move from Crystal Palace in the autumn of 2003 and was the quietly efficient kind of player that only really got noticed when making mistakes – and there were a few of those in the early part of his West Ham career as he was shunted around as a utility man. 'Mullins' replica shirts were rarely seen in Green Street on match days, but the 26 year old had made the holding midfield role his own by the time that promotion was won, and he was arguably the most improved player in West Ham's side in the early part of 2005–06. 'It's been difficult for Hayden, but he's come through the criticism and is well respected in the team,' said Pardew as he handed Mullins his deserved new contract.

With Harewood and Etherington also signing new contracts, West Ham were maintaining their recent tradition of ensuring all their key players were committed to the club for a lengthy period. The Hammers may have been criticised for making various mistakes down the years, but failing to recognise the implications of the mid-1990s Bosman ruling certainly wasn't one of them. Other clubs had seen valuable talent walk away on free transfers as they allowed their contracts to wind down and expire before signing on elsewhere – as Tottenham defender Sol Campbell famously did when defecting to arch rivals Arsenal in 2001.

If West Ham were going to continue investing in their productive youth system, they could ill afford to allow their best young players to sneak under the fence, and so they ensured that contracts were regularly extended. And if the policy saw individuals occasionally being paid more than they were perhaps worth on the field, it was a price worth paying, as it at least preserved the player's value in the transfer market. West Ham would obviously not have earned £29 million through the sales of Rio Ferdinand and Lampard if the players had not had several years remaining on their contracts. If there was nothing to buy out, the selling club would receive nothing. West Ham had even been prepared to put their promotion chances on the line in 2004 rather than lose out on £10 million in transfer fees by allowing Jermain Defoe and Carrick to see out their deals. Supporters were critical of West Ham being a selling club, but, with a few exceptions, the true market value was always received for players – and there were plenty of clubs that had been caught with their trousers down in that respect.

The most significant new contract drawn up in the autumn of 2005 did not land in the lap of a player, however, but the manager. West Ham had been punished for their 'cavalier' approach when losing 2–1 at Manchester City in mid-October, with Pardew admitting his side had been 'misguided' in trying to play 'too much football'. But they bounced back with a 2–1 home win against Middlesbrough that saw them enjoy an outrageous slice of good fortune when officials adjudged that the ball had crossed the goal line when it clearly had not. The Hammers were already 1–0 up thanks to Sheringham's penalty when a Konchesky free-kick was deflected goalwards by Boro defender Chris Riggott. Goalkeeper Mark Schwarzer comfortably held the ball before it reached the line, only for a goal to be bizarrely awarded. 'Sometimes you earn your breaks, and we deserved to win the game,' insisted Pardew afterwards. Indeed, the controversy over the second goal had 'taken the gloss' off the victory for the manager, who was disappointed his side might not 'get the recognition it deserved'.

Pardew was also unhappy a week later when it was pointed out that successive defeats at Bolton (in the Carling Cup) and Liverpool (in the Premiership) meant his team had lost their last three away games. 'That's a very negative comment,' he snapped, before admitting his decision to substitute Řepka at right-back had made it easy for winger Bolo Zenden to seal Liverpool's 2–0 win. 'We're all learning, and I could have been more patient, but we're making a big step up here,' he conceded. Just a few days later, it was confirmed that Pardew had signed a new five-year contract that would potentially extend his stay at Upton Park until 2010.

In many respects, the news of the deal came as no surprise. The manager had led West Ham back to the Premiership while significantly reducing the club's wage bill and raising money in the transfer market. He had implemented an entirely new structure behind the scenes, overhauling the coaching set-up and introducing many contemporary ideas, with a special emphasis on sports science. The club's upward trajectory – from the 2004 play-off final to promotion the following year – had continued with the team enjoying a strong start to the Premiership season. The first ten games had produced fifteen points to take them to ninth in the table, an impressive set of statistics considering that Sunderland, who had been promoted as convincing Championship winners, were rooted to the bottom with just five.

The team was also playing attractive football, while players such as Reo-Coker, Harewood, Etherington and Mullins were all increasing in value – as their new contracts affirmed. And Pardew's bosses were also impressed by the manager's ability to sign quality players without having to break the bank, with Carroll, Gabbidon, Benayoun and Konchesky all proving themselves worthy acquisitions. 'Alan has shown himself to be a shrewd judge in the transfer market, and I've been particularly impressed by the way he balances the success on the field against the business demands of this club,' said Brown.

Yet some supporters feared the West Ham hierarchy had been perhaps a touch hasty in handing Pardew a new five-year deal just ten games into the new season. The board had, after all, reportedly been close to sacking the manager the previous term when promotion appeared to have slipped out of the team's grasp. And what if the Hammers lost their next ten games and suddenly found themselves in a relegation battle? Would a change of management at any time in the future be prohibited by the cost of a settlement, as had appparently been the case three years earlier when the board had appeared reluctant to pay up struggling boss Glenn Roeder's contract? The good start to the season had certainly convinced some sceptical fans of the manager's abilities – untested in the Premiership before then – but it would still be a few more months before 'Alan Pardew's claret-and-blue army' would be sung with total conviction.

The cost of the big new contracts added more weight to a wage bill the club had fought hard to reduce in the two years following relegation in 2003. West Ham had lost £5.1 million in their promotion year, but, with the overall debt being reduced, the board insisted that the club was in a far healthier condition that it had been for some time. 'The fact that we are now in such good financial shape is because we took the pain early, doing what was necessary, and, in effect, changed the financial position of the company, which is vastly different to that of two years ago,' said Brown when the 2004–05 accounts were published.

The key difference this time around was that all the new contracts took into account the possibility of relegation – which had not been the case previously. That meant the club could afford to reward manager Pardew and the players for their successes, knowing their salaries would be reduced if the club were to drop out of the Premiership in the near future. Pardew was happy to accept the clause – partly in the belief that relegation was unlikely but also to exist on a par with his playing squad. 'If I'm giving that arrangement to the players, it's only right I have that in my contract as well,' he confided.

A further sign of the club's seat at football's top table came in the form of an international call-up for Konchesky. The shaven-headed left-back earned only the second England cap of his career when coach Sven-Göran Eriksson used him as a half-time substitute in the 3–2 friendly win against Argentina on 12 November. It was the first time a West Ham player had appeared for England in two years, with goalkeeper David James being the last to do so shortly before he left the club. Not only did the call-up reward Konchesky for his bright displays since his summer move from Charlton, but it gave hope to other members of the Hammers squad – particularly Reo-Coker, Ferdinand, Harewood and Etherington – that they could possibly sneak aboard the plane for the 2006 World Cup finals in Germany if they continued to impress during the domestic season.

Konchesky had been called up as a result of first-choice England left-back Ashley Cole being sidelined with injury, but it was Wayne Bridge, who had also been injured and played just an hour of Carling Cup football in the previous nine months, who was asked to start against Argentina. That hardly suggested that Eriksson had great faith in the West Ham left-back – who was sent on out of necessity after Bridge struggled in the first half – and he was later blamed for a goal scored by Walter Samuel. Konchesky failed to make another England squad and was privately told by Eriksson that he would not be going to the World Cup finals – many months before the squad was named. It was a strange display of man-management by the Swede, who could at least have kept Konchesky fully motivated in case circumstances changed. In that respect, Eriksson did West Ham few favours, but Konchesky persevered, despite receiving a blow to his confidence.

Surprisingly, it was the veteran striker Sheringham who was being touted for a return to the England set-up. His goal against Blackburn on the opening day of the season had seen him become the Premiership's oldest scorer – inheriting the record from former Hammer Stuart Pearce – and although he'd netted just four times, that was still four goals more than Liverpool striker Crouch had scored in sixteen appearances for club and country so far in the season. Sheringham was being mentioned in connection with a backroom role at the World Cup, but former boss Redknapp, who had bought and sold him for Portsmouth, responded by claiming the 39 year old 'could still do a job for the country as a player', although it was difficult to gauge how serious he was.

The Hammers lost the services of Reo-Coker for a six-game period in the run-up to Christmas because of an ankle injury, but, although Pardew had warned there could be 'sticky days' ahead, the team continued to be competitive. Ferdinand scored his first Premiership goal with an injury-time header to rescue a 1–1 draw at local rivals Tottenham, a result that represented one of the 'real highlights of the season' for Pardew, who knew how much it meant to the West Ham fans. They had suffered some miserable times over the previous three years, but days like that certainly paid off some of the debt.

The following weekend's home game against Manchester

United was significant not just for providing Ferdinand with his first opportunity to come face to face with brother Rio in a competitive game but for the fact it was the Red Devils' first outing since the death of their former idol George Best. It seemed somewhat appropriate that Sir Alex Ferguson's men should pay their respects to the Northern Irishman at Upton Park, given that televised footage of Best's mercurial magic in the late 1960s and early '70s invariably showed West Ham to be his victims. Best scored 11 goals in 16 outings against the boys in claret and blue between 1964 and 1971, not that Hammers fans held it against him, as they produced a minute's sincere applause – as opposed to the traditional 60 seconds of silence – in acknowledgement of his unique talents.

The noise had barely died down when Harewood shot West Ham into a first-minute lead, but second-half goals from England striker Wayne Rooney and Irishman John O'Shea gave the visitors a deserved victory as their superior quality became fully apparent. Pardew accepted the 2–1 defeat as a reality check, recognising his side had done well to frighten Ferguson's men early on and remain in the match until the end. 'It lived up to the tradition of great games between the two clubs, but in the end we were hanging on for dear life, and, even as a manager, there are times when you realise you've still got a long way to go,' he said.

West Ham remained in the top nine in the Premiership despite just two wins in their previous eight league outings, but a sequence of three successive away games – at Birmingham, Blackburn and Everton – was sure to prove pivotal to the club's prospects. The Hammers had won just one of their six away league fixtures, but Pardew had always highlighted the forthcoming trio of games as being vitally important. 'We drew up a list of teams we knew we had to compete with, and we had to win that particular league,' he said. 'Those three teams all sat in the table we'd put together, so we knew that was a massive period for us, and we really focused on it.'

Zamora obviously paid special attention to his manager, as the striker scored in all three games – having failed to net in his last four outings – producing arguably his best goal of the season in the 2–1 win at Birmingham after being asked to start at the expense of Sheringham. With Emile Heskey opening the scoring for the home side, Zamora levelled with a brilliant solo effort, flicking the ball over Matthew Upson and sidestepping the sliding challenge of Damien Johnson to fire home. Harewood then lashed in the winner in first-half stoppage time to seal West Ham's first top-flight victory at St Andrew's in 30 years.

But the Hammers were brought down to earth five days later when Blackburn avenged their opening-day defeat at Upton Park by claiming a 3–2 home win at Ewood Park in a real ding-dong affair that saw the visitors lose defender Gabbidon with a gashed knee. With the Wales international being carried off after being nudged off the pitch into the advertising hoardings and substitute Dailly being asked to plug the gap, West Ham made a series of defensive errors to return home empty-handed, despite Zamora's opener and Harewood's second-half header.

Gabbidon would be absent for the next half a dozen games, in which the Hammers conceded a further 13 goals with his presence sorely missed. Prospects looked particularly grim in the midweek game at Everton on 14 December as James Beattie fired the hosts ahead after just nine minutes. Heads could easily have dropped, but it was a sign of West Ham's character that they responded to the setback by producing possibly their best display of the season. Defender David Weir turned the ball into his own net, after Řepka crossed from the right, before Zamora confirmed his side's second-half domination by poking home star man Etherington's parried effort.

It was the match that really convinced Pardew his team

could be on the verge of achieving something special with the stylish win lifting West Ham up to seventh in the Premiership table. The manager admitted he was 'amazed' by some of his side's play and was left purring that his men had handed 'a footballing lesson' to Everton. 'That was our first genuine performance that made people sit up and say, "This team isn't bad, you know."' There were Everton officials saying things like, "You deserved to win today," and you don't get that very often at Goodison Park,' he said. Indeed, Pardew walked down the tunnel into the visitors' dressing-room and told his assistant Grant, 'That's as good as we'll ever be this season.'

Typically of West Ham, they then crashed to a 4–2 defeat at home to Newcastle – again paying the price for some dreadful defensive errors – as they embarked on a run of five games without a win. But there were positives, and the 1–1 draw at Portsmouth on Boxing Day proved to be yet another example of the team's ability to fight back and salvage games after going behind. Indeed, the hard-fought draw at Fratton Park represented the sixth time in the season that West Ham had conceded the game's first goal but recovered to claim one point (as also seen at Sunderland and Tottenham) or all three (as witnessed against Blackburn and at Birmingham and Everton).

Pardew was delighted with the spirit and character shown by his players on such occasions but was understandably frustrated at seeing the team regularly go behind to make their task so much more difficult – particularly away from home. 'It's something we've looked at recently, but hopefully we won't have to worry too much about it as the season progresses,' he said. Little did he realise that West Ham would go on to be crowned the comeback kings of the Premiership season, eventually pocketing 18 points from games they had gone 1–0 down in. Hammers supporters had long become accustomed to their side's Jekyll-and-Hyde nature from week to week, but now the erratic mood swings were taking place in individual games, with the team starting several games as if nursing a bad hangover before suddenly leaping into song and dance.

That had certainly been the case at Portsmouth, yet the year's final game at Charlton went completely the other way. West Ham dominated against Alan Curbishley's men for the opening 20 minutes, only to fall behind to a Shaun Bartlett header against the run of play. Darren Bent sealed a 2–0 win for the Addicks in the second half to leave Pardew pondering just how his men had ended up being well beaten on a day they should have won at a canter.

West Ham remained in the top half of the table, but the defeat annoyed the manager – and not necessarily because he'd lost to a club he'd played for while Curbishley had beaten the team he used to represent. Curbishley may have been schooled at West Ham to appreciate the flamboyant side of football, but his management approach was far more pragmatic – at least in Pardew's eyes. 'Charlton take a much more sensible approach than we do,' he said. 'And they get results on the back of it. We looked like we would take them to the cleaners, but Charlton nicked a goal, and, typically, they shut up shop and ended up getting a second one.

'We're always on the front foot, trying to win games, but on that occasion their tactical approach worked for them. Our approach didn't work for us, because we were bombing forward, and it cost us a second goal. It was a really bad defeat, but we learned something from that game, and it was something of a turning point.'

# 3

## 'WE WERE SO HUNGRY TO PROVE OURSELVES'

THE AIR was thick with conspiracy theories as the Norwich City team sheet passed through the hands of the media before the FA Cup third-round tie against West Ham on 7 January 2006. Dean Ashton's name was conspicuously missing from the Canaries' line-up, prompting suspicions that the striker had been sacrificed to avoid him becoming cup-tied – a handicap that could seriously affect his valuation if the club chose to acquiesce to those in pursuit of the 22 year old's services. Given it was West Ham who were keenest to secure Ashton's signature, it was a double boost for the visitors when they learned that a 'groin strain' had put him out of action – terrible luck considering he'd completed the previous 17 games and returned to start the following weekend. Indeed, according to one Hammer, there was a 'sigh of relief' in the dressing-room – and not just from manager Alan Pardew.

After West Ham's deserved 2–1 victory, in which Norwich had posed little attacking threat (their goal coming from the penalty spot), home manager Nigel Worthington wasted little time in telling journalists what they wanted to hear. 'He's gone,' he said, before waiting a few seconds for the news to be digested. 'Yeah, gone to hospital,' he added, quickly emphasising that he was talking about goalkeeper Robert Green, who had been stretchered off a minute from time with a worrying neck injury. That was, after all, what everybody was so desperate to know, was it not? Apparently not, because within moments Worthington was insisting that Ashton had been withdrawn with an injury – and he had 'the scans to prove it'. Regardless, he had no intention of selling the striker, who had been signed from Crewe just 12 months earlier for a fee of £3 million. It would take a 'crazy offer' for the Canaries to let their chief asset take flight, he insisted. And as far as the Norwich boss was concerned, that would price a certain east London club out of the market. 'There is no way in the world that West Ham could afford Dean, so you can knock that one on the head,' he had said before the season had started.

But Worthington had underestimated both the ambition of the Hammers and the determination of Pardew. With the club just inside the top half of the table in January, there were certainly no relegation fears, so some observers may have considered that the striker hunt – one that had seemed essential to West Ham's hopes of safety back in the summer – was not quite the priority it had once been. But it became apparent in the period leading up to the opening of the transfer window on 1 January that the £6 million originally set aside for a new forward had not been buried deep in the club's vaults. In the early part of December, Pardew had been asked if he had an interest in Crystal Palace striker Andy Johnson, who would certainly command a handsome fee. 'We'll be in the market for top-quality players next month, and Johnson certainly falls into that category. Should he become available, we would be very interested, and I imagine other clubs would be as well,' he admitted rather diplomatically.

While his response reassured West Ham supporters that the club was looking to move onwards and upwards, it did little to improve his relationship with Palace boss Iain Dowie, who complained that Pardew had no right to express an interest if no bid had been made. The West Ham manager subsequently found himself apologising for causing any offence and insisting he'd merely answered a direct question. The episode was conclusive evidence of West Ham's intentions, however, and, although the interest in Johnson faded – as it had done in Porto striker Benni McCarthy by that stage – the determination to sign Ashton intensified. Here was an old-fashioned type of centre-forward, an England Under-21 international, whose career was on a consistent upward trajectory, having scored eight, ten, sixteen, twenty and twenty-seven goals in his five full seasons of football so far. He'd also made his predatory instincts clear by scoring twice in Crewe's 3–2 home defeat by the Hammers the previous season. Not surprisingly, West Ham's first bid of £5 million was rejected, with Norwich well aware that Manchester City were also in the hunt. City's budget was just £6 million, however, and they were forced to drop out of the running before eventually investing that figure in Heerenveen's Greek striker Georgios Samaras.

City's withdrawal left the way clear for West Ham to agree a club record figure of £7 million plus a possible further £250,000 based on his success, with a 15 per cent sell-on clause also included. Indeed, Norwich had agreed to pay 20 per cent of any profit on the player to Crewe, meaning they had to divert £800,000 to Ashton's former club. The striker was also reportedly due a slice of the fee, although he apparently waived £150,000 to ensure the deal went through, as West Ham insisted they had hit the ceiling in terms of their bidding. In fact, Pardew had been forced to push hard for the board to go up to £7 million, considering the discussions with his directors a major test of their faith in him. Would they trust his judgement and back him?

Ultimately, Pardew convinced them there was little risk paying that sort of money for a player who would only increase in value. The manager may have claimed to be paying 'over the odds' when the transfer was announced, but a greater insight into West Ham's thinking was revealed when managing director Paul Aldridge, speaking like an estate agent, said, 'Dean represents an investment that can benefit the club for many years to come.' Fellow director Scott Duxbury then claimed the deal had been 'a steal', although it's doubtful he used such a term while the negotiations were taking place.

Other January arrivals came in the form of Maccabi Haifa forward Yaniv Katan – recommended to the club by Israel teammate Yossi Benayoun – and full-back Lionel Scaloni, signed on a deadline-day loan deal, with Czech defender Tomáš Řepka having returned to his homeland and former club Sparta Prague for family reasons. Former Hammer Glen Johnson, who had failed to establish himself at Chelsea, had also been linked, as had Tottenham's Stephen Kelly, but it was Argentina international Scaloni who would eventually be recruited from Deportivo La Coruña after a bid for Barcelona's Gabri fell through. Gabri's club teammate Maxi López had been another target for Pardew, who also confirmed his interest in former Manchester United skipper Roy Keane prior to his move to Celtic. Meanwhile, it was time to wave au revoir to Frenchmen Jérémie Aliadière and David Bellion after they made a handful of unconvincing outings since arriving on loan at the start of the season, with the latter complaining that he was 'sickened' by his treatment at the club.

Ashton was introduced to the West Ham crowd ahead of the game against Fulham, in which defender Anton Ferdinand and midfielder Benayoun both produced moments of striking magic to help secure a 2–1 win that ended a run of four successive home defeats. Ferdinand's stunning volley on the turn and Benayoun's delicate chip were described as 'masterpieces' by commentators as Řepka bid farewell to the Hammers in the

Sky televised game on 23 January. The result was West Ham's third victory in succession, with the FA Cup win at Norwich having been followed with an impressive 2–1 success at Aston Villa – yet another example of maximum points being won after going behind. Bobby Zamora's goal at Villa Park was his eighth of the season – all scored away from home – and he was rewarded in the form of a new four-year contract to join the growing list of players whose long-term futures at the club had been secured. Defender Danny Gabbidon's return to league action following injury was also reassuring, as was the fact that the win had been achieved with the same attack and midfield from the underachieving Championship years.

As far as Pardew was concerned, it was yet another example of his men enjoying the benefits of playing without the pressure that had cramped their style so much the previous season. The inventive Benayoun had been ruled out with a thigh problem, but some comfort was gained from West Ham's ability to impose themselves physically on opponents – not something they were traditionally famous for – with Villa manager David O'Leary complaining his team had been 'out-muscled'.

The 4–2 home FA Cup triumph against Blackburn maintained the team's winning run ahead of a difficult midweek trip to Arsenal at the beginning of February. It was to prove an astonishing occasion, not just because West Ham became the last visiting team to record a victory at Highbury – ahead of Arsenal's move to their new Emirates Stadium – but also because their success was overshadowed by Sol Campbell's bizarre half-time defection. The Gunners' England defender had twice been embarrassed as West Ham surged into a 2–0 lead. First, with 25 minutes on the clock, his miskick allowed Nigel Reo-Coker to run through and open the scoring. Just seven minutes later, he ended up on his backside as Zamora resisted his challenge on the edge of the penalty area, turned and brilliantly curled the ball into the far corner of the net. Campbell was spared any further blushes when he was substituted at the break, by which time Thierry Henry had pulled a goal back for the hosts.

The anticipated second-half onslaught from Arsenal never quite materialised, however, and Matthew Etherington's deflected strike ten minutes from time – after Ashton had forced an error on his debut as a substitute – ensured a late Robert Pirès effort was nothing more than a consolation as West Ham recorded a shock 3–2 win.

During the post-match inquiry, Gunners boss Arsène Wenger insisted it was 'difficult to understand' how his team had lost, while Pardew praised his side's 'fantastic performance'. The West Ham manager had studied Arsenal's style of play more than any other team, and he considered his success against them that season – taking four points from the two games – as evidence of his abilities to compete with the best. 'I felt we knew them perhaps better than anybody else,' he said, 'and that we could hurt them. We changed tactics two or three times, and, as a coach, it was a game you felt proud to have played a part in, although there's no doubt we had to fight for our lives.'

Not that West Ham received much in the way of credit for their fine achievement with the spotlight very much on the distressed Campbell after it was revealed that he had left Highbury at half-time. Wenger prompted the media frenzy when he referred to the 'exceptional circumstances' and the defender's 'mental shape', while midfielder Pirès claimed the player had 'a big worry on the private side'. Campbell subsequently went to ground for several days, and the continued speculation about his disappearance and state of mind ballooned to such an extent that the result of the game was only mentioned in the context of his mistakes. Campbell would not return to first-team action for another two months – due to 'an ankle injury' it was claimed

– when he started a game at Portsmouth, who he would soon join on a free transfer.

The victory at Arsenal had seen goalkeeper Shaka Hislop make a return to league action, having stepped in for five games earlier in the season while Roy Carroll recovered from a knee injury – sustained when catching his studs in the goal-netting, so journalists were told. This time around, the former Manchester United man was sidelined with a long-term back problem, and the reliable Hislop would stay in the side as the Hammers looked to continue their FA Cup run and finish as high up the Premiership table as possible.

West Ham had accumulated thirty-five points from their twenty-four league games and knew they would exceed the forty-point mark – the generally accepted safety level – if they won their next two fixtures, at home to struggling Sunderland and Birmingham. With bottom-of-the-table Sunderland doomed to relegation with an embarrassing nine points to their name, a home win seemed a formality – especially when Black Cats full-back Stephen Wright was sent off after twenty-three minutes following clumsy challenges on Reo-Coker and Etherington. But the visitors defended stubbornly as West Ham, still recovering from their exertions at Arsenal just a few days earlier, lacked inspiration and the creative verve that had been a characteristic of their season.

Just ten minutes of the game remained when Ashton – making his first start for the Hammers – pounced to slot home after substitute Marlon Harewood's shot was parried into his path. Goalkeeper Kelvin Davis then allowed Paul Konchesky's firm but somewhat speculative drive to squirm under his body into the net to seal the 2–0 result. But it was the predatory Ashton who won all the plaudits for a display that saw him not only make the vital breakthrough but go close to claiming a hat-trick, having seen a header tipped onto the bar and another effort fly just past the woodwork. West Ham fans who had previously seen little of him instantly recognised the 22 year old as a target man who knew where the back of the net was. Ashton may not have been blessed with the greatest of pace – indeed, he appeared rather unfit at first – but he read the game well and clearly had the instinctive knack of being in the right place at the right time.

'We needed to get more shots on target,' said Pardew, who identified Ashton as somebody who could play a key role in the building of attacks. 'I didn't really have that type of striker if Teddy Sheringham wasn't playing, as Marlon and Bobby are different kinds of players. Dean has fantastic technique and will certainly justify his fee.'

Ashton duly took his tally to two goals in as many Upton Park outings when hammering the final nail in Birmingham's coffin as West Ham cruised to a 3–0 win, set up by two Harewood strikes. More significantly, the triumph saw the Hammers equal their club record of seven successive victories, achieved when finishing a best-ever third in the 1985–86 season. Furthermore, the result lifted West Ham up to sixth in the Premiership table, level on points with expected title-challengers Arsenal and just five points off a Champions League place. Pardew was the highest-placed English manager in the league (with José Mourinho, Sir Alex Ferguson, Rafael Benítez, Martin Jol and Wenger above him), while his team had remained in the top half of the table from the opening day of the campaign, embarrassing the bookmakers who had listed West Ham as relegation favourites the previous summer.

It was no coincidence that the seven-game winning run had commenced with Gabbidon's return to the team at Norwich – and the manager knew it, too. 'We really missed Danny, and when James Collins came in alongside Ferdinand in the centre of defence the experience just wasn't there,' admitted Pardew.

'Gabbidon is a massive player for us, and that's shown itself in those seven games.'

The manager was also convinced that the fewer number of games in the Premiership – eight less than in the Championship – was a contributory factor in his side's success. Pardew placed great emphasis on pre-match preparation, and he believed that his methods were more successful when he had a full week between games, although some of the team's best results – such as the midweek wins at Everton and Arsenal – didn't exactly support his theory. 'The longer periods between games definitely helped us,' he said. 'There's much more time to prepare, and that suits the way I manage, in terms of the psychological approach to games. We've also had far better energy levels, and even if the players lose just 10 per cent they're not as effective. When they're at the top, they can actually overpower teams, but when we run into a period of continuous games we tend to struggle – as we saw in the Championship.'

A 0–0 draw at Bolton on 18 February may have ended the winning run but ensured the club was included in the FA Cup sixth-round draw, with Pardew demanding his players turn 'a good season into a great one'. There was a setback for the England hopefuls looking to make a late bid for inclusion in Sven-Göran Eriksson's squad for the World Cup finals that summer, however. Not a single West Ham player was named in the 23-man party ahead of the friendly international against Uruguay at the start of March, with Konchesky, Ferdinand, Reo-Coker and Etherington all left disappointed.

As usual, there were plenty of former Hammers included, with Joe Cole, Frank Lampard, Rio Ferdinand, Michael Carrick, Jermain Defoe and David James all given a chance to stake their claims for Germany 2006. Anton Ferdinand and Reo-Coker were both part of the England Under-21 squad to face Norway in a friendly, and, in reality, the World Cup finals were always going to be at least a year too early for them to seriously entertain ideas of making their way into the full team. And despite West Ham's lofty position in the table, it was never going to be easy to win the belief of Eriksson, who preferred to select players from the 'big four' clubs – Chelsea, Manchester United, Liverpool and Arsenal – whose players regularly experienced Champions League football. There was logic in the Swede's thinking: how could he be convinced that a player could compete with the world's best if they weren't at least performing on the highest stage at club level? But whereas it had previously been considered enough just to be playing in the top flight, Eriksson's policy left some players thinking that they had to play for the biggest clubs to be watched regularly and considered for selection.

Full-back Konchesky's exclusion from the squad, following his call-up earlier in the season, made it obvious that Eriksson had not been convinced by him, while fleet-footed winger Etherington needed to produce his best form on a more consistent basis if he was ever going to compete for a place on England's left side. But there was late hope for Ashton, with some members of the media keen for him to make a late surge into the World Cup reckoning – as former Hammer Geoff Hurst had done 30 years earlier – if he could continue the impressive start to his West Ham career.

Ashton scored for the third home game in succession in the 2–2 draw with Everton in early March but that would prove to be his last league goal of the season – as West Ham's focus gradually shifted towards their FA Cup run. Several Premiership games – most notably those at Bolton, at home to Portsmouth and at Middlesbrough – inevitably fell by the wayside as Pardew occasionally rested players to ensure his side's cup efforts were not undermined by the demands of the congested fixtures list. Bolton and Manchester City were successfully overcome to take the Hammers into their first FA Cup semi-final in 15 years, and, with UEFA Cup qualification potentially still available via the league, the team once again staged a comeback when Reo-Coker struck in the final minute to steal a 2–1 win at Wigan.

A third successive game in the north-west took West Ham to Manchester United on a Wednesday evening, but it was a subdued affair, with Pardew appearing not too unhappy with a 1–0 defeat. In fact, the manager admitted he'd been 'quite pleased' his side had remained in the game, although in reality they had never looked like denying the hosts the points after Ruud van Nistelrooy's goal in first-half injury time.

After Sheringham failed to celebrate his 40th birthday with a goal in the 0–0 stalemate with Alan Curbishley's Charlton, West Ham took advantage of a full week without a game by taking the overworked squad of players to Dubai for a low-key training camp. It did not prove to be one of Pardew's best decisions of the season. Indeed, the concept of choosing Dubai as a destination for a spot of 'team building' was seriously flawed, with Benayoun and Katan unable to travel because of Israeli citizens being denied entry into the United Arab Emirates. It would seem that the club had been oblivious of this, but it was decided to send the two excluded players on holiday with their families to Marbella in Spain rather than change the arrangement. Aldridge claimed that the trip had been 'planned in principal from very early in the season', although Pardew suggested that the idea had been generated more recently. 'We just sensed the players were in need of a rest,' he said.

Aldridge's suggestion that the Israelis 'did not wish to travel' ignored the fact they had little choice in the matter, while his claim that they were 'insistent the plans were not altered' failed to convince outsiders that the club had done the right thing. From a public relations point of view, the episode represented an embarrassing own-goal by West Ham, as well as potentially damaging the morale of the two players. Katan certainly didn't appear to be in the best of moods as he sat in Chelsea's media room the following weekend, looking lost and lonely as he pondered whether his one start and half-a-dozen substitute outings to date had merited his move from Israel. As for the Dubai debacle, he remained diplomatic. 'Sometimes the best thing is not to react,' he said.

West Ham's players may have enjoyed their week in the sunshine, but they looked anything but refreshed as they collapsed 4–1 at Stamford Bridge to a Chelsea side reduced to ten men for the majority of the game. Hopes of an unlikely seventh away league success for the Hammers – the bookmakers listed them at 9–1 for the victory – were improved when Collins headed in at the near post to give his side a shock tenth-minute lead. And those prospects looked to have received a considerable boost just seven minutes later when Chelsea midfielder Maniche was sent off for a lunge at full-back Scaloni. That's when things started to go wrong for West Ham – and Pardew appeared to be responsible.

The Hammers had lined up with five men in midfield in a bid to make life as difficult as possible for the Premiership champions. That strategy seemed to be working, but when Chelsea lost a man it was imperative that West Ham exploit their numerical advantage in midfield by pushing Harewood into his usual attacking position. However, Pardew persevered with a cautious approach, and by the time he had made the obvious change Chelsea had seized the initiative by scoring twice through Didier Drogba and Hernán Crespo. Second-half strikes by John Terry and William Gallas meant it was the first time West Ham had conceded four times to a ten-man Premiership side and left Pardew complaining about the lack of 'exuberance' from his team. 'The sending off seemed to inspire Chelsea,' he claimed, 'and certainly seemed to affect us more than it did them.'

If Pardew had enjoyed a rare bad day at the office in terms of his tactical strategy, the performance and result raised further questions about the wisdom of the club's warm-weather training break in Dubai. Ultimately, the manager was forced to concede the travelling might have taken something out of his players. 'I think we flew back a day too late,' he admitted. 'And we will have to examine the merits of the trip because things obviously didn't work out right.'

The failure at Chelsea, who would go on to retain the Premiership title, was in itself no disaster. Newly promoted outfits rarely budgeted to collect points at the very top clubs – it was just a bonus if they did. But the fear was that the nature of the defeat – to a ten-man side after having taken the lead – could demoralise West Ham and potentially damage their chances of success in subsequent games, in both league and cup. Such a worry was dispelled with the home victory against Manchester City the following weekend, with Shaun Newton claiming the game's only goal to lift the Hammers up to seventh in the table. Pardew was fully aware of how vital the victory had been for West Ham within the general scheme of things. 'The win was massive,' he later admitted. 'Our focus had begun to shift towards the FA Cup, and it was difficult to keep the players' minds on the Premiership games as well.'

Both Pardew and coach Peter Grant were desperate for the league form to be maintained, despite the distractions of the FA Cup. The semi-final draw had paired West Ham with Middlesbrough – with both sides knowing victory would guarantee them a place in Europe the following season as a result of Liverpool and Chelsea, the other two sides left in the competition, having booked Champions League spots. In those circumstances, it would not have been unusual to see a team in West Ham's position tail off in terms of Premiership performances. But the management had long targeted a top-half finish, and the

FA Cup became the bait they used to keep their players fully motivated. 'Everybody knows they're playing for their places,' said Grant, although, in reality, the team generally named itself, as most players were fully established in their positions.

It was a measure of their commitment, however, that they continued to perform to their maximum right until the end of the campaign. Harewood's spectacular strike proved enough to see off Middlesbrough at Villa Park on 23 April and take West Ham into their first FA Cup final for 26 years. The team would then win two of their final three league games before heading to Cardiff's Millennium Stadium the following month for the showdown with Liverpool. The 1–0 victory at relegated West Brom – with several enforced team changes – in the penultimate league match might have guaranteed West Ham a top-ten finish in their first season back in the Premiership. But circumstances would dictate that there would be no easing up against Tottenham as the league campaign came to a close in the most dramatic of fashions.

Tottenham had occupied one of the Champions League slots for the lion's share of the season – and knew that victory at Upton Park on 7 May would guarantee them fourth place at the expense of bitter local rivals Arsenal. Quite aside from the issue of bragging rights, Spurs were well aware of the financial significance of winning a place in Europe's elite club competition and the springboard it would provide for future success. They would probably need to beat the Hammers as well, with Arsenal just a point behind them and facing a home encounter with Wigan that looked something of a formality. But many fancied Tottenham to take advantage of West Ham's anticipated preoccupation with the FA Cup, especially when Pardew revealed after his side's victory at West Brom that there was 'no chance' of him naming his first-choice side. Indeed, many managers would never put out their best team in a relatively meaningless game less than a week before playing in a major cup final. But Pardew felt it was important to build momentum ahead of the meeting with Liverpool, and it's to his great credit that he named his strongest possible team against Spurs, with the exception of the injured Ashton and Etherington – who would both return the following weekend – plus Harewood who was rested until the second half. Indeed, Ferdinand, Konchesky and Benayoun were all brought back into the side following their absence at West Brom, with Pardew demanding 'a good performance against our local rivals'.

In many respects, Pardew's team selection for the Tottenham game was a risky strategy – and an unnecessary one. Record signing Ashton had been forced off at West Brom with a hamstring problem and was considered a doubt for the cup final. Etherington, Ferdinand and Benayoun had all picked up knocks in recent weeks, so many bosses would have wrapped up their key players in cotton wool rather than expose them to potential injury in a match that meant far more to the opposition. Tottenham, meanwhile, were sure to lack no commitment as they looked to book a Champions League place in their final game of the season. But Pardew was aware of his responsibilities to the Premier League, knowing how important it was that his men put up a convincing fight to ensure that a vital last-day issue was decided in a legitimate manner. The manager also knew the supporters – whose rivalry with Tottenham was far more intense than it was with Arsenal – would demand everything of the West Ham players to ensure Spurs went home disappointed.

The day itself was to prove more controversial than anybody could ever have anticipated. West Ham first became aware that it was going to be no ordinary occasion when they learned that Tottenham had contacted the Premier League to request that the match be postponed until the following day because of illness. Hammers officials were somewhat surprised by the news, given the golden rule was that the final round of games in any division must be played simultaneously to avoid teams benefiting from knowing other results. If Arsenal drew at home to Wigan, Tottenham would know they needed just a point at West Ham.

More pertinent to West Ham was the fact that any postponement would reduce their preparation time for the following weekend's FA Cup final, giving opponents Liverpool an unfair advantage. West Ham made their feelings known, but the Premier League had no intention of yielding to Tottenham's demands, which resulted from several players feeling sick on the morning of the game. The Spurs squad had stayed overnight at the Marriott Hotel in the docklands Canary Wharf development, but suspicion fell on their Saturday evening meal when around ten members of the squad complained of stomach problems and diarrhoea. It was a sign of the Premier League's sympathy towards Tottenham's plight that they were even prepared to consider a delayed kick-off, although police were prepared to grant a mere two-hour extension because of public-safety concerns.

Because a 5 p.m. start would serve no 'material medical benefit', it was agreed that the game would kick off as scheduled – with the Premier League arguing that Tottenham still had more than enough healthy players to fulfil the fixture. And so the match commenced, with supporters generally unaware of what had taken place. The Spurs line-up certainly gave few indications of selection problems, with just two changes having been made from the previous weekend's game against Bolton – Edgar Davids and Kelly replacing Danny Murphy and Paul Stalteri. Indeed, many of the 'sick' players were preferred to those who made no complaints and managed to see out the whole game, while an apparently fit and healthy Murphy remained on the bench.

Tottenham's performance was also spirited enough to suggest that their problems had been somewhat over-elaborated, despite falling behind early on. The game was just ten minutes old when Carl Fletcher – cementing his FA Cup final place after Hayden Mullins was sent off in the recent home defeat by Liverpool – fired West Ham into the lead with a fine 25-yard drive. Tottenham hit back before half-time, however, when Jermain Defoe marked his first return to Upton Park since his departure in 2004 with a well-placed shot on the turn. When former Spurs striker Sheringham failed to beat Paul Robinson with a weak penalty shortly into the second half, it looked as if West Ham were going to let the visitors off the hook – especially with Arsenal being held at that time by Wigan. But with the Gunners eventually going 4–2 ahead, Benayoun ended Tottenham's season-long hopes with just ten minutes remaining when he accepted Reo-Coker's backheel, switched the ball onto his left foot and fired home the winner.

After the final whistle, Tottenham manager Martin Jol blamed the result on his players being hit by illness, insisting that they were the victims of 'food poisoning'. It didn't take long for the conspiracy theories to be generated. Indeed, Jol appeared to suffer a memory loss when asked for the name of the hotel at which his squad had eaten the previous night, as if realising how unwise it might be to start apportioning responsibility without evidence. He eventually – and somewhat reluctantly – confirmed that Spurs had stayed at the Marriott and eaten from a buffet that included lasagne, but played down suggestions that 'foul play' had been involved.

That didn't stop Tottenham officials from calling in the police to investigate the matter – believing that legal action could possibly be taken even if sabotage was ruled out – while also submitting an appeal to the Premier League to have the 2–1 defeat by West Ham annulled and the game replayed. Spurs chief

Daniel Levy even sought the backing of his fellow top-flight chairmen, but his arguments fell on deaf ears as the Premier League insisted that there were no grounds for a replay.

It was never made clear when exactly West Ham were supposed to make themselves available for another game, but it would've had to have been some time after the FA Cup final the following week. It was at this point that the Health Protection Agency – working in conjunction with environmental inspectors from the Tower Hamlets council – confirmed that Spurs had not suffered from an attack of food poisoning at all but a form of gastroenteritis that had spread among the players. In other words, they had been hit by nothing more serious than a virus.

The game against Spurs had seen defender Gabbidon presented with the Hammer of the Year trophy. West Ham may have had long-standing traditions for producing free-flowing football but that never stopped the club's supporters from recognising the merits of great defensive work – with the likes of Steve Potts, Julian Dicks, Rio Ferdinand and Sebastien Schemmel all being successful in the end-of-season poll since the early 1990s. Gabbidon admitted he was 'a bit surprised' by how well things had progressed for the team over the previous nine months. 'We've all been so hungry to prove ourselves in the Premiership,' he said, 'and I think we've done that.'

Centre-half partner Ferdinand's contribution to West Ham's success during his first top-flight campaign was acknowledged in his Premiership Player of the Month award for January and his nomination for the PFA Young Player of the Year trophy, ultimately claimed by Manchester United's England striker Wayne Rooney. Ferdinand's hopes of representing his country at any level during the summer died when the Under-21s failed to qualify for the 2006 European Championship, while teammate Reo-Coker's fine season was recognised with a place on the standby list for Eriksson's full World Cup squad, only for the midfielder to withdraw with a persistent back problem.

And although Mourinho was named the Barclays Premiership Manager of the Year for leading Chelsea to back-to-back title successes, the achievements of West Ham boss Pardew – who claimed the Manager of the Month award in February – were acknowledged by Terry Venables for 'taking a team I thought would be relegated into Europe'. The former England coach described the Hammers' campaign as 'the major success story of the season' – a full week before the FA Cup final. The events in Cardiff on 13 May would do little to alter his opinion.

# 4

## 'THE FIRST TROPHY IS ALWAYS THE HARDEST TO WIN'

WEST HAM United might not have won the FA Cup in 2006, but they achieved far more than any straightforward trophy triumph would have represented – that would surely have been the view of Ron Greenwood had he lived long enough to witness the club's journey to the Millennium Stadium. The former West Ham and England manager, who claimed he would much prefer to see his teams 'lose an entertaining game 5–4 than win a dreary one 1–0', passed away on 8 February 2006 at the age of 84 and was sadly denied the chance of seeing the Hammers play in their first FA Cup final for 26 years.

Greenwood was the man who was famously photographed with the trophy on his lap at Tottenham Court Road underground station in 1964 – eleven years before his successor John Lyall enjoyed the first of his two FA Cup glories. When a heart attack tragically claimed the life of 66-year-old Lyall, just two months after the death of his close friend and mentor, it was clear that it was West Ham's destiny to head all the way to the final of the cup competition in which the two men had enjoyed such special success.

Thoughts of West Ham reaching the FA Cup final would have been considered far too ambitious when travelling to Norwich for the third-round game on 7 January. West Ham had lost their last three games – against Wigan, Charlton and Chelsea – and had collected just one league point from the last fifteen available. The Canaries had returned to the Championship following their brief flirtation with the Premiership the previous season, but West Ham's cup record against lower-league teams over the years left plenty to be desired, and they hadn't won at Carrow Road since 1973.

The chances of an upset, however, were greatly reduced when it was confirmed that Dean Ashton had joined injured Norwich strike-partner Darren Huckerby on the sidelines. Hayden Mullins duly eased any fears when he struck inside six minutes to put the Hammers on course for victory. Bobby Zamora then took full advantage of a mistake from goalkeeper Robert Green to nod West Ham 2–0 ahead shortly into the second half before Paul McVeigh gave Norwich late hope from the penalty spot.

Alan Pardew was unhappy his side had made life more difficult for themselves in the final 20 minutes following a needless handball from defender James Collins, but as he admitted, 'We don't do things comfortably at West Ham.' Yet the manager was pleased to see his men return to winning ways for the first time in nearly four weeks and had always considered the game pivotal to which direction the Hammers would head during the second half of the campaign. 'This game could determine whether a good season can become a great season,' he told his players in the build-up, believing a decent cup run was a 'realistic target' and would help them to rediscover their league form.

By the time the fourth-round tie at home to Blackburn Rovers came around towards the end of the month, West Ham had completed a hat-trick of 2–1 victories and looked to be very much back on course following their mid-season blip. The game promised no shortage of action, with the two league encounters between the sides producing nine goals – and supporters had to wait no longer than thirty seconds for David Bentley to put Rovers ahead with the day's quickest opener. The visitors were in generous mood, however, with Zurab Khizanishvili conceding a penalty – audaciously chipped home by Teddy Sheringham – and later scoring an own-goal after Matthew Etherington had put the Hammers 2–1 up. Lucas Neill reduced the arrears with a fine effort before Zamora sealed West Ham's 4–2 win.

Blackburn manager Mark Hughes needed no reminding of Sheringham's enduring talents, as the veteran striker had also scored in West Ham's 3–1 home victory on the opening day of the league season. Hughes had failed in his attempts to persuade the Hammers to part with the former England man the previous year, and Pardew was under no illusions as to how important the 39 year old was to the club – both on and off the pitch. 'Teddy has been fantastic, and we want him to stay next season. Maybe we can extend his role a bit onto the coaching side,' he said.

Sheringham was desperate to extend his Upton Park contract, which was set to expire in the summer, but he was less enthusiastic about taking on coaching responsibilities, believing the added burden would undermine his efforts to keep playing for as long as possible. And while his chances of starting games had diminished following Ashton's £7 million arrival from Norwich, the striker was content enough to resist joining former club Tottenham for a third time when they made an approach during the January transfer window. 'The manager made it clear he wanted me to stay, and I'm getting satisfaction here,' he said. In March, Sheringham duly signed a new one-year contract for the 2006–07 season, with Pardew stating, 'It's important for our young players that we have good senior professionals at the club, and Teddy has always set the right example.'

The Sheringham-inspired FA Cup win against Blackburn served a warning to West Ham that their support could not be taken for granted. The fourth-round game had attracted a crowd of just 23,700 – nearly 10,000 down on the league visit of Rovers at the start of the season and the lowest Upton Park attendance for an FA Cup tie involving fellow top-flight opposition since 1989. Season-ticket holders, asked to pay for cup tickets, were offered discounts of up to 20 per cent for admission, but the disappointing turnout was a sign of the times, with many fans using such games to show disapproval of the escalating costs of following their team. The low-key atmosphere did little to inspire the players in the early part of the game as they made a slow start, and Pardew was forced to admit, 'The crowd was not as big as usual and maybe that played a part.'

Less than a fortnight later, West Ham supporters were in mourning when it was confirmed that former boss Greenwood had died at his Sudbury home following a long illness. Having left Arsenal to succeed the ousted Ted Fenton in 1961, Ron led the Hammers to FA Cup glory against Preston North End before surpassing that achievement a year later in the European Cup Winners' Cup. West Ham's 2–0 win against TSV Munich 1860 in the Wembley final, courtesy of two Alan Sealey goals, was considered by many people to be the greatest game ever seen under the Twin Towers and served notice that the manager's progressive philosophies – largely influenced by the Continentals – were ready to take on the world. Indeed, his role in England's 1966 World Cup success cannot be underestimated, with his development of players such as Bobby Moore, Geoff Hurst and Martin Peters at Upton Park having a major influence on events at international level.

The win-at-all-costs ideology, so prevalent in the modern game, would have been considered anathema to Greenwood, who believed in discipline, dignity and decency. Former West Ham utility man John McDowell continues to recall the time he was admonished by his manager for conceding a penalty rather than allowing the opposition to score. The spot-kick was missed, and the Hammers won the game, but McDowell was warned his future at the club was in jeopardy. 'It's not the way we play football at West Ham,' lectured Greenwood.

The Hammers' league form was typically erratic under Greenwood's stewardship, but they succeeded in equalling their best-ever top-flight finish of sixth in 1973. And his move 'upstairs' to the position of general manager the following year – as he handed the first-team reins over to his understudy Lyall – was further evidence of his advanced thinking, showing great vision in creating a 'director of football' type of role that only became commonplace some 30 years later. As England manager, Greenwood guided his country to the 1982 World Cup finals – following a 12-year absence and the first they had played their way to since 1962 – but they failed to progress beyond the second group stage despite remaining unbeaten. Ron duly stepped down at the end of the tournament after five years in the post and announced his retirement from the game.

'He was a fine and tender man,' said former player Brian Dear, who joined the Upton Park crowd in paying their respects to Greenwood in a minute's silence before West Ham played Birmingham in a league game on 13 February. Ron would have approved of the football played as the Hammers secured a 3–0 win ahead of their FA Cup fifth-round trip to Bolton the following Saturday. It was an unappetising draw for West Ham, who had lost their last three visits to the Reebok Stadium by a 1–0 scoreline – including a Carling Cup third-round game earlier in the season – and could expect another tough test from a Wanderers side that played an unattractive but effective brand of percentage football. The victory against Birmingham took West Ham's winning run to a club-record-equalling seven games, but few of the five thousand travelling supporters seriously believed that figure would become eight – especially with Bolton having lost just one of their sixteen home games in all competitions that season.

Bolton manager Sam Allardyce certainly fancied his side's chances against a team he seemed to have little time for. He had ridiculed Yossi Benayoun's decision to sign for West Ham instead of Wanderers at the beginning of the season and paid little credit to the stylish play that bore little resemblance to his own team's bludgeon-them-into-submission approach. But he was left disappointed after the Hammers displayed all the dogged characteristics usually associated with Bolton to hold on for a 0–0 draw. Ashton was surprisingly wasteful when a good first-half chance presented itself in his first FA Cup appearance for his new club, while Bolton's Stelios Giannakopoulos was at the centre of two moments of controversy that left Allardyce complaining afterwards. The Greek midfielder first tumbled with great histrionics – after sensing minimal contact from Lionel Scaloni – in a bid to win a penalty and then saw a goal ruled out for offside. 'We should have had a penalty, but because Stelios made a meal of it and went to ground too theatrically he made the referee's mind up not to give it,' said Allardyce.

From West Ham's point of view, it was a case of mission accomplished, despite failing to create a club record of eight successive victories. 'We set our stall out to make sure we were strong defensively,' said Pardew as he reflected on a resilient performance from his side. But Allardyce hadn't finished lamenting his side's misfortune, insisting the replay at Upton Park – pencilled in for 7 March – would have to be pushed back because it would take place just two days before a UEFA Cup last-sixteen game. Bolton had yet to qualify for that stage and, with them needing to win in Marseille, few thought they would do so. But the FA Cup game was rescheduled for 15 March regardless – needlessly so, with Bolton crashing out of Europe as expected – and West Ham were forced to suffer their own fixture compression that would significantly reduce their chances of success while impacting on league results.

The three-and-a-half-week wait for the replay meant West Ham would have to return to the Reebok for a league encounter just days before meeting Bolton for the fifth time that season. Pardew was faced with a serious dilemma in terms of how to utilise his squad. Having worked so hard to keep the Hammers in the top half of the league, he was reluctant to throw away points but knew that some form of squad rotation would be required if his team was going to be at its best for the FA Cup. The manager was also painfully aware that if his men did get past Bolton in midweek, they would then have to play their sixth-round tie – at Manchester City – as early as the following Monday, just two days after a home league game against Portsmouth.

In that context, it was little surprise that Pardew made several changes for the league game at Bolton, dropping Ashton, Benayoun and Marlon Harewood to the substitutes' bench and leaving Nigel Reo-Coker out altogether. Perhaps more dangerously, he opted to hand Elliott Ward his first ever Premiership start in defence and move Anton Ferdinand into an unfamiliar midfield position. Bolton duly took full advantage of the weakened side, surging into a three-goal lead before the break with two goals by Stelios and another from Gary Speed. Sheringham pulled one back late on, but Henrik Pedersen wrapped up a 4–1 win for the hosts that ended West Ham's unbeaten run of nine games and condemned them to their heaviest defeat of the season. It hardly appeared to be the greatest of psychological boosts ahead of the fifth-round replay, but Pardew was unrepentant about his line-up decisions – if apologetic about the display. 'With three big games this week, I obviously needed to rest a few players,' he said. 'I thought the changes would make us stronger defensively, but we looked disorganised, and I have to take responsibility for that.'

Bolton boss Allardyce was left smirking in the Reebok corridors after the game. 'We'll smack their backsides again in the week,' he was heard to have said as he looked ahead to the following game. However, it was Bolton's faces rather than West Ham's backsides that were left reddened at Upton Park when defender Nicky Hunt's attempted clearance smashed in off floored goalkeeper Jussi Jääskeläinen to hand the hosts an early lead. But Wanderers hit back on the half-hour mark with a swerving Kevin Davies shot that deceived goalkeeper Shaka Hislop. Both sides worked hard to gain the upper hand but, as the game went into extra time, it was anybody's guess as to who would land the knockout punch. Harewood duly seized the moment, hooking in from Benayoun's right-wing cross in the 96th minute to seal the 2–1 win.

West Ham had often been considered a soft touch over the years when it came to physical battles. But the cup success against Bolton suggested the current team had attributes it would be dangerous to underestimate, and Pardew was fully aware of the test they had survived. 'From a physical point of view, that was the hardest game we'd had all season,' he later said.

As the dust settled, Allardyce insisted that Harewood had been offside in the build-up to West Ham's opening goal. And he showed little grace or diplomacy when insisting that Manchester City would win the sixth-round clash the following week. Next up for West Ham, however, was the game against struggling Portsmouth as former manager Harry Redknapp made his first return to Upton Park following his sacking five years earlier. Pompey had lost their last nine away games in the Premiership, but they realised that there was no better time to play West Ham than just two days before an FA Cup quarter-final – and three days after they had gone to extra time. This time Pardew made six changes to his starting line-up, omitting Hislop, Mullins, Benayoun, Ashton, Harewood and Etherington and deploying fringe defensive players such as Christian Dailly and Clive Clarke in midfield, while goalkeeper Jimmy Walker made his first outing since the play-off final the previous season. The back four may have been the manager's first choice, but the lack of initiative in front of them invited Portsmouth to go on the attack, and they duly strolled to an emphatic 4–2 success.

Pardew's post-match claim that he would 'take no pleasure if we win on Monday night after that' was unconvincing, although there's no doubt he was embarrassed by his team's lacklustre display. He stormed into the players' dressing-room and told them their performance had not been good enough. As far as he was concerned, the players coming into the side were capable of much better, while the regulars had let their focus drop ahead of the trip to City. Pompey boss Redknapp was understandably delighted to grab a second successive win that helped launch his side's successful battle against relegation. But he had great sympathy for West Ham, describing the scheduling for the FA Cup sixth-round game as 'scandalous'. He even found a surprise ally in West Brom manager Bryan Robson – whose men were eventually relegated instead of Portsmouth – who admitted that Pardew had no choice but to prioritise the cup game and rest players. Birmingham City, recently beaten 3–0 at Upton Park and who would also suffer the drop, were furious with the FA for allowing the quarter-final games to be spread over four weekdays for television purposes.

The situation was a result of the Premiership season ending a week early to give England coach Sven-Göran Eriksson more preparation time ahead of the World Cup finals in Germany. Once it became known that all four sixth-round games would be played on different days, it was inevitable that the top clubs involved – namely Chelsea and Liverpool – would be given the preferred Tuesday and Wednesday slots. West Ham supporters considered it somewhat typical that they should be handed the thin end of the wedge by having to travel up to Manchester on a Monday, while Pardew was as unhappy as City boss Stuart Pearce that such an important game would be played in such hasty circumstances. 'The build-up to a quarter-final game should be an exciting time but that has been robbed from everybody,' he complained. 'Both teams will have had no preparation for the game.'

The FA responded to criticism by insisting that the decision to play the quarter-finals in midweek had been taken the previous year after all Premiership clubs had been consulted on the matter. But it's unclear whether the four-day scheduling was made known, while there was no explanation as to why the teams playing on the Monday could not have postponed their preceding league fixtures. There was no reason why West Ham's game against Portsmouth could not have been rescheduled for the first week of April when both teams had a free week. Given that games were regularly called off just hours before kick-off because of poor weather, it seemed ridiculous that it couldn't happen with two days' notice.

West Ham suffered some mild criticism in the media for making Portsmouth's life so comfortable at Upton Park that weekend. But it went almost unnoticed that Manchester City had made even more team changes – eight to be precise – for their 1–0 home defeat by Wigan at the same time. 'City made more changes than we did, but we took the brunt of the criticism,' Pardew later complained. 'In circumstances like that, you have to protect your team and use your squad. What the result suggested was that our squad wasn't good enough.'

If one performance justified West Ham's club-record outlay on striker Ashton, it was at the City of Manchester Stadium on the evening of 20 March. The twenty-two year old scored his first two FA Cup goals for West Ham to take his tally to five in six starts for the club following his arrival in January. First, he produced a powerful left-foot finish inside the near post – after an intricate move involving Etherington and Reo-Coker – to break the deadlock just before half-time. He was then on hand to tap home West Ham's controversial second later in the game as Reo-Coker and Benayoun pulled apart the home defence. Ashton's brace saw Pardew comparing him to Hammers legend Hurst, describing the two efforts as 'proper striker's goals'.

Kiki Musampa's late volley for City ensured a tense finish, but West Ham held on for a deserved 2–1 win, although fortune appeared to favour them when it mattered. The home side, who wasted a great early chance when Musampa fired over and then lost defender Stephen Jordan to injury, faced an uphill battle when Sun Jihai was sent off in the 56th minute for swinging out at Etherington. The touchline spat seemed innocuous at the time, but referee Howard Webb deemed the China international guilty of violent conduct and brandished the red card.

It was the peculiar – some would say comical – nature of West Ham's second goal that suggested it might just be their night. Dailly, given the nod at right-back ahead of the stuttering Scaloni, whose defensive qualities were being increasingly questioned by his manager, surged down the flank only to collapse in a heap when trying to cross. City had the first opportunity to put the ball out of play to allow the distressed Dailly to receive treatment, yet they played on and West Ham regained possession. At that point, the home supporters started to jeer as the visiting players went back on the attack. City then won the ball back and pressed forward, prompting boos from Hammers fans, while both managers frantically waved their arms about as if directing air traffic. Meanwhile, Dailly remained face down on the turf and was clearly suffering from his injury. At this point, the pendulum swung in West Ham's direction again, and they brought play to a halt in the best way possible – by slamming the ball into the net. Reo-Coker fed Benayoun, who crossed for Ashton to score his second goal of the night. The home supporters were furious, believing West Ham had shown a lack of sportsmanship, although it couldn't be denied their own team had failed to stop play as well. City manager Pearce was left remonstrating on the touchline as his rival tried to calm him down. 'Stuart was cool about it,' said Pardew later. 'It was just one of those weird incidents, and nobody was at fault. Both sides should have kicked the ball out, but it somehow ended up in the back of the net.'

As the West Ham celebrations died down, Dailly was stretched off with a torn hamstring that would keep him out of action for more than a month, and Pearce was left to rue the fact that he'd dropped out of the race to sign match-winner Ashton earlier in the year. Pardew surprised many people when he failed to attend the press conference after the game, allowing assistant Peter Grant to face the media instead. Grant had played a major role behind the scenes since his arrival in 2004, and some observers saw this as an opportunity for the first-team coach to be recognised for his input. Yet there was also truth in the suspicion that an irritated Pardew had decided to shun journalists as a result of the disparaging coverage following the home defeat by Portsmouth. 'We had a wee bit of criticism at the weekend which we thought was undue,' said Grant tellingly.

While Ashton was guaranteed the headlines this time around, it was defender Collins who made a vital contribution while filling in for the injured Ferdinand. 'If players produce performances like that, it's going to be very difficult to leave them out,' said Grant after the game, throwing down the gauntlet for the rest of the squad to remain on their toes if they wanted to play in the semi-final.

West Ham's place in the last four of the FA Cup fully vindicated Pardew's selection decisions of the previous few weeks. 'Of course I protected players,' he said. 'As manager of

West Ham, I have to ask myself what I'm going to win. We're never going to win the Premier League, but we can win the FA Cup, so of course I prioritised. I've got to be honest: sixth place in the league doesn't enthral me as much as winning a trophy.'

At a time when so many club managers had shown contempt towards the cup competitions in favour of trying to stay in the Premiership, it was just what the West Ham supporters wanted to hear. Whether Pardew's position would have been different had his team been struggling near the foot of the table is an intriguing question. Indeed, it must be remembered that he selected a much-weakened side in the Carling Cup defeat at Bolton earlier in the season when top-flight safety was less of a formality. But given the fixture congestion that Pardew's team faced in March, the manager had little alternative but to take the approach he did.

West Ham supporters had further reason to celebrate when the draw for the semi-finals was made later in the week. With Liverpool and Chelsea disposing of Birmingham and Newcastle respectively in their sixth-round ties, the Hammers were desperate to avoid the two best sides left in the competition and meet either Middlesbrough or Charlton, whose game in London had gone to a replay. Their prayers were answered when it was confirmed that the big two had failed to avoid each other and West Ham had got the draw they wanted. The greatest significance of the draw was not that the Hammers had the easiest-looking game on paper, but that it guaranteed the winners of the semi-final tie a UEFA Cup place because of Chelsea and Liverpool heading towards the Champions League.

West Ham would have to wait another fortnight to learn who their opponents would be, giving their supporters plenty of time to debate who they would prefer to meet. The general view was that Charlton would provide the more attractive opposition, with the media relishing the opportunity to exploit manager

Alan Curbishley's past links with the Hammers. Meeting them would also increase the prospects of an all-London final. Boro, like Charlton, were in the bottom half of the Premiership table but were making fantastic progress in the UEFA Cup, which could work in West Ham's favour. Pardew at least had the opportunity to do his homework either way, with league fixtures against both outfits to be played before the semi-final on 23 April. Charlton proved they could blunt the West Ham attack in a goalless draw at Upton Park, but their defence collapsed at Middlesbrough as they crashed out of the FA Cup with a 4–2 defeat. And in a repeat of the fifth-round situation with Bolton, the Hammers would meet Boro in a league encounter less than a week before their semi-final clash at Villa Park.

Both sides made changes for the precursor at the Riverside Stadium on a bank-holiday Monday, but, with Middlesbrough halfway through a two-legged UEFA Cup semi-final tussle with Steaua Bucharest, Pardew was taken aback when key strikers Mark Viduka and Jimmy Floyd Hasselbaink lined up against his men. 'That shocked me,' he later admitted. 'But it was a phoney war in terms of the FA Cup, because there was always going to be a different level of focus in the semi-final.' Privately, however, Pardew used the disappointing 2–0 defeat – brought about by a Hasselbaink strike and a soft penalty converted by Massimo Maccarone – to wind up his troops, although they had no shortage of reasons to produce a better display the following weekend.

When former manager Lyall's death on Tuesday, 18 April 2006 was confirmed, it changed the whole perspective of the semi-final against Middlesbrough. For West Ham supporters, it gave them a chance to pay very public homage to a man that – like Greenwood before him – had done so much to shape the character of the club. For Pardew, it was an opportunity to prove he was capable of following in their footsteps – at least in terms of taking the Hammers to an FA Cup final. Lyall had accomplished that feat twice in his fifteen years as West Ham manager, initially at the end of his first season in charge in 1975 and again just five years later. The second of the two triumphs was by far the greater achievement, with the Hammers having to take on FA Cup holders Arsenal in the final as a Second Division team. Indeed, they remained the last club outside the top flight to lift the trophy.

That success was achieved thanks to Lyall's brilliant tactical strategy of deploying David Cross as a lone striker with partner Stuart Pearson dropping deep in a withdrawn role – a commonplace idea in the modern game but scarce enough in 1980 to leave the Gunners totally perplexed. Trevor Brooking's early header won the match as Lyall established himself as one of the best managers of the time, having also led the club to the European Cup Winners' Cup final in 1976. Lyall would also take the Hammers to the final of the 1981 League Cup – in which they took Liverpool to a replay – and return them to the top flight in the same year. In 1986, West Ham explored new territory when they challenged for the league title until the final weekend of the season before finishing third.

When the club was relegated just three years later, West Ham attracted huge criticism for dispensing with the services of an honest man who had remained loyal for 34 years after joining straight from school. He led Ipswich into the Premiership in 1992 but retired a couple of years later and gradually distanced himself from the game. His legacy at West Ham lives on, though, with his appointment of Tony Carr as youth coach in 1980 yielding huge dividends over the next three decades as the club's academy produced talents such as Tony Cottee, Paul Ince, Rio Ferdinand and Joe Cole, among a host of others.

Pardew was pleased the Hammers had a high-profile game that weekend to highlight how much both Lyall and Greenwood had meant to the club. But he was also concerned that the demands of the occasion could prove too much for his players. 'We were desperate to win the semi-final for John and Ron's families, because the two men did so much to build the football beliefs of the club,' he said. 'But the players were under enough pressure to deliver for the fans.'

With Liverpool beating Chelsea 2–1 in the other semi-final at Old Trafford the previous day, West Ham knew they would be facing the reigning European champions in Cardiff if they could get past Middlesbrough. Pardew realised that his men had their work cut out, however, with Steve McClaren's side proving their expertise on such occasions with the fact that this was their 24th cup outing of the season. But he suspected that tiredness from those endeavours could undermine Boro's efforts, especially late in the game, while the second UEFA Cup meeting with Steaua four days later might also prove a distraction for the Teessiders.

The 'cauldron of noise' that Pardew had demanded from his supporters came somewhat prematurely when the planned minute's silence for Lyall before kick-off evolved into a well-meaning chant of the former manager's name. But it was Pardew's name they were singing at the end of a tense and emotional game after the West Ham boss had masterminded yet another great cup triumph. Not that the match started well for the Hammers, with Middlesbrough enjoying far the better of the first period, although they suffered a setback just before half-time when goalkeeper Mark Schwarzer was forced off with a fractured cheekbone following a collision with Ashton.

Middlesbrough had beaten the Hammers with a 4–4–2 formation in the league six days earlier, but McClaren had elected to play three at the back and deploy five in midfield for the cup meeting. His strategy appeared to get the better of West Ham in the first half, and Pardew was tempted to adapt his side's 4–4–2 line-up. Before the game, his only dilemma had been where to utilise the fit-again Ferdinand, opting to bring him in at right-back to avoid having to drop centre-half Collins, who had performed so impressively in the previous round. But now he was torn between making radical changes to address Boro's midfield superiority and gambling on his original game plan coming good in the second period. At the break, he sat his players down and said, 'Their system is dictating to ours, but it doesn't have to be that way.'

Retaining the system but ordering his full-backs to push up further, Pardew's faith in his players began to reap its rewards as West Ham started to impose themselves on the match. Ashton saw a looping header hit the bar, Reo-Coker fired just wide and then came the match-winner with only 12 minutes remaining. Ashton headed Ferdinand's long ball forward, and Harewood held off defender Gareth Southgate to produce a venomous shot that left substitute goalkeeper Brad Jones with no chance. The West Ham striker celebrated his 16th goal of the season by ripping off his shirt and hurling it to the ground, while his manager embarrassed himself with a comical jig in front of his delirious supporters. Hearts were then in mouths as Middlesbrough produced a late flourish, never more so than when defender Chris Riggott spurned a golden opportunity in injury time.

But West Ham survived, and Pardew took great satisfaction from knowing he'd beaten three bosses – Allardyce, Pearce and McClaren – who were in the running to replace Eriksson as England manager. 'The easiest thing is to change tactics when things aren't going well, but sometimes the bravest thing is to stick with what you've got,' he reflected. 'We played to our strengths and banged into gear at the crucial time.' The post-match celebrations were the kind usually reserved for trophy-winning occasions, but, in many respects, the game had represented a cup final with a place in Europe the prize. 'We knew what was at stake,' he said, while remaining adamant that West Ham fully deserved to be heading to Cardiff. 'We've beaten four Premiership sides, and every one of them brought a sigh of disappointment when they came out of the hat. They were awful draws, and we really have earned the right to be there.'

By strange coincidence, West Ham's next league match – just three days after the semi-final – was against their FA Cup final opponents Liverpool. The supporters were understandably buoyant, and it was considered appropriate to pay tribute to Lyall with a minute's applause in the first game back at Upton Park following his death. Hopes that West Ham could gain a vital psychological boost for the final, however, were shattered as French striker Djibril Cissé scored either side of a Reo-Coker tap-in to secure a narrow victory for the visitors.

But the result paled into insignificance when Hammers midfielder Mullins was sent off – along with Liverpool's Luis García – with just eight minutes of the game remaining. It was a mild confrontation between the two players, but, with García throwing himself to the ground claiming a facial injury, referee Webb – yes, him again – felt obliged to show both men the red card. Mullins had indeed caught García with his hand, but without the amateur dramatics from the Spanish midfielder it's likely they would have both escaped with a booking. Instead, they were handed three-match bans for violent conduct and could forget about playing in the FA Cup final.

It was a cruel blow for Mullins, who had recovered from an erratic start to his West Ham career to become one of the team's most-improved and important players. He may have lacked García's star quality, but it was arguable that he was more central to West Ham's general play than the Spaniard to Liverpool's. An FA Cup final appearance was probably a once-in-a-lifetime opportunity for him, whereas García stood far more chance of winning silverware with the Reds. Pardew's calls for 'clemency'

– supported by rival manager Rafael Benítez – were more in hope than expectation, however, and both players were ruled out of the big occasion on 13 May.

Pardew's planning and preparation for the meeting with Liverpool at the Millennium Stadium – West Ham's third visit to the venue in three seasons – was meticulous. The manager believed that breaking Liverpool's offside trap would be the key to victory and worked particularly hard in training on ways to get behind their defence. The main ploy was for Harewood to exploit space around centre-half Sami Hyypiä, which would be created by tempting full-back John Arne Riise out of position. Pardew also felt his side could take advantage of Liverpool's zonal-marking system at set-pieces and developed a series of well-rehearsed moves ahead of the game.

Pardew also knew his team would need to nullify the threat of Steven Gerrard. The West Ham manager was of the opinion that the Liverpool skipper's right foot was his strongest weapon, so his plan was to pressurise him onto his left-hand side wherever possible. That was if the England midfielder was fit to play, however, because Pardew had been privately warned that Gerrard was allegedly nursing a small groin problem that few knew about. It was unlikely to jeopardise his place in the team, but the story made its way back to the West Ham manager through a source that claimed to have spoken to Liverpool striker Fernando Morientes, who didn't expect to play in the final and was set to leave the club. Pardew was also advised that Benítez was likely to play around with his formation and line-up – not that this was a revelation given the Spanish manager's habit of rotating his squad and adapting the team's system.

Come the last few days before the final, Pardew's biggest concern was establishing whether playmaker Xabi Alonso would recover to face his men after damaging an ankle in a game at Portsmouth. The West Ham boss was compiling a highly technical presentation for his players three days before the game, and keeping Alonso quiet was a key part of his strategy. Doubts about the Spaniard's participation created an uncertainty for Pardew, who expected the midfielder to play but hoped to use his possible absence to galvanise his troops.

West Ham had their own injury concerns with striker Ashton having suffered a hamstring problem at West Brom in the penultimate league game and winger Etherington struggling with an ankle knock. Pardew was upbeat, though, believing the 2–1 win against Tottenham in the final league game of the season was evidence that his side's energy levels were peaking at the right time – with the much-criticised break in Dubai a month earlier now paying dividends. The West Ham manager also consciously used the media – giving them the material they wanted – by emphasising his team's role as underdogs and Liverpool's need to avoid failure. Meanwhile, he challenged his side to end the sequence of the recognised big four of Manchester United, Liverpool, Chelsea and Arsenal being the only clubs to win the FA Cup in the previous ten years. 'We have an opportunity to stem the tide,' he declared.

West Ham were listed at 9–2 to win the trophy in ninety minutes – incredibly generous odds given that just six league places separated the two sides in the Premiership table. But Liverpool had won 11 games in succession and still had the European Cup in their trophy cabinet, while the Hammers were a newly promoted club whose last FA Cup final success was in 1980. The Reds had also just completed the league double over Pardew's men, but West Ham had a habit of avenging Premiership defeats by winning FA Cup games, as Blackburn, Bolton, Manchester City and Middlesbrough could testify.

The match itself was magnificent. Both managers were able to name their preferred line-ups – save for the suspended Mullins and García – while Pardew decided that Scaloni and Ferdinand should remain in their more familiar positions. For many supporters, the game had a somewhat surreal quality, not least when West Ham raced into a two-goal lead within the opening half an hour. After 21 minutes, Ashton released Scaloni on the right, and when the Argentinian drilled in his cross Liverpool defender Jamie Carragher could only run the ball into his own net. Just seven minutes later, the Hammers doubled the lead when Reds goalkeeper José Reina – whose handling had been questioned by Pardew behind closed doors – fumbled an Etherington shot and Ashton was on hand to bundle the ball over the line.

West Ham knew there was too much football to be played to start taking anything for granted. Liverpool had proven they could never be written off in the most amazing style the previous year when they recovered from a three-goal half-time deficit against AC Milan to draw 3–3 and win the Champions League trophy on penalties. Could they stage yet another remarkable comeback? They needed to hit back quickly – and they duly did so within four minutes when the unmarked Cissé volleyed past Hislop following Gerrard's long ball into the box.

At that stage, West Ham knew that they couldn't afford to relinquish the lead before the half-time break, and it is to their credit that they continued to take the game to Liverpool. Free of the tension that surrounded their must-win play-off final against Preston 12 months earlier, the Hammers were able to reproduce their traditional free-flowing football in the knowledge that this was an occasion to be enjoyed. And Pardew was happy to see his side return to the dressing-room at half-time with their one-goal advantage intact.

Harewood and Benayoun were both denied by Reina just after the restart, and it was Gerrard who brought Liverpool level on 54 minutes, smashing home from 15 yards after Peter Crouch had nodded down Alonso's free-kick. With a two-goal lead having evaporated, West Ham would surely struggle to contain a side that now had the momentum firmly in their favour. But they had other ideas, and they regained the lead in bizarre fashion just past the hour mark when full-back Paul Konchesky's cross sailed over Reina into the far corner of the net.

All three of West Ham's goals had come in fortuitous fashion, prompting the suspicion that maybe it was their destiny to lift the FA Cup in memory of their two most treasured former managers. But this was a day when all the scripts – plus much of Pardew's game plan – were being torn up and rewritten, and when the match moved into the final two minutes Hammers fans feared there was perhaps one last twist in the tale. Scaloni planned to kill some valuable time by 'sportingly' knocking the ball out of play when Cissé pulled up with cramp. But when play resumed, Scaloni's rushed clearance simply returned possession to Liverpool, and, with ninety minutes and ten seconds on the clock, Gerrard produced a right-foot, thirty-yard thunderbolt that exploded into the net to make it 3–3 and stun the entire stadium.

At that moment, West Ham supporters knew an FA Cup final victory just wasn't meant to be. If confirmation was needed, it came in the final moments of extra time when Reina tipped Reo-Coker's header onto the woodwork only for the injured Harewood – very much a passenger after being caught by Gerrard – to agonisingly miscue the loose ball wide. Few fancied the Hammers when it came to the penalty shoot-out, believing that Liverpool's greater experience of the big occasion would make it easier for them to hold their nerve. And so it proved. Although substitute Sheringham gave his team hope when making it one apiece, Zamora, Konchesky and Ferdinand all failed to beat Reina as Liverpool claimed a 3–1 triumph thanks to Dietmar Hamann, Gerrard and Riise's successful spot-kicks. It had been an incredible afternoon, but after two-and-a-half hours of sensational drama it was suddenly all over – and West Ham were left empty-handed.

Gerrard was understandably showered with superlatives following his two spectacular strikes. Some newspapers dubbed the match the 'Gerrard final', and the right foot that Pardew had been so fearful of certainly proved to be his side's undoing. Reina also received huge credit for the late heroics that atoned for his earlier misjudgements. But while Liverpool marched off with the trophy, it was West Ham who won thousands of new friends for helping to produce one of the most entertaining and thrilling cup finals of all time. Only once since 1953 had an FA Cup final produced six goals, although on this occasion the Hammers would obviously have preferred the scoring to cease at five.

West Ham led for a total of 59 minutes and were never behind in the game itself. Many experts considered them the better side on the day, with Ashton, Benayoun and Gabbidon singled out for their fine displays. And Greenwood and Lyall would surely have been immensely proud of a performance that exemplified all the good things associated with the club's famous footballing philosophies.

Inevitably, Pardew was bitterly disappointed to see the trophy slip from his players' grasp with just a few minutes of injury time to be played. 'I felt comfortable towards the end of normal time and thought we'd won the game,' he said, although it wasn't a feeling shared by Peter Grant alongside him. 'Even when we were 2–0 up, I knew we didn't have the players to dictate the game,' he said. 'As a boxer we were putting our jabs in, but we'd have needed to knock the opposition out, because we never had the control. Gerrard could hardly move his legs at the end of normal time, and that's why he was so deep when the ball came to him for his second equaliser. It's disappointing not to have won the game, but the drama we helped produce is what everybody wants on cup final day.'

Pardew insisted that 'both teams were winners' in what was 'a fantastic spectacle for English football'. And he was at pains to stress that the FA Cup final heartbreak was not the end of the road but just the start of a journey as West Ham looked to establish themselves as a club that could compete with the best. 'The first trophy is always the hardest to win, but this team will come back,' he said. 'The next time we're in that position we'll be better placed to actually cross the line. Ashton, Reo-Coker, Gabbidon and Ferdinand proved the spine of this team is in very good health, and those players are only going to grow over the next few years. Hopefully we can go one better next time by claiming a trophy.'

Such thoughts were echoed by many of the West Ham first-team squad as they reflected on a successful first season in the Premiership and looked ahead to the following term, which would of course include the challenge of European football. Having finished ninth in the league and gone within moments of winning the FA Cup, the management and players believed they had arrived as a top-flight force. That conviction would prove to be the team's Achilles heel in the coming months.

# 5

## 'IT WAS GUARANTEED … THERE WERE NO GET-OUT CLAUSES'

'WEST HAM United are delighted to announce the double signing of Argentinian World Cup stars Carlos Tévez and Javier Mascherano from Brazilian club Corinthians. The pair have been signed on permanent contracts with the club this afternoon. All other aspects of the transfers will remain confidential and undisclosed.'

Official confirmation that West Ham had pulled off one of the most stunning coups known to British football appeared at 4.52 p.m. on 31 August 2006, the summer's transfer-deadline day. For most observers, it seemed too good to be true. Here were two world-class superstars, valued at £20 million when they signed for Corinthians in 2004 and recently linked with a number of top English outfits, including Manchester United, Chelsea and Arsenal, being snapped up by a club that clearly wouldn't usually have had the financial resources to purchase them outright and could not even offer them Champions League football. Striker Tévez, dubbed by many as 'the new Maradona', had won the South American Player of the Year award on the previous three occasions. Midfield anchorman Mascherano, labelled 'a monster of a player' by Maradona himself, was such a key element of the Argentina team that he played in every minute of their five

World Cup games that summer. For West Ham supporters, seeing the pair of 22 year olds arrive at Upton Park was as likely as rock legends Bob Dylan and Bruce Springsteen turning up on their doorsteps and asking to come in for a cup of tea.

It was Tévez himself who was the first to break the news of the deal, announcing on his personal website that he and Mascherano, who had both suffered problems with Corinthians, had signed contracts 'to play for West Ham United of England'. The official verification on the London club's website, revealing no information in respect of transfer fees paid or length of contracts, only served to deepen the sense of mystery and intrigue by cloaking the deals in what could be termed an Irons curtain of secrecy. If West Ham believed they could announce the signings without prompting wild speculation, they were sorely mistaken.

The lack of information led some newspapers to suggest the two Argentinians had simply been secured on loan, although news that both players were 'owned' by a company named Media Sports Investment Ltd – as opposed to their former club Corinthians – became public knowledge very quickly. In reality, the economic rights of the two footballers were spread across four corporate entities – MSI, Just Sports Inc., Global Soccer Agencies Ltd and the perhaps rather appropriately named Mystere Services Ltd. The nature of third-party ownership of players, although popular in certain other countries, particularly in South America, was an alien concept in Britain, and the lack of knowledge of such arrangements, especially on the part of the media, resulted in a plethora of misunderstandings and misinterpretations that would blight West Ham far more than they could possibly have feared.

Kia Joorabchian, an Iranian-born businessman who had discussed a possible buy-out of West Ham in 2005, was the front man for MSI. And when his involvement with Tévez and Mascherano became known, several theories began to circulate as to why he had brought the two players to Upton Park. The most popular belief was that the Argentinians were effectively being 'parked' at West Ham for a limited period, thought to be one year, in order to generate concrete interest from the top Premiership clubs or major European outfits. It was suggested that both men had 'exit clauses' in their contracts, allowing them to jump ship when it suited their owners. Tévez had been linked with a move to Chelsea earlier in the year – with Joorabchian reportedly talking about a buy-out clause of 'between £69 million and £83 million' – and the suspicion was that, having eventually adapted to the Premiership and the English way of life, the striker would then find himself plying the tricks of his trade over at Stamford Bridge the following season.

Indeed, there was even newspaper speculation that billionaire Chelsea owner Roman Abramovich had links with MSI, although that notion was firmly dismissed by Joorabchian. Meanwhile, it was claimed that Manchester United had rejected a deal involving Tévez but had 'first option' on Mascherano and that the Hammers would receive only a fraction of any future transfer fee, with the third parties pocketing the rest. All that Joorabchian would confirm was that the deal was 'complex and involves many aspects'.

All the theories failed to trouble West Ham supporters, who were simply grateful that their club had the opportunity to utilise the star players, however short their stays might be. Not only could they revel in the excitement of watching two mercurial talents perform their magic on the Upton Park stage, but West Ham would also reap the benefits of their services and hopefully challenge at the top end of the Premier League. In fact, one bookmaker slashed the club's odds of topping the table, minus the 'big four' of Manchester United, Arsenal, Chelsea and Liverpool, from 20–1 to 9–1 on the strength of the signings. The supporters were entitled to be pragmatic; if exit clauses allowed the Argentinian duo to leave after one season, it was no different to taking them on a year's loan, and the majority of clubs would have jumped at that opportunity.

It was also suspected that West Ham were handed Tévez and Mascherano as 'a sweetener' for a possible second takeover attempt by Joorabchian, an idea that gained momentum when it was subsequently confirmed that the businessman did indeed hope to buy the club. This motive was denied, but many observers thought it was too much of a coincidence that the players had arrived at Upton Park just days before takeover talks commenced.

Ironically, Hammers manager Alan Pardew had previously joked about trying to sign Brazilian superstar Ronaldinho, admitting, 'I'm not sure the chairman can stretch [his finances] to get him, but we'll have to see.' So he was pleasantly bemused when told by Terence Brown that 'the opportunity to go for Tévez and Mascherano' existed. 'You don't turn that kind of chance down,' he insisted, adding that he didn't have to sell West Ham to the two players, as Lionel Scaloni, their international teammate who had just completed a four-month loan period at the club, had spoken very positively about the set-up. 'They knew all about our success last season and our style of play. This will give us a real chance to compete with the very best teams in the Premiership and Europe,' he said.

Brown, meanwhile, hailed what had been 'a momentous day' for the club and described the deals as 'the biggest in our history'. He added, 'I must give a mention to [managing director] Paul Aldridge and [commercial and legal director] Scott Duxbury, who worked through the night to ensure the transfers went through.'

Tévez and Mascherano were officially unveiled as West Ham players at an Upton Park press conference on Tuesday, 5 September. By this time, it had been confirmed that the club had entered into 'exploratory discussions' regarding a possible takeover bid, but they insisted 'there is no contractual link' between the signing of the two Argentinians and the buy-out talks. Although no mention of Joorabchian was made, the statement effectively confirmed that he was behind the takeover initiative, and Pardew's comment to journalists that the situation was 'intriguing' suggested the manager knew little about the mysterious manoeuvres that had been taking place behind closed doors. He did, however, dismiss notions of 'shady dealing' and claimed, 'I've put the terms of the deal to the back of my mind. I've got two world-class players at West Ham, and I just want to work with them.'

What Pardew did let slip was the length of the players' deals, to the best of his knowledge, which had previously been kept officially undisclosed. 'They've signed four-year contracts, and I can assure you they will not be leaving in the next transfer window,' he said. 'And I will never be forced to play either of them, otherwise I wouldn't be here any more.'

Pardew was aware that the recruitment of Tévez and Mascherano – clearly a move that had been instigated at boardroom level – might be seen as undermining his authority at the club. Unlike the Continental system, which saw club presidents make the major decisions about playing personnel and first-team coaches simply work with the squads at their disposal, the accepted rule in Britain was that the manager decided which players he wanted at the club and the directors tried to deliver them. The Tévez and Mascherano signings bucked against this established trend, so it was important to Pardew that he retained his credibility with supporters by insisting he not only had the power to veto the deal but would also come under no outside pressure to use the two players.

Peter Grant supported these claims. 'We were given the option of taking the players, and I don't care what anybody says:

if any manager is offered Tévez and Mascherano, they would take them.' Pardew did, in fact, initially speak to his assistant about the two stars, only for Grant to understandably question West Ham's ability to afford them. 'No, it can be done,' assured Pardew, who allegedly insisted to his bosses that the third-party ownership must not allow for the players to be moved on without his agreement. 'It was guaranteed to Alan that there were no get-out clauses in their contracts for a minimum of a year,' said Grant. 'That was the one thing Alan stipulated. If he was going to start building a team around the two players, there was no way he was going to accept them waving goodbye at Christmas.'

Whether the third-party owners of Tévez and Mascherano did, in fact, retain the power to move the players on without the club or the manager's agreement – mid-season or otherwise – would be revealed in due course. But for the time being, both Pardew and Grant were delighted that the club had been able to secure the Argentinians' services. 'As coaches, all we were interested in was having the best players available for our team,' said Grant. 'From a business point of view, as far as we were concerned everything was above board.'

West Ham fans would not have to wait long to see their new star players in action on English soil, with Argentina playing a friendly against rivals Brazil at Arsenal's Emirates Stadium just a few days after signing their contracts. Not since Argentina's 1978 World Cup winners Ossie Ardiles and Ricky Villa signed for Tottenham had there been so much excitement and anticipation over two South American imports. The novelty and glamour of foreign arrivals may have diminished since those days, but for Hammers supporters, who little more than a year earlier had been fretting over fixtures against Crewe and Rotherham, the idea of watching Argentina in the knowledge that two of their stars would soon be gracing Upton Park was beyond their wildest dreams.

Both men started against Brazil, although it wasn't an enjoyable day for them with their side slumping to a 3–0 defeat. Tévez charged around like an angry dog whose bone had been stolen, prompting fears that he might struggle to survive games if he failed to cool his temperament. Meanwhile, Mascherano failed to impose himself on the game and was taken off at half-time. Within the next few days, more of the players' recent histories came to light, with both of them talking about their difficult experiences at Corinthians. 'I have to thank Alan Pardew,' said Mascherano, who, like his long-time friend Tévez, had suffered at the hands of the unforgiving Brazilian fans when their club was struggling and they fell out with its management. 'My family were becoming ill, and West Ham came and saved us. When I heard the transfer had gone through, it was the happiest moment of my life.'

Tévez added, 'I never want to go through what happened at Corinthians ever again.' Not that the latter had lived a closeted existence, having been brought up in poverty on the rough streets of Fuerte Apache in Buenos Aires. He bore a dreadful scar on his neck after being burned with boiling water as a child but had since resisted the temptation to have surgery. 'The scar is a reminder of where I came from,' he said. If West Ham supporters thought they had seen a true maverick in Italian striker Paolo Di Canio several years earlier, Tévez would surely prove himself a worthy successor in terms of capturing their imagination and igniting their fervour.

Dean Ashton was signed for £7 million back in January, but West Ham supporters had been expecting the club to exploit the FA Cup final display and top-half finish in the Premiership with a number of big-money signings. That failed to come to fruition, with Pardew attempting to solve his right-back problems – following the departure of loan signing Scaloni and Tomáš Řepka before him – with the acquisition of Tyrone Mears, John Pantsil and Jonathan Spector for fees that totalled around £2.5 million. The manager also bolstered his squad by signing midfielder Lee Bowyer for a nominal amount, landing Sunderland left-back George McCartney for a payment of £600,000 that saw fringe full-back Clive Clarke head in the opposite direction and securing England Under-21 striker Carlton Cole for a fee of £2 million from Chelsea.

The most significant purchase, however, was that of goalkeeper Robert Green, who was recovering from a groin injury sustained on an England B outing against Belarus at the end of the previous campaign but had agreed a £2 million move from Norwich. Green would have to recover before establishing himself as West Ham's first choice, but his contribution would later prove to be invaluable – not something that could be said for too many of the new recruits.

Bowyer had been the first to arrive earlier in the summer, insisting his return to the club was a case of 'unfinished business' after his initial 11-game spell at Upton Park – undermined by an ankle injury – had failed to prevent West Ham from being relegated in 2003. Bowyer's career at Charlton, Leeds United and, more recently, Newcastle United had been blighted by a succession of on- and off-field problems to the point that many people, including Pardew, admitted the midfielder was drinking in the last-chance saloon. 'Lee needs to have a clean bill of health,' said Pardew following the 29 year old's arrival, although his suggestion that the player's 'best years are still to come' was difficult for many observers to imagine. Bowyer had been labelled damaged goods after being involved in a high-profile court case – in which he was accused and acquitted of assaulting an Asian student outside a Leeds nightclub in 2000 – and his initial signing for West Ham had attracted a certain amount of criticism. His return three years later was greeted with rather less disquiet, but it remained to be seen if he could live up to Pardew's expectations.

Ghana international Pantsil was a character that had provoked controversy in a very different way when he waved an Israeli flag in celebration of one of his country's victories at the summer's World Cup finals. As a Hapoel Tel Aviv player he felt entitled to display thanks to the Israelis who had travelled to Germany to support him, but the Ghana FA were forced to apologise on his behalf and insist he was not taking sides in the conflict with Palestine after he was heavily criticised in the Arab world. Rather more amusingly, the 25 year old insisted West Ham had incorrectly spelt his surname by calling him Pantsil instead of Paintsil, as had been on his Ghana shirt at the World Cup. West Ham were obliged to stress that the name 'Pantsil' appeared on his official documentation – which he hadn't bothered to question – and so 'Pants' it would have to be.

West Ham had missed out on their main full-back target with Luke Young eventually deciding to sign a three-year contract at Charlton after holding talks with new manager Iain Dowie. This had been a great disappointment for Pardew, as the 26 year old, who had just forced his way into the England frame, appeared to be the ideal candidate to make the right-back position his own. The Hammers boss had been confident that Young would consider a move across the Thames as an upwards step, particularly because of the ascendancy the club had enjoyed in the previous 12 months, but this would appear to have not been the case.

Pardew could at least take consolation from the fact that he was able to hold onto his best players during the summer of 2006. While a top-half league finish, an FA Cup final appearance and UEFA Cup qualification made West Ham an attractive proposition for possible recruits, the flip side of the coin was that success would expose the very top clubs to the talent on display at Upton Park. Supporters were only too aware of how difficult – and ultimately futile – it generally was for West Ham to fend off the interests of the bigger outfits once their better players had been targeted. There were growing fears that youngsters such as Anton Ferdinand and Nigel Reo-Coker could be lured away, while there was also concern that Yossi Benayoun might be tempted by a move to Liverpool, who were clearly interested in the playmaker. West Ham offered the Israel international a new contract, and although many people believed he had put pen to paper the reality was that the deal remained unsigned.

The Hammers did, however, say goodbye to goalkeeper Shaka Hislop, who joined FC Dallas on a free transfer, young defender Elliott Ward, who had understandably become frustrated with a lack of first-team opportunities, having played a key role in helping the club to promotion ('We wouldn't be here without him,' said Pardew when sanctioning a £1 million sale to Coventry), and midfielder Carl Fletcher, who was allowed to sign for Crystal Palace in a £400,000 deal. Other departures included goalkeeper Stephen Bywater to Derby, striker Yaniv Katan back to Maccabi Haifa on loan and youngster Petr Mikolanda, who had been loaned to a number of lower-league clubs before being released.

West Ham prepared for the new season with a series of friendly games that included trips to Sweden and Greece as well as a home clash with Olympiakos. Ashton looked particularly sharp, having worked hard during the summer after being placed on a special fitness programme. The 22 year old had made such an impact following his club-record move from Norwich that Newcastle were believed to be set to make an offer in the region of £12 million as they looked to replace the retired Alan Shearer. The West Ham of old might have been tempted to consider an instant £5 million profit on a player, but Pardew was building a team and not breaking one up. And to have cashed in on Ashton so swiftly would have sent out a terrible message about the club's ambition – or lack of it.

Yet the reality was that Ashton had not arrived at the club in the fittest of conditions and occasionally appeared somewhat leaden – not that his manager ever publicly acknowledged it. Both Pardew and Grant knew how important Ashton would be for the team in the new campaign and were delighted with his fitness during the pre-season games. Grant led the expedition to Greece, while Pardew remained in England, and he worked the striker particularly hard. 'The games were played in 100 degree heat,' said Grant, 'but I kept Dean out there in a central midfield position, and he was outstanding. He looked as fit as ever.'

New England manager Steve McClaren, who had succeeded Sven-Göran Eriksson following the disappointing World Cup quarter-final elimination, duly named Ashton in his first squad for the friendly against Greece on 16 August. Everybody at West Ham was naturally delighted with the player's first full call-up. 'We've worked hard at changing Dean's body shape and making him more mobile,' said Pardew as the news broke. 'He looks fantastic and now has all the attributes of an England player.'

Ashton was set to start against the Greeks at Old Trafford, with McClaren insisting the player 'deserved his opportunity having come through the England Under-21 side and done so well following his big-money move to West Ham'. But the striker was to suffer appalling luck when he was hurt in a collision with Chelsea winger Shaun Wright-Phillips during a training session the day before the game. Those who witnessed the clash immediately feared the worst, and hospital scans quickly confirmed that Ashton had broken his right ankle. If this was bad news for England, it was devastating for West Ham, who had lost their key man just four days before the new

Premiership season kicked off. Grant discovered the news from physiotherapist Steve Allen, who told him, 'Dean's been taken off with an injury, and we think it's a bad one.' The Hammers coach was understandably distressed. 'It was a massive blow,' he said. 'Dean was going to be the focal point of our team, and if there was one person we couldn't afford to lose it was him.'

Initial estimates were that Ashton would be sidelined for at least 12 weeks, but Pardew put on a brave face and insisted that his squad had the resources to compensate for the forward's absence. 'We still have four quality strikers at the club,' he said, with reference to Cole, Marlon Harewood, Bobby Zamora and Teddy Sheringham. And it was Harewood and Zamora who won the nod from the manager as West Ham lined up for their opening league game against Charlton on 19 August.

Ironically, the Hammers began their 50th season of top-flight football in exactly the same manner as they had commenced their 49th: with a home game that saw them recover from a half-time deficit to record a 3–1 win against opposition that finished with just ten men. Bowyer was the architect of the victory, setting up two goals for Zamora and one for Cole, who sealed the result just seconds after coming on as a last-minute substitute, although visiting defender Djimi Traoré's sending off just ten minutes after Darren Bent's penalty opener undoubtedly made things easier for the Hammers.

Three days later, West Ham again bounced back after giving their opponents a one-goal start when securing a 1–1 draw at newly promoted Watford that took them to the top of the table for twenty-four hours, with Zamora once again on target. And the striker was credited with his fourth goal in just three games the following weekend when his attempted cross deceived Liverpool goalkeeper José Reina – hardly faultless in the FA Cup final three months earlier – who could only parry the ball into the net. However, hopes of a first win at Anfield since

1963 and some small form of revenge for the defeat in Cardiff were dashed when Daniel Agger and Peter Crouch gave the home side a 2–1 half-time lead that was only threatened when Bowyer somehow scuffed wide in front of an open net close to the end.

Four points from the opening trio of games seemed a decent return, and the promising form suggested that West Ham had continued from where they had left off the previous season. There was no doubt the loss of Ashton would seriously undermine hopes of pushing for a top-six place in the Premiership – the next logical step after finishing ninth last time around – but the Hammers had remained in the top half of the table for five months prior to the club's record signing arriving in January, and it was hoped they could do so once again. When the shock captures of Tévez and Mascherano were announced three games into the new campaign – followed by news of a possible big-money takeover – the expectations ballooned to an unrealistic level.

By sheer luck, West Ham's next game – at home to Aston Villa on 10 September – had been scheduled for live coverage by Sky Sports, and champagne corks were surely popping at the company's London headquarters in celebration of the event coinciding with the debuts of two Argentina internationals. It seemed the rest of the country was just as desperate as the West Ham supporters to witness the two players making their Premiership debuts, placing considerable pressure on Pardew to include them in his starting line-up. An international break, however, would restrict Tévez and Mascherano to just a couple of days' training with their new teammates, and so Pardew had the perfect excuse when it came to pointing them towards the substitutes' bench when the game came around, insisting that it was a 'football decision'.

Nevertheless, the media interpreted the omission of the two

players as a deliberate statement from Pardew – that he alone dictated first-team affairs at West Ham – and an opportunity for him to assert his authority. There was an element of truth in that. But there was another message the manager considered equally as important: that he had a loyalty to the players who had performed so well for him over the last 18 months. Hayden Mullins had worked diligently in the holding midfielder's role and had established himself as a key component of the team, so was it right he should lose his place because Mascherano had arrived at the club as a consequence of a boardroom initiative?

Pardew had the same dilemma in attack if he wanted to accommodate Tévez. Ashton's injury might have been a major setback, but Zamora had taken full advantage of his run of starts by topping the Premiership goal charts, albeit after just a handful of games. And although strike-partner Harewood had failed to open his account for the new campaign, it was surely just a matter of time before the club's top scorer from the previous season rediscovered his goal touch. So while the supporters and media were disappointed with the unspectacular and somewhat familiar look of the West Ham team that lined up against Villa, Pardew had at least suggested the Argentinians would enjoy no favouritism or preferential treatment.

For those expecting the game to represent the start of an exciting new era, it was something of an anticlimax. If anything, all the usual characteristics were on display, with West Ham falling behind, Harewood failing to take his chances and Zamora scoring with a goal that had an element of luck about it. Tévez replaced Harewood for the final 30 minutes and immediately impressed with his tenacity – possibly trying too hard at times – although the striker looked surprisingly heavy. From the initial evidence, it appeared that it might take some time for West Ham to see the best of him. Little did anybody realise, however, that the same could have been said about the entire team.

# 6

## 'IF YOU GAVE THEM THE BALL, THEY RARELY GAVE IT BACK'

THE SWARM of black clouds had an ominous look about them as they suffocated the highest reaches of Mount Etna on Sicily's east coast. It was appropriate that West Ham's management staff and players should take in such an imposing view as they flew into Palermo for their UEFA Cup first-round second-leg game in the final week of September. Having lost 1–0 at home to the on-form Serie A outfit a fortnight earlier, West Ham had certainly left themselves with a mountain to climb if they were to make further progress in the competition.

There had been a great sense of anticipation ahead of the club's first European adventure for seven years. Back in 1999, Harry Redknapp's Hammers had beaten Finland's FC Jokerit, Heerenveen of Holland and French side Metz to win the Intertoto Cup and qualify for the UEFA Cup for the first time in the club's history. But after cruising past Croatian outfit NK Osijek in the first round, West Ham met their match when losing 2–0 on aggregate to Romanians Steaua Bucharest.

This time around, the draw in Monaco on 25 August 2006 was always going to be difficult for the Hammers with their lack of recent European pedigree – their last Cup Winners' Cup run had been in 1980–81 – leaving them unseeded and guaranteed to meet one of Feyenoord, FC Basel, Rapid Bucharest, Osasuna and Palermo. The latter, who had initially finished eighth in Serie A and qualified for the UEFA Cup after Lazio were banned for their role in Italy's match-fixing scandal, were something of an unknown quantity for many. But they had reached the last 16 of the competition the previous term and would start the new season in excellent form.

West Ham manager Alan Pardew knew little about Palermo, although he admitted it was a 'difficult draw'. The Serie A season had yet to start at that point but coach Keith Peacock – a recent recruit who had just severed a 35-year association with Charlton – and scout Roger Cross travelled to Italy to watch Palermo's opening league game at home to Reggina on 10 September, as the Hammers were in action against Aston Villa that day. The Sicilians were 3–0 up within half an hour and eventually won a thrilling game 4–3, prompting the West Ham men to return home with a glowing report. 'If they play like they did in the first half, don't bother turning up!' was the message given to Pardew, who had been hoping Palermo's lack of competitive games would work against them.

The West Ham boss was further disappointed when he was handed the visitors' team sheet on the evening of the first leg on 14 September. Just six names had survived from the Reggina game – and just one of the goal scorers – to render much of his Palermo dossier redundant. Pardew hoped rival coach Francesco Guidolin had named a weaker side, but there was little doubt his players were going into the unknown and would have to learn quickly – especially as only goalkeeper Roy Carroll and midfielders Yossi Benayoun and Lee Bowyer had any experience of European club competition under their belts.

Being drawn to play the first game at Upton Park also didn't help, so Pardew had done everything he could to ramp the event up, insisting on the club reducing ticket prices to ensure as full a house as possible. And while he knew his side would probably need to win at home if they were to progress, he was aware they couldn't afford to allow Palermo to score an away goal that could prove the difference. European football was a new experience for Pardew, as it was for many of his players, and he arrived at the game having made some tough decisions.

These included handing Carlos Tévez and Javier Mascherano their first starts in West Ham colours. Palermo boss Guidolin had admitted he 'feared' the two players, and their pre-match emergence from the tunnel – at the expense of Marlon Harewood and Hayden Mullins – naturally helped buoy the home support. The shape of the team suggested that Pardew had approached the game too cautiously, however, with the usual 4–4–2 formation being abandoned for something resembling 4–1–4–1 in the early stages. Whereas Mullins was a defensive midfielder who generally played alongside Reo-Coker, Mascherano was accustomed to sitting much deeper, and he occupied the position immediately in front of the back four. Tévez, therefore, was asked to fill in on the left of midfield, leaving Bobby Zamora somewhat isolated in attack.

It was an unfamiliar ploy that took some getting used to, and many observers believed it surrendered the initiative to Palermo, who scored the only goal of the game in fortuitous fashion. Tévez had been urged into attack late in the first half and nearly opened his West Ham account with a shot that was blocked by goalkeeper Alberto Fontana. Some felt he should have been more clinical, and the Argentinian was left to rue his failure when just moments later Palermo took full advantage of hesitancy in the home defence. The ball looked to have rolled out of play, but the Sicilians ignored West Ham's appeals, and Aimo Diana crossed for Andrea Caracciolo to poke home just seconds before the half-time whistle.

If Pardew was unhappy with the nature of the goal, he was

furious with the leniency of Swedish referee Stefan Johannesson, who was content to turn a blind eye to Palermo's strong-arm tactics and booked just three of their players. Tempers eventually flared late in the second half when West Ham attempted to take a corner after Fontana had thrown the ball out and collapsed to the ground with an apparent 'injury'. A 20-man melee ensued with Tévez and Zamora at the centre of the aggravation before order was ultimately restored. Confirmation that it was never going to be West Ham's night, however, came when Harewood, a 77th-minute replacement for Tévez, hit the post with a close-range effort. 'The referee was disappointing and let far too much go,' complained Pardew, who also bemoaned his side's poor luck. 'We just didn't get the breaks. But this tie isn't over yet.'

The events of the game left a bitter taste in the mouth of many Hammers supporters. The evening had begun in good spirits with joint West Ham–Palermo scarves being sold outside the Boleyn Ground, but it was easy to imagine scissors being taken to some of them with the Sicilians winning few friends. Guidolin did little to improve relationships after the match by questioning West Ham's sportsmanship. 'In our country when a player is injured, the other side gives the ball back. That is normal, but it obviously isn't in England,' said the coach with more than a hint of sarcasm.

Pardew immediately went to work, insisting that the tie was still 'evenly poised' and claiming that Palermo would have a psychological dilemma as to whether they should defend their lead in the second leg or play more openly. 'Either way will suit us,' he declared. But the clubs would experience contrasting fortunes in the fortnight between the two legs. While Palermo won two of their three Serie A games to continue their great start to the campaign, West Ham suffered 2–0 defeats at home to Newcastle and at Manchester City to extend their winless run to six games.

Mascherano and Tévez had kept their places for the visit of Newcastle – although both were substituted – but the latter was dropped to the bench in Manchester as Harewood was recalled. Aside from having doubts about their fitness, Pardew became aware that the attempted integration of the two Argentinians was proving less successful than anticipated. 'In terms of the spirit in the squad, there has been a change,' he acknowledged, although the admission was perhaps unwise, as it gave the media the ammunition they needed to accuse the signings of Tévez and Mascherano of undermining team morale. West Ham had failed to win any of their four games since their arrival, and many people jumped to the conclusion that this was no coincidence – especially when an upturn in results had been expected.

Pardew was equally as candid in confessing that he was becoming increasingly unsure as to what his best line-up was as he sought to rediscover the winning formula. Whereas the team had almost picked itself the previous season, the influx of nine new players during the summer had solved certain problems but created several others. 'If you put me on a lie detector and asked for my best team, I'd have a problem answering,' he said. Injuries had solved some of the manager's dilemmas at the start of the season, with returning midfielder Bowyer being accommodated because of the absence of Matthew Etherington, for example. But when the winger was fit, the fact that Benayoun (against Newcastle) and then Bowyer (at Manchester City) made way for him reflected Pardew's general uncertainty.

There was even greater disruption in defence, not that the manager could be blamed for that. Tyrone Mears and John Pantsil had each played at right-back in the early games, but, with both of them out injured, Christian Dailly was forced to fill in at City. When Anton Ferdinand limped out of that game with a hamstring problem, Dailly switched to centre-back and

Mullins took over at right-back. And the problems intensified when Dailly subsequently picked up a knee injury.

It meant that West Ham travelled to Palermo for the second leg of their UEFA Cup tie with huge uncertainty about the team that Pardew would – or could – select. The manager put on a brave face in the media suite of the Excelsior Palace hotel the day before the game, however, and challenged his players to rediscover the fighting spirit they had displayed in the FA Cup earlier in the year. Their backs were certainly against the wall, with Pardew revealing that James Collins – who'd figured just once so far that term and had been sidelined with a groin problem – would probably have to play at centre-half, while Jonathan Spector looked set to be thrown in for his debut at right-back. Local journalists spoke to their English counterparts in a bid to establish the shape and make-up of the West Ham team, and it was easy to suspect that the information would find its way back to the Palermo camp.

It was a surprise that the West Ham party had chosen to stay in the heart of Palermo, what with the capital being the noisiest and dustiest city in Sicily as it sprawls away from the northern coast under the peak of Monte Pellegrino. The city has suffered social and economic decline over the decades, with the regeneration programme following the heavy bombing of the Second World War having allegedly been undermined by the constant diversion of funds towards Mafia-controlled organisations. The ongoing fight against organised crime is reflected in the fact that the city's Falcone Borsellino Airport is named after two anti-Mafia investigators who were murdered in 1992. Unemployment and petty crime in the city is rife, with Vespa-riding youths – many of whom will succumb to corrupt influences – using the streets of the old and new towns as their playground.

Many of the 2,500 West Ham fans that travelled to Palermo

did so by independent means, choosing to resist the club's offer of a £310 one-day trip for the sake of enjoying several days in Sicily for a similar outlay. The bars around the Teatro Massimo were accommodating on the evening before the game, although the local juveniles were rather less so, storming into the square to hurl a variety of missiles at the visiting supporters, some of whom inevitably fought back. Scarves obscured the Sicilian faces as they engaged in battle and then disappeared into the night before helmeted police officers arrived to mop up the mess, focusing their attentions on the English tourists. Twenty West Ham fans were arrested and six were injured, yet just one Italian was held – indicating that the true perpetrators of the violence had long fled the scene. The British media predictably had their script already written, however, with one BBC office contacting an English journalist in the town centre the following day for information, only to reveal they weren't particularly interested in whether Palermo fans had instigated the trouble.

The Sicilian authorities responded to the scenes by declaring that security for the game would be significantly increased. It was therefore no surprise that the Stadio Renzo Barbera resembled Fort Knox in the hours before the match on 28 September, with a number of heavily guarded gates needing to be negotiated before access to the ground could be gained. However, the extra measures failed to prevent one coach of West Ham supporters having its windows smashed by Palermo fans before the game – or a group of English journalists smuggling a ticketless supporter into the stadium. It seemed that for all the militant posturing on the part of the armed *polizia*, there was no substitute for intuition and courage.

West Ham's players displayed similar qualities as they sought to recover their one-goal deficit but fortune, yet again, would remain hidden. Pardew had bravely named Tévez, Harewood and recent signing Carlton Cole in attack, but luck was very much against them as Palermo goalkeeper Fontana produced a number of brilliant saves to keep the Londoners at bay in the opening half an hour. The Italian tipped a Tévez shot away for a corner, flew across goal to block Harewood's overhead kick and then denied both Cole and Collins as the visitors dominated the early part of the game. The key moment came just ten minutes before half-time, however, when Paul Konchesky was penalised for what appeared to be a legitimate challenge and Greek referee Georgios Kasnaferis generously allowed Palermo to retake the free-kick after they had lost possession with a hasty first attempt. When Fabio Henrique Simplicio's shot appeared to take a deflection to find its way into the bottom right-hand corner of the net, it was obvious that fate was against West Ham performing on a level playing field.

After Cole was stretchered off having seen a header hit an upright, Simplicio ignored offside calls to extend Palermo's lead just past the hour mark before David Di Michele rubbed salt in West Ham's wounds with his side's third to complete a flattering 4–0 aggregate success. The victory was celebrated by a home support that was allowed to fire flares and firecrackers at riot police without punishment while Hammers fans were penned into a corner of the stadium under close scrutiny. Later in the season, all Italian football would be suspended for more than a week after 38-year-old policeman Filippo Raciti was killed when Palermo visited Sicilian rivals Catania, suggesting the country still had much to learn about the governance of football followers and the troublemakers who attached themselves to many Serie A clubs.

Pardew succeeded in keeping his eyes away from the bevy of local beauties adorning the Palermo media quarters after his side's defeat to apologise for the brevity of West Ham's European endeavours. Once again, he found himself complaining about the lack of 'breaks' and the need for a change of 'luck'. 'We always felt the first goal would be crucial,' he said, 'and that's how it proved. A 4–0 aggregate scoreline flatters Palermo, but after a result like that I can't really claim we were the better team.' Coach Peter Grant was equally disappointed. 'We really felt we could be successful in Europe, and over the two games we deserved more, there's no doubt about that,' he said. 'But Palermo were a very good team on a technical level, and if you gave them the ball, they rarely gave it back.'

The 'Cockney Boys On Tour' T-shirts were plentiful in the bars overlooking the sun-baked beach of Mondello a few miles along the coastline the day after the game, yet the reality was that West Ham's UEFA Cup campaign was less of a tour and more of a trip. The club's minimum aim had been to qualify for the subsequent group stage – as Premiership rivals Tottenham, Blackburn and Newcastle all succeeded in doing – but the irony was that going out of Europe was very much a blessing in disguise.

Pardew had insisted his club was 'in it to win it', but the revised format of the competition meant any team lifting the trophy would have to play an energy-sapping and focus-distracting 15 games to do so. Middlesbrough had reached the final the previous year, but their league form had suffered as a consequence, and the likelihood is that prolonged participation in the tournament would have cost West Ham vital Premiership points further down the line.

Palermo failed to live up to their UEFA Cup promise by going out at the group stage, which saw them lose 1–0 at home to Newcastle. The Hammers, meanwhile, were left wondering how long it would be before they would return to European competition – something that would be high on the agenda if the proposed takeover of the club was successful. Like many things involving West Ham, however, the process would be anything but straightforward.

# 7

## 'CERTAIN THINGS WERE NOT AS I THOUGHT'

WEST HAM United may be located in the heart of *EastEnders* territory, but the dramatic events of September 2006 were less the type seen in a soap opera and more those expected from a Cold War documentary or spy movie, in which mystery and intrigue cloak every move and clandestine figures lurk furtively in the shadows. Few could ever have imagined the remotest connection being made between the Hammers and former KGB agent Alexander Litvinenko, whose murder in London later in the year created huge publicity, but the creation of such a link from Green Street to Red Square proved possible as the identities of the potential investors in the club became the topic of intense media debate.

Just a few days after West Ham had issued a statement to the Stock Exchange revealing that discussions regarding the possible sale of the club had begun, Kia Joorabchian admitted he had revived his interest following the failure to secure a price agreement with chairman Terence Brown the previous autumn. During those initial talks, Joorabchian had publicly declared his intention to plough £200 million into the club, with half of that figure being spent on new players. 'There is no point buying West Ham unless you are going to invest in turning them into one of the top teams in the country,' he said. Such a claim may have been music to many West Ham supporters' ears – indeed, manager Alan Pardew eagerly admitted he 'could do a lot with £100 million' – but there were other observers who were suspicious of the entrepreneur's use of the media while takeover talks were still taking place.

Joorabchian's Media Sports Investment Ltd firm had previously purchased a 51 per cent stake in Corinthians, who enjoyed a huge revival and won the Brazilian title in 2005 following the arrival of Argentinian duo Carlos Tévez and Javier Mascherano from Boca Juniors and River Plate respectively. But there was conjecture about how the estimated £20 million investment in the club – on a ten-year lease – had been funded, with Joorabchian claiming that MSI was 'backed by a diverse group of powerful men with interests in oil, the media and entertainment'. The speculation was that those men included Russian oligarch Boris Berezovsky and Georgian businessman Badri Patarkatsishvili, with whom Joorabchian had reportedly become acquainted when forging a career in the oil trade in the late 1990s. Some reports claimed that he was involved in the purchase of *Kommersant*, Russia's most influential newspaper, before it fell into the hands of Berezovsky and then Patarkatsishvili, although Joorabchian has denied having any direct business involvement with the two men.

The net result of these links – whether substantiated or not – was that many believed Berezovsky and Patarkatsishvili were behind Joorabchian's renewed attempts to take control of West Ham. Patarkatsishvili was reported as saying, 'At this time, I am not involved in any possible bid for West Ham, but I am thinking about it.' This not only prompted sensational images of a Chelsea-style revolution at Upton Park, with huge amounts of money being invested to turn the club into Premier League and Champions League contenders, but fears that something more cynical was afoot in terms of billionaire businessmen using football for their own ends.

On the same day that West Ham confirmed takeover talks were taking place (1 September 2006), London's *Evening Standard* ran a detailed article warning of 'an impending cataclysm in the world's favourite sport' and suggesting that Berezovsky and Patarkatsishvili were the 'architects of a scheme to revolutionise the way football is run'. The evidence that a plan existed to 'control an international soccer network' was 'circumstantial but compelling' it said.

Berezovsky, formerly the richest man in Russia before being forced to seek exile in London following accusations in Moscow of fraud and embezzlement, was once the owner of oil firm Sibneft before offloading it to partner Roman Abramovich. That connection had some people speculating that the latter – who funded the £300 million transformation of Chelsea after buying the club in 2003 – had a distant interest in the MSI bid to take control of West Ham, with some newspapers referring to an obvious conflict of interest and expressing the fear that the east London outfit could become some kind of secret nursery for their more illustrious neighbours.

Joorabchian was quick to deny some of the reported links with the Russians. 'I have never done business with Berezovsky, although I count him as a friend. I've never done business with Abramovich,' he said. That didn't stop Ian King, editor of *The Sun* newspaper's financial pages, from claiming, 'If this takeover [of West Ham] goes through, it will mean three Premiership clubs [including Chelsea and Portsmouth] are directly or indirectly backed by Russian money.' Two months after the West Ham takeover speculation threw images of Berezovsky onto the British sports pages, his name resurfaced as the poisoning with polonium-210 and subsequent death of Litvinenko dominated the news headlines. As a senior operational officer of the FSB (formerly the KGB) in Moscow, Litvinenko had been assigned the task of protecting Berezovsky – who held a major government position – but later claimed he'd been ordered to murder him. Both men would eventually secure political asylum in London.

By the time the past relationship between Berezovsky and Litvinenko was being acknowledged in November, speculation of MSI's links with Russian oligarchs had diminished – but so had the company's chances of purchasing West Ham. Joorabchian had launched his bid by expressing his belief in the potential of the club. 'West Ham can be bigger than Chelsea,' he said. 'What is so impressive about the club is that when they have hit bad times the passion and loyalty of the fans has seen them through thick and thin. Sometimes when I look at Chelsea, despite their recent success, it's all a bit cold. They talk more about the brand than the football club.'

Such words proved the 35 year old at least related to the product he was seeking to purchase. But the lack of transparency in terms of who was financially involved with MSI did little to discourage the speculation that kept surfacing at that time. Reports the firm had been investigated for suspected money-laundering activities in Brazil as a result of their investment in Corinthians did little to improve their public relations, although no charges were brought against them at that time. Britain's sports minister Richard Caborn expressed his concern about mysterious characters buying into football by saying, 'Those involved should be as open and transparent as possible. The Premiership is not a millionaires' playground.'

West Ham had yet to play a match since news of the possible takeover had broken. So, when they returned to action against Aston Villa on 10 September, the anticipated debuts of Tévez and Mascherano were not the only issues in the minds of the media, who would intrinsically connect the arrival of the 'West Hamigos' – as they were dubbed – with their owner Joorabchian's efforts to gain control at Upton Park. The public hysteria over the new signings was matched by the media's growing contempt for the takeover initiative, not helped by the fact that local mayor Sir Robin Wales had reportedly arranged for the Argentina flag to be flown at Newham Town Hall. 'Even the local council can't wait for the sell-up of the jewel of its own community's heritage,' said the *Daily Express*, who referred to emerging signs of 'a dramatic reshaping of West Ham's precious soul'. Other newspapers echoed the theme, with the *Daily Mirror* talking of West Ham being 'the most traditional of clubs, working class through and through, where cockney folk-tale memories of the Blitz spirit sit hand in hand with tales of the Boys of '86'. As a postscript, they added, 'Something has changed at Upton Park, and it will never be the same again.'

Manager Pardew helped fuel the fears in the wake of the 1–1 draw with Villa by claiming he would fight off the threat of outside forces. 'Whoever comes in will have a wall up against them, because it's my job as manager to protect the integrity and history of this club,' he said. 'From the Trevor Brooking era through to the Tony Cottee era and right through to the Hayden Mullins and Marlon Harewood era, we've done things the right way. We must never lose the history of the club.' Rather comically he added, 'The two new guys were the icing on the cake – but the cake has to taste nice in the first place.'

It was impossible for West Ham supporters to disassociate Tévez and Mascherano with part-owner Joorabchian. But there was another man who had been pulling the strings in the background, and without his influence it's likely the Argentinians would never have arrived at West Ham. That man was Pinhas Zahavi, the Israeli football agent who was seen by some as being an almost Godfather type of figure, with his tentacles of power and influence spreading right across the globe. Zahavi knew the West Ham hierarchy, having represented England defender Rio Ferdinand and Israel midfielder Eyal Berkovic during their times at the club, and it was apparently his initiative to bring the Joorabchian/Tévez/Mascherano package to Upton Park.

'I bring people together and get paid a commission if a deal is struck – only this time it's caused World War Three,' he said. 'It was my idea to bring the players to West Ham – they don't need the pressure of big clubs in their first season in England. The idea was to keep them together and play them together. If the players are a big success, I make money – and not just if they leave. West Ham is a club I believe can go from zero to big football success.'

Zahavi was forced to deny suggestions that he was a potential investor in West Ham. But it soon emerged that another Israeli was, with property developer Eli Papouchado confirming his intention to plough funds into Joorabchian's bid after Zahavi had put the two men together. 'Mr Joorabchian has spoken to me about leading a consortium of investors in football projects, and I have agreed if he decides to go forward,' he said. It was claimed by a business associate that he 'wouldn't know West Ham from West Brom' but Papouchado – who reportedly had to ask Zahavi how many players there were in a football team – made no secret of the fact he saw the Hammers purely as an investment opportunity and would play no management role if a takeover was completed.

Indeed, it was speculated that Papouchado's interest was as much in the land that West Ham's Boleyn Ground was located on as the football club itself. The club did own the site, having even bought nearby school buildings to accommodate their ground redevelopment schemes, which included the new 15,000-capacity Dr Martens West Stand and hotel complex, completed in 2001. The land would later be estimated to have a value of £18 million, which would increase substantially if it were sold for housing or commercial-property ventures. It was also anticipated that the whole Upton Park area was set to enjoy a regeneration over the following decade, with the nearby Canary Wharf complex and the staging of the 2012 Olympic Games making London's East End far more valuable and attractive to investors.

As the possibility of the club falling into new hands continued during the early part of the 2006–07 season, the team suffered an appalling loss of form that saw them sink towards the bottom of the Premiership table. The 3–0 defeat in Palermo, as West Ham's UEFA Cup dreams blew up in smoke, was the team's fourth in succession, while the 1–0 loss against Reading just a few days later meant that they had been beaten in their last three home games. Their fortunes failed to improve on the road with the Hammers losing at Portsmouth, Tottenham and, most embarrassingly, to League One strugglers Chesterfield in the Carling Cup to extend their run to eight successive defeats – a new club record in one campaign. The 1–0 loss at Tottenham was their seventh game without a goal to their credit and dumped them one place off the bottom of the Premiership table, sparking fears of a relegation battle, with the team having registered just five points from their first nine games.

This was not the environment in which the club's board of directors wanted to be negotiating a possible sale, knowing that the threat of relegation would undermine their chances of securing the figures they were looking for. If West Ham dropped out of the Premiership for the second time in four years, the club would seriously diminish in value and would face the problem of paying off debts with a much-reduced income. Some people felt that it was somewhat premature to start seriously considering the threat of relegation, but there was obviously huge pressure on Pardew to lift the team out of its slump.

Outside observers came to somewhat rash conclusions as to why West Ham were struggling so badly. Many blamed Tévez and Mascherano for having upset the equilibrium and team spirit in the camp, although Joorabchian quickly denied suggestions that the club was under any obligation to play them. 'That is totally the manager's choice,' he stated. Pardew's team selections would prove the point, with both men failing to hold down regular places and looking off the pace. But the manager did little to quell suggestions that their influence had not been entirely positive when he admitted, 'Those two players arriving has put some noses out of joint.'

The media also promoted the theory that doubts about the club's future ownership was creating uncertainty that made it difficult for Pardew and his players to focus on football. Again, the manager helped perpetuate such an idea by saying, 'The sooner the takeover talks are over, the better it will be for everyone feeling more comfortable in their positions at the club. The chairman is aware of that.' Further down the line, towards the end of October, he said, 'I have seen first hand the damage that the uncertainty can do.' Striker Bobby Zamora also claimed the speculation was an issue when he admitted, 'I'm not using it as an excuse, but we'd like to concentrate on the football.'

Yet the notion that takeover talk was a distraction for the team has been shot down by Peter Grant, who said, 'For any player to claim that a takeover had an effect on them would beggar belief really. As a player, that would never have affected me. Players are just interested in getting picked for the team on a Saturday.' Grant left the club to take up the manager's position at Norwich City in mid-October, but he denied that he had allowed speculation about the potential changes at the club to particularly worry him. 'If Alan Pardew and Peter Grant had to move on and a new management team was brought in to take the club onto another level, sometimes you just have to hold your hands up,' he said.

There had indeed been leaks as to who might be moved into the Hammers hot seat if Joorabchian's takeover initiative succeeded, with former England boss Sven-Göran Eriksson, Portugal manager Luiz Felipe Scolari and Alan Curbishley – on a sabbatical from football management after leaving Charlton Athletic earlier in the year – being linked with the post. The idea of Eriksson being appointed horrified many West Ham supporters, who believed the Swede had hugely underachieved during his six years with England and would never be in a position to relate to the history of the club and its traditions.

Such conjecture was particularly difficult for Pardew to contend with, especially as he realised that there might be considerable substance to the rumours. 'I'd like to think it didn't affect me, but there was so much speculation about my future,' he admitted. 'I even heard people in the corridor outside my office discussing whether I was staying.' Meanwhile, there were many observers who believed his chairman should not have allowed the continuing uncertainty over the club's future to potentially threaten its immediate prospects on the field.

Brown certainly had his critics after succeeding Martin Cearns in 1992, two years after joining the West Ham board. Manager Billy Bonds wasn't happy when he was asked to move upstairs into a 'director of football' type of role – an offer he rejected – to allow his assistant Harry Redknapp to take control of the first team in 1994. Many supporters were then disturbed to see Redknapp sacked in 2001 – after he'd kept the club in the Premiership for seven years – and replaced by novice Glenn Roeder. And when West Ham paid the price for that decision with relegation two years later, the inevitable consequence was the sale of the club's best players, much to the anger of the loyal supporters who believed their team had been mismanaged out of the top flight. Brown admitted the 'belt tightening' of the previous summer had 'maybe not been the right move' and was criticised by some fans who questioned his leadership and resented his high earnings – he'd reportedly backdated a

£50,000 pay rise to take his salary to £492,000 a year prior to accepting a post-relegation salary deferral.

One group of rebel shareholders, under the name of Whistle, launched an initiative in 2003 to oust Brown and managing director Paul Aldridge from their positions. However, they failed to gain sufficient support from larger shareholders to stage an internal coup and were eventually threatened with legal action after making allegations about the state of the club's finances before being forced into a climbdown.

Brown was furious with what he perceived to be deliberate attempts to destabilise the club as the team was trying to win promotion in 2004 and was angered the following year when news broke that former striker Tony Cottee was fronting a consortium exploring the possibility of launching a takeover bid. Cottee's services as a match-day host were immediately dispensed with, and the group's interest came to nothing once West Ham's promotion back to the Premiership priced them out of the picture.

It was the second promotion the club had enjoyed under Brown, and the chairman, who was a qualified accountant and had run a holiday-homes firm in Sussex, could rightly point to the fact that West Ham had played in the Premiership for the majority of his reign, produced a wealth of talented youngsters, redeveloped the Boleyn Ground, qualified for the UEFA Cup in 1999 and broken their transfer record on a number of occasions. 'The club was on its knees when I joined,' he said when reflecting on a yo-yo period that saw West Ham relegated in 1989 and 1992, manager Lou Macari survive just six months and the club shoot itself in the foot with the ill-advised Bond Scheme that asked fans to pay for the right to buy a season ticket.

By those standards, the next dozen years or so represented a period of stability. But Brown, who by nature was a private individual, suffered from his low profile, with even Pardew admitting that his chairman wasn't 'particularly good with the media' before adding, 'The fans hammer him, but he has held his hands up to some of those criticisms.' Brown himself acknowledged his lack of popularity after the play-off final win in 2005 by saying, 'I hope Alan has shut up his critics, but I doubt I've silenced all of mine.'

Brown was hugely relieved to have presided over West Ham's return to the Premiership and was fully aware of the difficulties both he and the club would have faced had they lost the parachute payments that summer. Yet with promotion having been won, some were surprised that Brown was prepared to consider selling the club when Joorabchian made his first approach that year, although staying up was by no means a formality. The new season had not even kicked off when Brown admitted, 'Any serious proposition will be carefully studied. I am not about protecting my position. I know I am a mere custodian of the club.'

At that point, in August 2005, it was reported that Joorabchian was prepared to pay £45 million for West Ham, some way short of the £60 million that Brown, who owned around 36 per cent of the club's shares, was allegedly looking for. One year later, however, with the club's profile having been considerably boosted by their FA Cup final appearance and top-half league finish, the asking price had increased, and it was believed that at least £70 million would need to be paid.

The accounts for the year up to 31 May 2006 certainly provided evidence of West Ham's upward trajectory, with pre-tax profits of £6 million being announced against a virtual doubling of turnover to £60.1 million. Meanwhile, club debts had been reduced by over £7 million to £22.5 million. 'The financial prudence shown by the club during those two seasons in the Championship enabled us to make a major investment in the playing squad during the summer and again in the January transfer window,' said Brown, who made no reference to either the arrivals of Tévez and Mascherano or the provisional takeover talks in his statement.

It was unrealistic to expect negotiations about the ownership of the club to be concluded overnight. But, with the team still struggling, that didn't stop the *News of the World*'s Martin Samuel – no doubt one of the critics Brown had referred to – from accusing the chairman of 'wrecking three years of hard work by destabilising Pardew while holding out for the £29 million that would be his share of Kia Joorabchian's takeover'. And the manager's calls for the whole matter to be wrapped up quickly only added to the pressure, although there was no truth in the rumour that Pardew had threatened to resign over the affair.

But no formal offer had yet been received from Joorabchian, despite him having negotiated a possible purchase price of £70 million. There were also reports that he was disputing the size of West Ham's debt, suggesting that it might be £15 million more than claimed, although this could have been a ploy to bring the price down if he was struggling to raise funds. This may have been the case, with backer Papouchado reportedly beginning to lose interest in the project.

The West Ham board had a meeting in early October at which it was agreed a deadline would be set for Joorabchian to make a definite offer, provide proof of funds and propose an acceptable business plan. Within a week, however, it was confirmed that a new proposed buyer had arrived on the scene in the shape of Icelandic businessman Eggert Magnússon. The 59 year old had impressive sporting credentials, having been president of the Football Association of Iceland since 1989, following a five-year period as president of Valur Reykjavik. He had also held a seat on UEFA's executive committee for four years.

A West Ham statement was issued to the London Stock

**Time for take-off:** West Ham celebrate their promotion to the Premiership at the Millennium Stadium

**Happy Hammer:** Goal hero Bobby Zamora holds the play-off final trophy aloft

**Man with the plan:** Manager Alan Pardew plotted West Ham's ascent

**Ash landing:** Dean Ashton is submerged by his teammates after scoring in the FA Cup sixth-round tie at Manchester City

**Hare we go:** Marlon Harewood (right) is acclaimed by Anton Ferdinand following his FA Cup semi-final winner against Middlesbrough

**Two easy:** Dean Ashton leaves Liverpool goalkeeper José Reina floored after putting West Ham 2–0 ahead in the FA Cup final

**Kon trick:** Paul Konchesky is the centre of attention after putting the Hammers 3–2 up in the FA Cup final

**Mystery and intrigue:** Alan Pardew introduces Argentina duo Carlos Tévez and Javier Mascherano as West Ham players (© Getty Images)

**No Pal of mine:** Javier Mascherano tries to shake off the attentions of Fabio Simplicio during West Ham's UEFA Cup defeat in Palermo

**Reasons to be cheerful:** Former chairman Terence Brown earned around £30 million from the sale of his West Ham shareholding

**Baptism of fire:** Manager Alan Curbishley (left) and his assistant Mervyn Day
endured tough times after taking over

**Ham and Egg:** Eggert
Magnússon had a lot on
his plate after becoming
West Ham chairman

**Valley of nightmares:** Alan Curbishley shakes hands with rival boss
Alan Pardew after the Hammers collapse 4–0 at his former club Charlton

**Gold Trafford:** Carlos Tévez scores the winner at Manchester United
as West Ham retain their Premiership place

**Escape artist:** Carlos Tévez celebrates
Premiership survival at Old Trafford

**Money man:** Kia Joorabchian
(© Getty Images)

Exchange on 12 October, although Joorabchian was suspicious of the emergence of a rival party, apparently believing the approach was a 'red herring' to push the process through. Magnússon claimed to have been following the events at Upton Park for some considerable time, however, and he responded by saying, 'If there are any red herrings, it is the other bids. We are looking at this very seriously.'

It's possible, though, that Magnússon's interest was provoked at the start of September when UEFA expressed concerns about football clubs being owned by mysterious corporations. Treasurer Mathieu Sprenger said, 'I have heard the news reports concerning West Ham. Our proposals are that all clubs must show who owns them. It will not be enough to show that a company owns them. They will have to show who is behind that company as well.'

West Ham's fortunes on the pitch had improved, with successive home wins against Blackburn and Arsenal lifting the team out of the relegation zone. The speculation about Pardew's position continued, however, with Eriksson's name returning to the frame if the Joorabchian initiative succeeded. This was a result of Joorabchian's associate Papouchado being spotted while dining with the former England boss and agent Zahavi in Israel. Papouchado then flew to London to meet Joorabchian, although Athole Still, Eriksson's agent, denied that the name of West Ham was ever mentioned during their conversations.

Once again, rumours of Eriksson being lined up to take over at West Ham worried the club's supporters, who generally favoured the Magnússon bid, despite the Icelander making no bold statements about how much he would spend on new players if he took charge. There were no reports of links with Russian oligarchs or Israeli property developers, no stories of expensive Swedes coming in to manage and no fears about the Icelander's motives for wanting to buy the club.

But Magnússon was no less ambitious, and he left Pardew impressed by his plans for the club when they met in the early part of November. 'I was enthused coming out of the meeting, just as I was when I met Kia Joorabchian,' he said. 'Both men have sound views on what they want to do, and I am all ears to that because I want to take this club forward and hopefully into the Champions League.' Magnússon, dubbed a 'biscuit baron' by the media because of his past ownership of a bread and biscuit manufacturing company, had been granted permission to inspect the club's accounts.

An opening bid had been rejected, but he was soon able to prove he had the funds to increase his offer when it was revealed that billionaire financier Björgólfur Gudmundsson was backing the move. Gudmundsson was the chairman of Icelandic bank Landsbanki, had business interests in a number of different environments and had football credentials himself, having played for his country's oldest club, KR in Reykjavik, where he later became chairman. The Icelandic interest – funded purely from equity rather than loans – was beginning to look increasingly more attractive.

There were members of the West Ham board that reportedly favoured the Joorabchian initiative, although Brown has denied he had any preference, having an obligation to the club's shareholders to seek out the best deal. Under Joorabchian's proposal, however, it was likely that both he and managing director Aldridge would be allowed to remain in their positions at the club. This was fully understandable; they had the expertise of running West Ham together for several years, and it made sense for Joorabchian to keep them in place. 'The Kia lot needed management,' said Brown later.

However, if Magnússon took control he would inevitably want to succeed Brown as the club's chairman. There were others on the West Ham board that allegedly did not look forward to the idea of working under Joorabchian, with some observers suspecting that finance director Nick Igoe and commercial and legal director Scott Duxbury – both employees as opposed to major shareholders – would leave the club if that move went through.

By mid-November, the negotiations had taken the price up to an eyebrow-raising £85 million, plus responsibility for the £22.5 million debt, which Joorabchian failed to match. Although there was speculation of some late American interest – prompted by US tycoon Randy Lerner's recent £63 million purchase of Aston Villa – it was inevitable that Magnússon's generous bid would be accepted. That decision was confirmed to the Stock Exchange on 21 November with Magnússon securing agreements to purchase 83 per cent of the club's 20,202,352 ordinary shares (the West Ham directors' beneficial holdings representing 45 per cent and the remaining 38 per cent coming from other shareholders) at a price of 421p each, with a recommendation being made to the remaining stakeholders to accept the offer.

'The offer reflects fair value for West Ham, considering its significant history, recent performance and prospects, and its position as a leading London club,' stated Brown. As anticipated, Magnússon would succeed Brown – who would stay on as non-executive deputy vice-chairman – while fellow consortium members Thór Kristjánsson (a board member of Landsbanki) and Gudmundur J. Oddsson (a partner of Logos legal services) would join the West Ham board. Chief backer Gudmundsson, meanwhile, was handed the position of honorary life president. Furthermore, it was announced that outgoing directors Charles Warner and Martin Cearns – whose ancestors founded the Hammers in 1895 – would become associate members to 'ensure the traditions of the club are preserved'.

Brown was adamant that the club was being 'passed into good hands' and added, 'I think Eggert will be tremendous for West

Ham.' Magnússon immediately made his intentions crystal clear. 'I want to be competing for places in the Champions League – that is my ultimate ambition. But we will take it slowly and build on the foundations that are already here.' It's fair to say not too many West Ham fans shed tears over Brown's departure as chairman, and they had at least been reassured that the new owners were credible and had the financial capacity to advance the club.

Magnússon immediately resigned from the Icelandic FA and confirmed his wish to relinquish his UEFA responsibilities as he pledged to concentrate his energies on lifting the Hammers out of their present mire and into the upper echelons of the Premiership table. 'Eggert will make West Ham successful,' said Ólafur Gardarsson, an Icelandic agent and lawyer who had known Magnússon for nearly a decade. 'He's enthusiastic, powerful and is usually successful in whatever he does. It's difficult to stop him once he gets involved in a project.'

The Icelandic acquisition of West Ham attracted some mild concern in the media with some pundits becoming increasingly fearful of the number of Premiership clubs falling into foreign hands. Americans had bought Manchester United and Aston Villa, while Liverpool would soon join them. Portsmouth, like Chelsea, was owned by a Russian, while Fulham was under the control of Harrods owner Mohamed Al-Fayed, an Egyptian. The trend would continue with former Thai prime minister Thaksin Shinawatra buying Manchester City in the summer of 2007 and Birmingham City, Blackburn Rovers and Arsenal being targeted for potential takeovers by foreign investors.

It was perhaps inevitable that the huge amount of money generated by England's top clubs – largely thanks to the television revenue provided by media-mogul Rupert Murdoch's Sky network – would attract increasing interest from parties based abroad. If the smell of money is in the air, the vultures will circle. Yet the purchase of a Premiership club was not a cheap business, and there was little point in acquiring one if the funds could not be supplied to invest in the playing squad.

So it was no coincidence that all the top English clubs moving into foreign ownership enjoyed a substantial boost in spending power. Chelsea owner Abramovich may have been accused of treating the London club as a plaything – with huge losses being incurred on the balance sheet in the quest to achieve profits on the field of play – but his supporters were not complaining as the team was crowned League Champions for the first time in half a century. Few could dispute they were buying success and inflating the football market in terms of transfers and wages, but the money remained within the game and filtered down through many levels. Indeed, West Ham had themselves benefited from Chelsea's lavish rebuilding programme in 2003 with £12.6 million being received through the sales of Joe Cole and Glen Johnson in the aftermath of relegation. Chelsea was very much an anomaly, however, with few clubs under new ownership being able to match the spending power of Abramovich, despite offering renewed hope to their supporters with an initial injection of funds.

In West Ham's case, fans were pleased to discover that Magnússon had quickly made contact with Chelsea about the possible availability of winger Shaun Wright-Phillips when the next transfer window opened. It was a clear statement of intent, with the 25 year old having cost the Blues £21 million when signing him from Manchester City the previous year. The Icelander was also looking to the long term by announcing his desire to relocate the club to the new Olympic Stadium in 2012 if possible.

Magnússon was introduced to the West Ham supporters ahead of the home game against Sheffield United on 25 November and was given a warm reception. 'I'm not going to let these people down,' he promised. He was duly rewarded with the club's third home win in succession, with Mullins – re-established in midfield at the expense of the unfortunate Mascherano – scoring the winner in a game that would ultimately have huge significance at the end of the season. Yet the post-match headlines were as much about a hot-tempered Argentinian as a cool-headed Icelander, with Tévez storming out of the Boleyn Ground in disgust after being substituted midway through the second period.

Tévez had just completed a full Premiership game for the first time in seven attempts in the previous week's 1–0 defeat at Chelsea and was West Ham's most dangerous player at Stamford Bridge, despite playing wide on the right. But he experienced less joy against the Blades – in terms of opening his goal-scoring account for West Ham or lasting the full 90 minutes – and his frustration was obvious as he disappeared in a huff. It was not the wisest of actions on the striker's part, with it being speculated that both he and Mascherano would be moved on at the earliest opportunity as a result of Joorabchian's failure to buy the club. Pardew, who admitted he 'needed to meet up with Kia' to establish what his plans were for the two players, had no problems revealing his thoughts on the Tévez walkout by complaining about the Argentinian's 'disrespectful' behaviour.

Within a week of Magnússon's arrival, it was confirmed that Aldridge had left the club 'by mutual consent', with Duxbury being promoted to deputy chief executive in his place. Few outside observers were surprised, although it was interesting that the original statement issued by WH Holding Ltd – the company formed by the Magnússon consortium for the purchase of West Ham – had declared that Aldridge would remain in his position. 'It was a very difficult decision to decline the opportunity to join the new West Ham board,' said Aldridge, although Magnússon's declaration that 'this is a natural moment for a change' indicated little regret about the departure. Aldridge, who had spent ten years at Upton Park and succeeded Peter Storrie as managing director in 1999, could at least console himself to some extent with the £235,339 he earned from the sale of his 55,900 shares in the club.

It had gone virtually unnoticed that *The Guardian* had a few days earlier run a profile piece on the 'real power behind West Ham' in which they revealed how financier Gudmundsson had made much of his money in Russia – along with son Björgólfur Thor Björgólfsson – after having been convicted in 1991 of minor accounting offences in his homeland following the collapse of shipping line Hafskip. 'The conviction was a long time ago,' said a spokesman for the man who was listed as the 799th-richest person in the world. 'Mr Gudmundsson has come a long way and is well respected in Iceland.'

As Gudmundsson remained in the background, Magnússon wasted little time in dirtying his hands as he got to grips with his new responsibilities at the Boleyn Ground. But having got his feet under the table, it was what he discovered under the carpet that began to alarm him. 'Certain things were not as I thought regarding the club and the team,' he candidly admitted. 'I cannot go into details, but some things have surprised me.' Unlike the majority of foreign businessmen buying English football clubs, Magnússon had a wealth of football experience and expertise. But it's clear that wasn't enough to prepare him for everything he had to contend with.

He was clearly unhappy with the irregular arrangement that had brought Tévez and Mascherano to the club. 'I would never have entered into a contract where a club doesn't own a player; it's out of the question,' he scoffed as he discussed the situation in the Boleyn Ground's trophy room. The plot regarding the Argentinian duo would thicken over the following months, with copies of documents appearing in two *News of the World* stories that focused on the negotiations with Joorabchian, both in terms of the takeover and the acquisition of the two players.

Former chairman Brown denied any wrongdoing, but the question was how these documents had fallen into the hands of a newspaper. Magnússon was concerned about the possibility of leaks at West Ham, and he confided, 'We have been having serious discussions at the club about where this has been coming from.' The newspaper reports sought to discredit the former West Ham hierarchy, but some of the conspiracy theories being developed were illogical, as it couldn't possibly have benefited the club to have suspicions raised about any of its activities.

Magnússon was also forced to contend with other issues in his early days at Upton Park, of course. It had been stated in the sale agreement that 'WH Holding's intention to retain Alan Pardew as manager is one of a number of factors that has gained the favour of the [existing] board'. That may well have been Magnússon's original hope, but he would soon be forced to revise his opinion.

# 8

## 'THERE WERE REASONS WHY I HAD TO DO IT'

'I THINK Alan Pardew is a great manager, and he has done great things with West Ham. Last season was a great year, and I fully believe he will help me take West Ham to the next stage.' So said Eggert Magnússon within a few days of taking control at Upton Park towards the end of November 2006. Yet the team would play just four more games before Pardew's employment at the club was ruthlessly terminated, leaving many shocked by how quickly the chairman had reappraised the situation and lost faith in his manager.

Pardew had first begun to publicly question his West Ham future after the 2–0 defeat at Portsmouth on 14 October. The result saw the Hammers set a new club record for failing to score in six successive defeats and dropped them back into the relegation zone. Pardew looked understandably downcast as he made his way along Fratton Park's cold corridors after the final whistle. 'I think any manager who has lost six successive games has to have a certain amount of fear for his job,' he said, although there was a feeling he didn't really believe that there was a serious threat of him being relieved of his duties. Nevertheless, the admission allowed the media to produce the 'Pardew fears the chop' headlines they were looking for.

The West Ham manager had fully anticipated the tabloid

treatment he would receive ahead of the following weekend's trip to Tottenham. 'The media attention on the players and myself leading up to the Spurs game will be very strong, and we've got to be big enough to take it,' he said. That was all very well, but the signs from many of the players were that they were struggling to cope with the growing criticism, having enjoyed nothing but praise for their efforts over the previous 18 months. And Pardew virtually acknowledged as much when calling for his men to take a reality check after the 1–0 defeat at White Hart Lane extended his side's goalless and pointless run. 'We've got to face up to the fact we're in the bottom three and need to roll our sleeves up,' he said. 'Certain players can reach higher levels than they have.'

The media focused on two possible reasons why that might have been – the speculation surrounding the club's protracted takeover and the theory that the shock arrivals of Carlos Tévez and Javier Mascherano had knocked the team out of its stride. But the reality was that there were two *groups* of reasons why the team was seriously underperforming – the ones that were publicly evident and the ones that were not. The ones that were visible could potentially be addressed, while the ones that were more latent were left neglected and acted as a corrosive force beneath the surface, explaining why they would prove so damaging and difficult to erase. Pardew would eventually become a victim of those influences, while his successor Alan Curbishley would fight long and hard to overcome them.

The first obvious sign that West Ham's season was never going to be what was anticipated came in the form of the serious ankle injury to striker Dean Ashton. It was immediately evident that the record signing would not be fit to return to action until the Christmas period at the very earliest, which would inevitably jeopardise the club's chances of building on the previous season's achievements. Peter Grant was acutely aware of how sorely

Ashton was missed in the early part of the campaign when just a few goals from the hit man could have made a huge difference. 'We just couldn't score,' he reflected. 'Dean was a natural, and I'm sure he would have got goals in that period to turn things around. We were playing quite well, but the natural instinct to put the ball into the back of the net wasn't there, and as we lost games the confidence started to drain.'

West Ham's passing style of football required a decent amount of confidence to be successful, and it's true that heads gradually began to drop as results – and whatever luck was going – went against them. There was a degree of poor fortune in the early games, with Palermo scoring disputed opening goals in both UEFA Cup legs, Tévez hitting the bar against Newcastle with the match still goalless and Tottenham scoring their winner in the third minute of first-half injury time after just one minute had been signalled. Spurs striker Jermain Defoe somehow avoided being sent off after bizarrely choosing to bite a grounded Mascherano – an incident that made front-page headlines – while Reading stole a 1–0 win at Upton Park with their first and only shot on target in the game's opening minute.

A number of players had also suffered injuries that deprived them of a proper month's pre-season training. Anton Ferdinand had spent the summer recovering from a double-hernia operation that prevented him from being added to England's standby list for the World Cup finals and was then sidelined with a hamstring strain. Fellow defender Danny Gabbidon and skipper Nigel Reo-Coker missed the three friendly games in Sweden with groin and back problems respectively, while midfielders Yossi Benayoun (thigh) and Matthew Etherington (knee) also had their pre-season preparations wrecked. All except Etherington were fit enough to start the season's opening game against Charlton, but none of them could claim to have been at their best. Players such as Paul Konchesky and Marlon Harewood also started the campaign in disappointing fashion, for reasons best known to themselves.

There were problems at both ends of the team, with the defence having to wait until the 14th game of the season to keep a clean sheet and the attack failing to score in seven successive outings. Pardew complained that games would always be an uphill struggle while West Ham were conceding the opening goal – as they had done in ten of their first eleven fixtures. Further injury problems made it difficult to keep a settled defence. But matters weren't necessarily helped by the manager's constant shuffling of cards in a bid to find a winning hand.

This was particularly apparent up front, where Pardew deployed his five strikers in an astonishing eleven different permutations, including substitutions, in as many games. First, he started with Harewood and Bobby Zamora, then it was Tévez and Zamora. In Palermo, Tévez supplemented Harewood and Carlton Cole before Zamora replaced Cole and Teddy Sheringham replaced Harewood. Then Tévez and Cole started, followed by Zamora and Sheringham. Substitutions saw Cole partner Sheringham, Harewood and Zamora on different occasions, while Harewood also played with Sheringham.

If this was disorientating for the supporters, it was just as confusing for the players, who were being asked to immediately develop an understanding with whomever they were being thrown in with. It was believed that several members of the squad became increasingly unhappy with the situation, not least Harewood and Cole. The former had top-scored with sixteen goals the previous term but failed to hit the net in his first ten outings of the new season. After starting the first four games, he was exiled to the substitutes' bench for the sake of Tévez and then recalled before being dropped and called up again. He wasn't playing well, but Harewood would no doubt argue that it was impossible to do so when he was in and out of the team and partnering different players.

Cole was another face of discontent, having left Chelsea in the summer due to a lack of opportunities only to suffer the same fate at Upton Park. He couldn't have done much more than score on his debut – against Charlton with his first touch – but he started just two of the opening eleven games and would fail to do so again under Pardew's management. It's fair to say that wasn't what he expected when he joined the club. 'I've got to try and find the right formula,' said Pardew as he explained the constant rotation. 'Whether I start with the same two next week or change it again, that's my decision.'

The manager was faced with an obvious dilemma. Players were underperforming and the team was losing games, so it was natural to want to make changes. But nothing appeared to be working, and the lack of stability seemed to be doing nobody any favours. 'It's difficult,' admitted Pardew. 'We need to find the right balance without shuffling things too much.' But the experimentation continued, almost at random it seemed, with the manager throwing ideas at the tactics board with increasing desperation.

The names of Tévez and Mascherano could be added to the growing list of unhappy players. The former's exceptional talent may have made him versatile, but he didn't appreciate being asked to play in a variety of different positions – on the few occasions he was selected. 'I'm here to help, but playing out of my role puts me under pressure,' he complained. Mascherano had also found opportunities very limited. 'It's been very tough,' he admitted, somewhat bemused that he should have lost his shirt to Hayden Mullins. To see the two players being neglected was somewhat mystifying – especially with West Ham struggling so badly – but Pardew managed to avoid heavy criticism for his failure to integrate the two Argentinians into his team, even though many managers would love to have had such talent at their disposal. The situation would have been strange enough had the team been winning, but the Hammers were crying out for inspiration and an injection of quality.

The team was no different to a functioning machine, and the pieces of equipment needed to fit together for it to work properly. Grant believed West Ham would have needed to dismantle their usual 4–4–2 construction to accommodate the two Argentinians on a regular basis. 'Javier couldn't play in a central two in midfield,' he said as he looked back. 'He had always played in a sitting role with two other midfielders in a 4–3–3 system, in which case he was a fantastic player. He could have played in Chelsea's team standing on his head. But in a two he couldn't get close to the opposition.' Grant was also of the view that Tévez would have been more comfortable playing with Ashton, who he considered more adaptable, whereas the likes of Zamora and Harewood played as a more conventional pair. 'With a different type of striker available to us, such as Ashton, things could have been very different,' he said.

Ashton had already suffered injury by the time the option to sign the Argentina stars became available. Few managers would have rejected the opportunity, but the fact remained that players were usually recruited to fulfil a specific function. Team building was about finding the missing pieces of the jigsaw. If the manager had not initiated the recruitment drive, it was inevitable he was going to find himself with spare parts that didn't necessarily fit and end up having to ram square pegs into round holes. Such would appear to be the case in terms of Pardew struggling to incorporate the unfortunate Tévez and Mascherano, who inevitably felt increasingly alienated by the whole experience.

Pardew potentially had reason to feel isolated himself when sidekick Grant was allowed to leave West Ham to move into full management with Norwich City in the middle of October. The Scot was eager to return to the Championship club he'd represented as a player for two years after leaving Celtic in 1997. And his departure from Upton Park was another setback for the Hammers, as he had played a key role behind the scenes. West Ham attempted to accommodate for his loss by promoting Keith Peacock – who had joined the club as senior coach in the summer after leaving Charlton along with Curbishley – to the position of assistant manager, while Kevin Keen was promoted from reserve-team boss to first-team coach.

Grant left Upton Park believing West Ham would soon recover from their poor start to the campaign. He knew the players were capable of doing so much better but recognised there was 'a lack of confidence' in the squad. 'Some of the boys were not playing well and not doing the things they were good at as individuals. It only takes a 1 per cent drop in the performance levels of each player and you've lost 10 per cent across your team – and we weren't good enough to carry that drop,' he said. Grant had particularly recognised that skipper Reo-Coker's form was not what it could have been. The England Under-21 international had played his part as the Hammers enjoyed a great first season back in the Premiership, showing plenty of industry and developing a strong partnership with Mullins in the centre of midfield. He was far from being the finished article, of course, with his final pass occasionally letting him down and showing little threat in front of goal. But his career was on a consistent upward trajectory, and the feeling was that he would only become more influential as he continued to mature.

Indeed, Reo-Coker's contribution towards West Ham's success had not gone unnoticed by both Arsenal and Manchester United, who had been tracking his progress with interest. It was inevitable that a bigger club would make a move for the

22 year old at some stage, but it still surprised many when it emerged that West Ham had received enquiries about him on the final day of the summer transfer window. The news was almost buried amid the hullabaloo over the signings of Tévez and Mascherano, and it was believed that no definite bid was made.

West Ham made it known that they were not interested in doing business at that stage, much to the dismay of Reo-Coker, whose contract reportedly allowed him to talk to one of the 'big four' clubs if a certain fee was offered. Grant was of the view that Reo-Coker wasn't yet ready to make the step up to one of England's top outfits anyway. 'If Nigel wanted to play for the Arsenals or Manchester Uniteds of this world, he knew he had to improve,' he said. 'He's got power and pace, but the best players are judged on their final selection of pass and how many goals they score.' Grant was sceptical of how definite the interest was, knowing that agents frequently claimed that managers were chasing players without any follow-up. 'There was no conversation between Alan Pardew and [Arsenal boss] Arsène Wenger,' he said.

West Ham supporters quickly identified that Reo-Coker had appeared to let his head drop in the early part of the season. A group flying back from the UEFA Cup defeat in Palermo in September were unhappy with the midfielder's apparent lack of commitment, and that type of conversation would become prevalent among Hammers followers as the campaign progressed. Grant believed it was inevitable that Reo-Coker's 'head was going to get twisted a bit' as a result of such transfer speculation. But he attributed the player's disappointing form to other factors and felt his demeanour on the field of play was often misinterpreted. 'Nigel needed the team to be playing well for him to perform at his best,' he said. 'If he was winning the ball and had nowhere to pass it because there were a lack of runners, he was going to get caught in possession, and the fans would then get on his case. He could be a moody little boy and had that sulkiness about him anyway, but he wasn't playing well and got frustrated about that.'

Reo-Coker's 'sulkiness' appeared to do little to improve the morale of the squad during a period when their captain should have been inspiring and motivating his fellow troops. But that was just one of the problems that was bubbling beneath the surface in the West Ham dressing-room. The confidence gained thanks to the team's ascendancy over the previous 18 months had started to evaporate on the pitch as the results deteriorated. By that stage, however, egos had ballooned and feet had long left the ground, with several players – particularly the younger ones – becoming increasingly intoxicated by their success and growing wealth.

Many of them had attacked the previous season's campaign feeling they had a point to prove. West Ham had fought hard to win back their place in the Premiership and that wasn't going to be easily relinquished. The team had also been written off as relegation fodder, and there was the added motivation of trying to make the critics eat their words. Youth brought with it innocence and a lack of fear, and the Hammers benefited from that mentality in the 2005–06 season. One year later, however, too many players thought they had truly established themselves as Premiership stars, which created a culture of complacency that would nearly ruin the club from within. The players wouldn't admit it at the time – indeed, many of them couldn't recognise it – but the decay had begun to set in from the moment they left the Millennium Stadium on FA Cup final day back in May.

It was something that a few members of the squad were able to acknowledge in retrospect, however. 'Maybe the players thought we were better than we really were,' admitted Gabbidon.

'We definitely haven't worked as hard as a team. The hunger we had last season has not been as evident. Maybe there was a complacency there.' That view was supported by teammate Christian Dailly, one of the most experienced players in the camp. 'There's no doubt some of the boys took their foot off the gas. We have a lot of young players at West Ham, and it was a learning curve for them. If you begin to ease up, then you can end up in trouble,' he said.

Grant, however, believed the players had continued to display the right work ethic as they prepared for games. Indeed, he and boss Pardew attempted to 'raise the bar' on the training field to ensure that there was no slackening. 'I don't think we had good enough players to be complacent,' he reflected. 'They knew that everything relating to their success was geared to the fact they had to put total effort and commitment into it. The reality is that they still had a lot of improving to do.' Nevertheless, at a subconscious level, a change of attitude would seem to have taken significant hold and undermined the team for a prolonged period of time.

There were also suspicions that Pardew was not immune to being consumed by West Ham's success either. As the first season in the Premiership had come to a close, he had insisted stability of mind was the key to constant development. 'I don't let any of my staff get carried away, and we've got to stay on the same level,' he said. But Pardew appeared to enjoy his growing celebrity status, and it was inevitable he would start to display the trappings of success.

It was reported that the manager had shocked his players by arriving for training in a Ferrari. It was also alleged that he put a few noses out of joint by referring to his wealthy status – he'd reportedly earned over £1.5 million including bonuses over the previous year or so – when talking to his players after the home defeat by Newcastle. It was considered acceptable for the club's dizzy-headed first-team stars to brandish their wealth if they wanted to, but the manager was an authority figure and needed to retain the respect of his players. Preserving that relationship was vital to the chemistry within the camp.

Evidence that the manager had perhaps lost his focus came in the shape of the Carling Cup third-round tie at Chesterfield on 24 October. The Spireites were struggling in League One, but they had shown fighting qualities in cup games, squeezing past Championship outfit Wolves on penalties in the first round and then claiming a major Premiership scalp in the form of Manchester City. So, with West Ham travelling to Saltergate on the back of seven successive defeats, the game was less of a banana skin and more of a giant oil slick. Pardew knew he could not afford to take Chesterfield lightly, but the team sheet he handed out on that freezing-cold night was somewhat bewildering.

The selection of 18-year-old winger Kyel Reid – for his first and only Hammers outing of the season – might have been enforced by Yossi Benayoun and Lee Bowyer being injured and Matthew Etherington only being fit enough to make the bench. But in handing George McCartney his debut at full-back it meant that the entire left-hand side of the team was completely untried and tested. Central midfielder Reo-Coker had failed to impress when asked to play on the right flank at Tottenham a few days earlier, but Pardew decided to keep him out there for a second game, which was unlikely to reap dividends. And the idea of deploying the ultra-defensive Dailly alongside Mullins in midfield resulted in an obvious lack of attacking initiative in the centre of the park.

This was always likely to play into Chesterfield's hands, and perhaps the only surprise on the night was that West Ham managed to bring an end to their 672-minute goal drought when they took an early lead through Harewood's instinctive strike. They failed to capitalise on that boost, however, and Chesterfield gradually gained a foothold in the game as they realised the visitors had little to offer. Roared on by a sell-out crowd, the Spireites turned up the pressure and were eventually rewarded when Colin Larkin levelled shortly after the break. Hammers goalkeeper Robert Green, making only his second start for the club after eventually displacing Roy Carroll, could only force Caleb Folan's curling shot onto the woodwork, and Larkin gleefully latched onto the rebound. With Dailly instinctively dropping back to act as a third centre-half to repel the flurry of balls into the penalty area and West Ham offering little in the way of an attacking threat, it was only a matter of time before the defence cracked again. It duly obliged with just three minutes of the game remaining when Folan poked home following Jamie Lowry's free-kick into the box.

West Ham's embarrassment in front of a live TV audience was complete. So much for the Tévez-and-Mascherano-inspired revolution mocked the critics – the two Argentinians were nowhere to be seen as the Hammers made it a straight eight in terms of losses. Terence Brown's presence in the tight tunnel area by the visitors' changing rooms prompted claims that the chairman had ridiculed the players by telling them they had 'played like a pub team'. That description might not have been far short of the truth. But Brown responded to the reports by insisting he'd simply put a comforting arm around his manager and told him that 'everything would be fine'.

After facing the TV cameras, Pardew stepped out onto the edge of the pitch to discuss what had gone wrong. 'We never really got going,' he said, ignoring the fact that his side could hardly have enjoyed a better start than Harewood's fourth-minute opener. He failed to acknowledge his team would have benefited from having skipper Reo-Coker in his traditional central-midfield role or that Konchesky would have offered more experienced support to novice Reid on the left. As far as the media was concerned, this was now a fully blown crisis for West Ham, and the subsequent headlines all focused on Pardew's position, with it being reported that victory in the home game against Blackburn a few days later was essential to the manager's survival.

This was not the case, however. There had been all sorts of debate about the club's impending takeover creating a destabilising atmosphere that could potentially cost Pardew his job if he failed to deal with the pressures, but the reality was that the likely change of ownership actually helped protect the manager, with the existing West Ham hierarchy unlikely to wield the axe before handing over the club's keys to a new party. That would have been highly illogical, even if the board had decided that Pardew's achievements of the previous two seasons could not disguise his current problems. With Grant now gone, there was nobody on the coaching staff keen to assume control, even on a temporary basis. And who would want to succeed Pardew knowing that the club's next owners would probably want to recruit their own management team?

Predictably, however, veteran striker Sheringham was deemed to have 'saved' Pardew's neck by scoring the opener against Blackburn to set up West Ham's 2–1 victory – the team's first in a dozen outings. The 40 year old made the most of only his second start of the season, and Pardew was acclaimed for showing faith in the former England international. But Sheringham's inclusion at the expense of Harewood was a surprise, because the latter had expected to start after scoring his first goal of the season at Chesterfield. The striker was left feeling that if he couldn't hold onto his place after hitting the net, then his prospects were obviously diminishing. Zamora, meanwhile, had retained his starting place for all but two games, despite not scoring in his previous eight outings – and never really looking like doing so.

The backing that Pardew received from the West Ham supporters during the Blackburn match proved two things: first, that it would take some time to forget the journey he had taken them on over the previous three years; and second, that they largely blamed the underperforming players for the club's current woes. That was obvious by their reaction at the final whistle at Chesterfield when chants of 'you're not fit to wear the shirt' rang out loud and clear.

Before the kick-off against Blackburn, they sang 'there's only one Alan Pardew' to leave the manager feeling genuinely humble. 'I'm not the most emotional of people, but I was a little bit choked at the start,' he confided. 'They showed the quality that some grounds can't get, and I thank them for that.' Pardew had always played the crowd particularly well, knowing how to stoke them up when a big atmosphere was needed, when to thank them during the good times and how to appease them during the bad. Some observers took the cynical view, arguing that he often manipulated public opinion to keep the fans on his side. The vast majority, however, had faith in his integrity and considered his words to be never less than sincere.

Victory against Blackburn lifted West Ham out of the relegation zone, but a far sterner test awaited them in the following week's visit of Arsenal – a game that won Pardew support in more ways than one. The use of Zamora as a lone forward in front of a five-man midfield perhaps suggested a lack of ambition on the manager's part, although there's little doubt fans would have been happy with a point given most of the season's results. But having been content to soak up the best the Gunners had to offer on the day, West Ham stepped up a gear with the introduction of strikers Sheringham and Harewood just past the hour mark – and the latter subsequently grabbed a vital last-minute winner.

As had happened after the previous season's win against

Arsenal, however, the 1–0 success was overshadowed by controversy, with Pardew and Gunners boss Arsène Wenger becoming embroiled in a bizarre touchline spat as West Ham celebrated Harewood's goal. Pardew appeared to do little wrong as he punched the air in delight, but Wenger took umbrage and induced a shoving match with his counterpart while some colourful language was exchanged.

Wenger further embarrassed himself by refusing to shake hands with Pardew after the final whistle and then failing to appear for the post-match press conference. The West Ham boss graciously apologised if his celebrations had unwittingly offended Wenger, but in truth he had nothing to be pardoned for. He had suffered far more misfortune than most managers that season and had conducted himself with a dignity that Wenger sorely lacked at Upton Park. 'It's always the same with Arsenal. You get in and about them, and they don't like it. There's an arrogance about them,' said defender McCartney.

There was more to the bust-up than met the eye, however. Wenger hadn't been happy when Pardew questioned how much pride Britain could take from Arsenal's progress to the Champions League final the previous term given that the majority of their players were foreign. It was a fair point, yet Wenger's response was to accuse the West Ham boss of making xenophobic remarks. 'We have "Kick Racism Out Of Football", yet racism starts here,' said Wenger. Pardew was deeply unhappy, putting out a statement in which he said, 'I was not being racist or xenophobic. But I maintain we need to have young British players coming through if we are to have strong national sides.' He would later reveal his belief that 'taking four points off Arsenal [in 2005–06] is probably why Wenger had a go at me'.

It wasn't the first time Pardew had found himself involved in a war of words with an opposing manager. Earlier in the year, he had accused Graeme Souness of talking 'nonsense' after the Newcastle manager had reportedly claimed West Ham's defenders were scared of striker Michael Owen, who bagged a hat-trick in his side's 4–2 win at Upton Park. The press inevitably exploited such conflict between managers, and Pardew became increasingly aware – especially as the club's profile continued to grow – of the dangers of speaking too openly. 'You have to be on your guard, because the media can often take just one little sound bite from an interview and make you look foolish,' he later said.

But the manager was also of the view that West Ham's public relations left much to be desired. Some observers believed that the club had been slow to adapt to the growing demands of the media, with one overworked press officer dealing with general enquiries, overseeing administration and editing the match programme for several years prior to promotion. Yet football had moved on, with public and media interest intensifying and expanding as a result of Sky's marketing of the game, the increased money in the sport and the development of the Internet.

Pardew recognised a football club was no different to any other product in a competitive marketplace in respect of image and presentation being key elements of its appeal. He claimed West Ham's PR to have been 'a disaster' in past years and worked hard at trying to build solid bridges with the media. A key part of the club's new strategy was to recruit former *News of the World* editor Phil Hall as a media consultant. The move wasn't just about controlling press accessibility to players – this didn't necessarily become easier, although the process was more professional – but managing and manipulating the media to ensure a positive image. This was easier said than done, however, because the nature of a football club's coverage was largely dictated by results – which couldn't be governed – while it was impossible to stop some stories from finding their way into the public domain.

The successive home victories against Blackburn and Arsenal ultimately proved to be a false dawn, with West Ham losing at Middlesbrough and Chelsea by 1–0 scorelines. The home win against Sheffield United towards the end of November was timely in terms of coinciding with new chairman Magnússon's arrival, but if Pardew believed all his troubles were behind him, he was sadly mistaken. West Ham were unlucky in their next game at Everton when they failed to capitalise on their early dominance – with Zamora extending his goalless run to 13 outings – as they fell to a 2–0 defeat. Indeed, they forced twelve first-half corners to Everton's one but could not avoid yet another blank away day.

After three successive victories at Upton Park, it at least appeared that West Ham's home form would offer them hope, but a dismal 2–0 midweek defeat by Wigan – in which they mustered just one shot on target – left them feeling as if they were back at square one. 'We were second best all night, and I wouldn't have thought Mr Gudmundsson is very pleased,' admitted Pardew after the game, the club's new main backer having witnessed the depressing display up in the stands. The manager would not have liked what was being said between Gudmundsson and Magnússon had he been party to their conversations during the match.

In fact, Magnússon spoke to Pardew before he left Upton Park that evening, warning him that the performance against Wigan had been unacceptable – although the manager hardly needed telling. In his defence, he could have pointed to the previous season's corresponding fixture, which had produced the same result following an equally disappointing display. But the context was very different on this occasion with West Ham now back in the relegation zone and new owners demanding to see an improvement.

The last prospect Pardew would have relished at that time was a trip to Bolton for a Saturday evening game shown live on Sky Sports. But that is what followed as West Ham prepared for their third game in six days. A weakened Hammers side had crashed 4–1 at the Reebok Stadium earlier in the year, and hopes of being stronger defensively this time around were dealt a heavy blow when an ankle injury forced Ferdinand to join fellow centre-half Gabbidon – who had missed the last two games with a hamstring problem – on the sidelines. A makeshift partnership of McCartney and James Collins was always likely to struggle against the Trotters, and so it proved, with Kevin Davies scoring in the 18th and 53rd minutes to put the hosts well in control before El-Hadji Diouf and Nicolas Anelka poured salt into West Ham's wounds to seal the 4–0 result.

The expression on Gudmundsson's face in the stands was that of a businessman watching a very expensive acquisition diminish in value as the seconds ticked by. Next to him, partner Magnússon simply sunk deeper into his seat with his head gradually disappearing into his overcoat in a bid seemingly to cover his embarrassment. With the Bolton fans chanting that Pardew was 'getting sacked in the morning' – yes, that old chestnut again – it was easy to imagine what the two directors were thinking as they watched West Ham set a new club record of ten successive away defeats in a single season. The team may have had its injury problems, but there was no excuse for the lack of concentration and commitment by the West Ham players as they meekly surrendered the points and waved the white flag.

Pardew weighed into his players in the dressing-room, but he sensed it was probably too late to make a difference in the grander scheme of things. He looked ashen-faced as he appeared in the media room, and his usual bullishness in defeat was noticeably absent. He spoke in more philosophical terms, talking about coming through times of adversity and enjoying success only if difficult periods such as this were survived. But by declaring 'we're a lot better than we're suggesting', he was admitting his failure to get the best out of his players.

Pardew was asked to attend a meeting at Upton Park on the morning of Monday, 11 December 2006 when he was officially informed that his services were no longer required. 'We can say you're leaving by mutual consent,' offered Magnússon, but Pardew rejected the idea, believing that it would appear as if he was throwing in the towel. 'I wasn't going to accept that, because I thought I could turn things around,' he later explained. A severance agreement, reported to be worth around £1 million, was offered on the remaining three-and-a-half years of his contract, and Pardew made his way to the Chadwell Heath training ground to clear his desk and say his goodbyes. 'Half the players had left when the manager told everyone he was leaving,' said Reo-Coker. 'We had no idea he was going to get sacked.'

The news was made public on West Ham's official website at 1.50 p.m., with a formal statement explaining, 'The chairman and board have been concerned by the performances of recent weeks and feel it is the right time to make a change in the best interests of the club.' A personal note then followed from Pardew:

> I'm proud of my achievements at West Ham. When I took the helm, they were in the Championship and struggling to find direction. In two consecutive seasons, we qualified for the play-off final, ultimately achieving the Premiership status the club so richly deserves. I am also proud of our first season back in the top flight in which we finished ninth and came so close to winning the FA Cup. The supporters have stood by me, and I will always cherish memories of their support and loyalty. They really are a special set of fans.

It was a rather formal summary of Pardew's three years at the club, and it disguised the pain he felt at having been tipped out of his position, prematurely in his view. 'I felt aggrieved that I left West Ham too early. I felt there was no situation where they would get relegated,' he later said. But his dismissal wasn't just about the threat of relegation, although that fear was very real with the club sitting third bottom with 14 points from 17 fixtures. Pardew had lost 13 of his last 16 games, and the reality was that few managers survived that kind of statistic.

There was inevitably some criticism of the decision, with the club's new Icelandic owners being accused of panicking about the potential loss of TV revenue should the club be relegated – the new £1.7 billion Sky–Setanta TV deal commencing from 2007 would be worth an average of £40 million to each club every year – and ignoring just how close Pardew had come to winning the FA Cup just seven months earlier. The point was also made that sacking managers just wasn't in keeping with West Ham's traditions, with Pardew being only the tenth permanent boss in the club's history. John Barnwell, chief executive of the League Managers' Association, said it was a 'worrying' state of affairs, while John Madejski, the Reading chairman and Pardew's former boss, went so far as to describe the culling as 'brutal'.

Pardew had fought hard to secure his escape from the Royals back in 2003 after they had rejected West Ham's initial overtures, resigning before being put out on gardening leave while an out-of-court settlement between the two clubs was reached. But it wasn't only the loss of what he'd recently had at Upton Park that grieved him so much: it was the realisation that he would now be deprived of the once-in-a-lifetime opportunity to transform the club thanks to its new-found wealth. The feeling of regret, of missing out on the chance to potentially lead West Ham into the Champions League in years to come, was sure to have caused him considerable anguish.

Former assistant Grant was shocked and disappointed by the way Pardew had been treated, believing the club's new owners had ignored what had been achieved over the previous three years. 'It left a bitter taste in my mouth,' he said, 'and it seemed the change had been made without looking at the full picture, which was rather strange.' To some observers, it was ironic that the Icelanders had brought an end to Pardew's reign, given that his position had been considered to be under more threat if Kia Joorabchian's takeover bid had been successful. But the new owners had made it clear that they had big ambitions for West Ham, and from their point of view they were simply displaying courage and leadership. The Hammers had paid the ultimate price in 2003 when chairman Brown allowed manager Glenn Roeder to steer the team towards relegation, and, at the very least, it was clear these new people meant business.

The media predictably accused Pardew of 'losing the dressing-room' and suggested he'd been undermined by the takeover speculation and the surprise arrival of Tévez and Mascherano. But it seemed there could have been unpublicised reasons why Pardew had lost the support of Magnússon and Gudmundsson so quickly.

Magnússon was occasionally guilty of using a poor choice of words when talking about Pardew. As he took office, he reportedly referred to the manager's 'throat' being 'cut' if he failed to produce results, and he made later mention of 'a cancer we had to cut off'. The latter statement was subsequently denied, however. 'I never said that,' he insisted. 'But there were reasons why I had to do it [sack Pardew], and I will keep those to myself. You have an obligation to make the change if things are not right.'

There was a mixed reaction to Pardew's departure in the dressing-room. The manager's influence may have waned, but some of the players were still sorry to see him go. His dismissal came as a shock to some members of the team, and coach Keen, asked to oversee training for a few days until a successor was found, had the task of lifting spirits. But other players did not seem to be too disappointed to see Pardew leave, not least Tévez and Mascherano. 'He was a good man but kept asking me to play out of position against my will. I was surprised to see how long he held on to the job in the end,' said Tévez. Compatriot Mascherano, meanwhile, questioned Pardew's attitude towards the two Argentinians. 'His manner with Tévez and me was not the same as with the rest of the team. I don't think he could accept our arrival,' he said.

Keen would not have to hold the fort for long, as Magnússon had already decided that former Charlton manager Curbishley was his number-one choice to succeed Pardew. He was the obvious candidate for several reasons: he fully understood West Ham's unique traditions, having made 96 midfield appearances for the club in the late 1970s after coming through the youth ranks; he'd proved himself as a manager having twice got Charlton promoted, establishing the club as a Premiership entity during his 15 years there; and he was available, having left The Valley at the end of the previous season after agreeing to take a sabbatical.

Curbishley had rejected other opportunities to manage West Ham over the years, having been approached when Harry Redknapp and Roeder departed in 2001 and 2003 respectively. On both occasions, he'd decided that the time wasn't right to leave Charlton, displaying a sense of loyalty towards the south London club that had no intention of releasing him anyhow. But the forty-nine year old was now looking for new opportunities, having completed a six-month rest period – which some suspected may have been a contractual agreement – after departing from The Valley. He'd retained a profile in football with the occasional appearance on Sky Sports as a match analyst – and ironically had been on duty for West Ham's humiliating defeat at Bolton.

Just two days after that debacle, Magnússon – having reportedly taken advice from former England manager Sven-Göran Eriksson – contacted Curbishley and a three-year contract worth a reported £7.5 million was agreed. The speed of the negotiations had some observers questioning whether Pardew's successor had been sounded out in advance, but Curbishley insisted otherwise. 'I've found out how quickly Eggert likes to move,' he said. 'He does not stand about, and he was bossing the situation.'

There was much for Curbishley to be excited about. Not only was he returning to his spiritual home – despite his lengthy association with Charlton – but he knew that major funds would be available to help West Ham avoid relegation and subsequently challenge for honours. 'West Ham have been a big part of my life, and the affection never goes away,' he said. 'They're my club.' Yet he needed to satisfy himself about a few issues before signing on the dotted line. He wanted assurances he would have the autonomy at Upton Park that he had previously enjoyed at The Valley. He was worried about taking over 'midstream' but knew the opportunity to manage West Ham would probably never come along again. He even sought the advice of Manchester United manager Sir Alex Ferguson. 'You've got a good opportunity to be successful there, so take it,' said the Scotsman.

Curbishley was officially appointed as West Ham's new manager on Wednesday, 13 December 2006, with Mervyn Day – his right-hand man at Charlton and another ex-Hammer – being confirmed as his assistant. With yet another former

Charlton coach in Peacock already on board, Curbishley could not claim he didn't have his own men around him. Or that he didn't have the full support of the West Ham fans, who immediately embraced him as one of their own – the same could not have been said of Pardew three years earlier.

Many people viewed Curbishley as a safe pair of hands – on both a professional and personal level. But there were still some observers who questioned the appointment, believing that West Ham represented a very different challenge to the one he'd had at The Valley. The manager had worked with a limited budget at Charlton to regularly achieve mid-table safety – but were those credentials appropriate for a manager of a club that was planning to invest heavily in the quest for regular European qualification? By his own admission, however, Curbishley's short-term aim was simply to avoid relegation, and few people doubted his ability to achieve that goal in a comfortable manner – not least his predecessor.

Former midfielder Pardew had been one of Curbishley's first signings as Charlton boss in 1991 when, ironically, the homeless club were tenants at Upton Park. And the latter was sympathetic towards the plight of his old colleague. 'I feel so disappointed for Alan, because he did a great job and turned this club around,' he said. Yet in a bizarre twist of fate, Pardew would soon return to management at Charlton, who had struggled badly since Curbishley's departure and sacked bosses Iain Dowie and Les Reed. Indeed, they were immediately below West Ham in the Premiership table, just one place off the bottom.

The feeling was that both Curbishley and Pardew were back in their natural environments, and it was intriguing to see how they would both fare. Pardew certainly believed West Ham would have no problems. 'There are a lot things that are going to work for Curbs,' he said. 'He's inherited a great squad, he's got money to spend in the transfer window and he's got Dean Ashton coming back.'

As Pardew should have realised, however, nothing could be taken for granted in football, and time would emphatically prove that point in the most dramatic of fashions.

# 9

## 'LET'S NOT GET AWAY FROM IT: I HAVEN'T DELIVERED RESULTS'

IT WOULD have been naive of Alan Curbishley to assume he was walking into a club that did not have problems. West Ham would not have been in the bottom three of the Premiership table if that were the case. Chairman Eggert Magnússon, while convincing Curbishley of the huge opportunity that was open to him, could not pretend that everything at Upton Park was sweetness and light. Removing manager Alan Pardew from the equation might have been seen as a step in the right direction on the club's part, but nobody was under any illusions that other key issues did not need addressing.

One matter, in some people's opinion, was packaged in the form of the number 20 shirt. Nigel Reo-Coker had looked unhappy all season, and this was evident in his lacklustre performances. The captain had inevitably attracted some criticism – along with several other players – but it appeared a huge overreaction on his part when he publicly complained that he was being blamed for Pardew's dismissal. 'Everyone keeps saying I should be sacked and it's all my fault that we've been doing so badly,' he said. 'I've really been getting it in the neck. And now Pardew has gone it's only going to get worse for me with people pointing the finger.'

It had been commented that if West Ham's key players had

performed to the levels of the previous season, then Pardew might have stood more chance of keeping his job. It seemed a fair point but one seemingly too damaging for Reo-Coker's fragile ego, and the 22 year old's reaction only served to increase the suspicion that he was too young to have been handed the club's captaincy. His complaints did little to win sympathy from the West Ham support, a section of which felt compelled to boo the midfielder's name before the kick-off against Manchester United in the next game on 17 December. As should have been anticipated, however, Reo-Coker scored his only goal of the season, and West Ham claimed a shock 1–0 win against the Premiership leaders in Curbishley's first game in charge.

The goal provided the player with the perfect opportunity to repair his relationship with the fans by sharing in their joy. Instead, he chose to cup his right hand to his ear in front of the Bobby Moore Stand, not allowing even the faintest hint of a smile to cross his face. Being occasionally jeered might have hurt his feelings, but had he displayed some humility by admitting his form had dipped he would have discovered that not 'everyone' was as against him as he believed. This wasn't an easy situation for Curbishley to deal with upon his arrival at Upton Park, but he tried to be supportive by claiming Reo-Coker had 'answered his critics' with the goal.

When it was revealed that Reo-Coker had become the subject of 'hate mail', many people were suspicious of his motives for allowing the news to be made public. Curbishley certainly wasn't concerned by what was apparently just one unsigned letter, simply telling the midfielder to 'bin it' and concentrate on his football. The manager had known truly great West Ham captains such as Bobby Moore and Billy Bonds in his days as a player and was not likely to have been impressed by the 'wounded soul' antics of somebody who appeared to be building leverage for a move. This was identified by former Hammers skipper Julian Dicks, who said, 'Certain players don't want to be at the club, and Reo-Coker, who seems to have spat his dummy out, is one I'd get rid of.'

However, Curbishley had no intention of allowing Reo-Coker to be sold when the January transfer window opened, despite the player reportedly making it clear just before the home FA Cup third-round tie against Brighton on 6 January 2007 that he wanted to leave. Reo-Coker was subsequently omitted from the squad, prompting suspicions he'd not been 'rested' – as the manager claimed – but left out to avoid him becoming cup-tied should an irresistible offer materialise. If Curbishley was going to try to keep the player, however, he needed to win his confidence and get him back onside – and he did so in controversial fashion.

The 3–0 win against Brighton gave the manager the chance to focus media attention on several positives, such as Mark Noble's first senior goal for West Ham, the growing influence of Carlos Tévez and the encouraging debut of new signing Luís Boa Morte. But Curbishley spurned that opportunity, deciding to attack reporters for the 'outrageous' criticism of Reo-Coker, who had not even played in the game. 'Every time I pick up the papers, it seems to be Nigel's fault we're in this situation. I want everyone to get off his back,' he ordered. If this was a way of keeping Reo-Coker's name out of the newspapers, it was an unconventional way of going about it, putting several journalists' noses out of joint. Yet Reo-Coker was eventually pacified by his manager's public show of support. 'Nigel wasn't happy with the way he was being portrayed,' said assistant boss Mervyn Day, 'but he started to warm to us after Alan came out in the press and said, "This is wrong. He's young. You should leave him alone."'

Curbishley's reign as West Ham manager could not have begun in more sensational fashion than the victory against Manchester United, who had been unbeaten in their previous

12 Premiership games. It was the first home win against Sir Alex Ferguson's men since 1992, when an all-but-relegated Hammers team helped finish off their opponents' title aspirations thanks to Kenny Brown's famous goal.

And although the visitors enjoyed – and wasted – most of the chances, West Ham got full reward for their determined efforts when Reo-Coker poked home from close range following Marlon Harewood's cut-back with 15 minutes remaining. Curbishley was modest enough to avoid claiming much tactical credit, having spent minimal time with his squad before the game. He'd simply asked the players to give everything they had, and they'd duly obliged, although there was never likely to be a lack of commitment given the glamorous opposition and the fact that a new manager needed to be impressed.

When a 0–0 draw at Fulham ended the lengthy run of away defeats the following weekend, the assumption – on the part of the supporters and media – was that West Ham were off and running under Curbishley, even though they remained in the relegation zone. But the first two results of the new manager's reign perhaps brought about a false sense of security. Two home defeats in the space of five days over the Christmas period – against Portsmouth and Manchester City – indicated that the corner had not yet been turned, while disaster was waiting as the New Year arrived.

The dominant feature of West Ham's two previous trips to Reading had been the home crowd's hostility towards their former boss Pardew, who had been forced to look on in embarrassment as his side conceded three goals on both occasions in defeat. The Pardew factor was removed from the game at the Madejski Stadium on 1 January 2007, but Royals fans had much more to revel in as West Ham crashed to a humiliating 6–0 defeat – their biggest for six years since a 7–1 collapse at Blackburn. If Curbishley learned a lot about his underachieving players during the game – and he made sure they all knew his feelings in the dressing-room – he also discovered that he had to be very careful about how he discussed defeat after the final whistle.

The manager spoke of how Reading – playing in the top flight of English football for the very first time – had displayed the 'newly promoted hunger' that West Ham had demonstrated the previous season. 'They have the commitment and desire of wanting to be in the Premiership and driving the Baby Bentley,' he said. 'If Reading come ninth this year, they won't be going around in an open-top bus, they'll just be looking forward to the next season. At Charlton, I was used to getting to that kind of position and seeing the same hunger and spirit in the team.'

It was abundantly clear what Curbishley was saying: that his players thought they had arrived as established Premiership performers and the previous season's success had eroded their appetite and commitment. In other words, they had got too big for their boots. The 'open-top bus' reference was in relation to the club's initial plans to recognise their FA Cup achievements the previous term – an idea that was subsequently scrapped. Both Curbishley and chairman Magnússon, who said, 'Football is about winning not losing,' when he heard about the suggestion, believed that the proposal reflected the wrong attitude on the part of the club.

Yet Curbishley was unhappy with how his views were presented by the newspapers, who claimed the manager was criticising his players' 'big-time Charlie' mentality. Indirectly he was, of course. But Curbishley complained that his words had been unfairly distorted. 'I was talking about the Baby Bentley in terms of Reading, but it was spun around so that it looked as if I was having a go at my own players,' he said.

A similar situation occurred when Curbishley made the point that the majority of the previous summer's signings had failed to establish themselves as first-team regulars. Several newspapers, quite understandably, referred to those players as 'flops', but that sent Curbishley into a rage. As well as upsetting many of the recent recruits, it was suspected that Pardew was also unhappy and may have personally complained about what he felt was a direct attack on his transfer-market judgement.

Curbishley hit back at reporters at his next press conference. 'I'm loyal to my players, so I'm very disappointed that some of them think I've had a go at them,' he said. 'I'm not blaming any of the players who were brought in during the summer – and I'd like you to report that,' he said before storming out of the club's media room. 'Pathetic!' muttered veteran journalist Brian Glanville as Curbishley dashed past him towards the exit. 'Well, you should try printing what I say in future,' he retorted.

Curbishley may not have scored an own-goal as a West Ham player, but it had not taken him long as the manager, with reporters believing that the outburst was evidence of him succumbing to pressure. He was accused of 'throwing his toys out of his pram' and of lacking 'media savvy'. Some journalists made the point that it was maybe just as well he had not been successful when interviewed by the FA to succeed Sven-Göran Eriksson as England manager the previous year if this was how he responded to West Ham's current crisis.

Curbishley had not helped his relationship with the media by imposing an interview ban on West Ham's players during his early weeks at the club. That didn't stop quotes occasionally appearing, however, with Yossi Benayoun offering the view that his teammates had 'played like a bunch of drunks' in the thrashing at Reading. The club suggested that the comments came via a phone conversation the Israeli midfielder had with a reporter in his homeland, but it's believed they appeared on his personal website and were circulated by its owners to gain publicity – the very kind that Curbishley had been looking to block.

The rout at Reading had been 'on the cards' according to Curbishley. Both he and Day knew there were serious problems at the training ground and that things could get worse before they got better. Morale was low and some of the players were in turmoil. 'We had one or two people [Reo-Coker included] knock on the door and ask for transfers,' said Day. 'The camp was a bit polarised, with one group over here and another over there. We had all sorts of things to deal with while trying to get to know people at the same time.'

Luck certainly wasn't on the new management team's side – continuing the trend that had become established under Pardew in the early months of the campaign. Having been given a heavy pasting at Reading, the FA Cup match against League One outfit Brighton at least allowed West Ham to stagger to their feet and recover their senses, and it was to the players' credit that they produced fighting performances at home to Fulham on 13 January and at Newcastle the following weekend. The disappointment was that just two points were gained from matches that should have seen the Hammers collect all six available.

West Ham had fought back from a goal down against Fulham to lead 2–1 and then 3–2 with just under half an hour left to play. The skies darkened in the seventy-fifth minute when striker Bobby Zamora was dismissed for an unnecessary lunge that cost him a second yellow card, but the Hammers appeared to have weathered the storm as the game moved into injury time. But referee Graham Poll surprisingly indicated five minutes of added time, and West Ham paid the price as Fulham scored a controversial leveller shortly before the final whistle. It was a devastating blow to see two vital points snatched away at the death in a game in which little had gone right. Defender Anton Ferdinand had already been ruled out with a groin problem, and James Collins and Danny Gabbidon joined him on the treatment table as West Ham lost both centre-halves – and striker Tévez – to injury during the game.

Curbishley then patched up his team to head to Newcastle, and a first away victory of the season appeared to be on the cards when Carlton Cole and Marlon Harewood put West Ham two goals ahead in the opening twenty-two minutes. The last thing they needed was to concede before the break, but referee Uriah Rennie played a big role in throwing Newcastle an ill-deserved lifeline in the final minute of the first half. James Milner's shot found the far corner of the net, but with Scott Parker jumping over the ball in an offside position the linesman inevitably flagged to disallow the effort. That was until Rennie overruled his assistant on the unlikely insistence that Parker had not been interfering with play. It was just the fillip the home side needed, and they levelled from the penalty spot in the second half after Boa Morte inexplicably handled. Fellow new signing Calum Davenport then looked to have headed home the winner before being harshly penalised for an alleged push.

At any other time, a 2–2 draw at Newcastle would have been considered a good result, but in West Ham's position – third bottom and two points adrift of safety – they could not afford to let a two-goal lead disappear. Curbishley rued his dreadful luck. 'If we were mid-table, the offside verdict would have been given and our third goal would have stood, but when you're at the bottom you don't get those decisions,' he said. And to rub salt into his wounds, the returning Ferdinand was forced off with a hamstring injury that would sideline him for three games.

The failure to beat either Fulham or Newcastle further sapped the morale in the camp as the winless run extended to seven games. If there was a ray of light for West Ham and their supporters, it was that Curbishley had at least been promised generous funds to spend during the January transfer window. The manager had appeared to pull off a major coup by persuading Fulham captain Boa Morte to complete a £5 million move across London early in the month, but efforts to land Chelsea winger Shaun Wright-Phillips and Watford forward Ashley Young floundered, despite near £10-million fees being agreed for each player. Neither relished a move to Upton Park, however, with a lengthy battle against the drop facing them. 'That 6–0 defeat at Reading killed us,' said Day. 'We made a lot of enquiries only to be met with the response that certain players didn't want to get involved in a relegation fight.'

Curbishley had identified a lack of aggression in the centre of midfield and sought to solve the problem with a £1.5 million swoop for West Brom's Nigel Quashie. The 28-year-old Scotland international knew plenty about relegation fights but little about winning them, having dropped out of the top flight with QPR, Nottingham Forest, Southampton and the Baggies during his career. But from the middle of January onwards, Curbishley was forced to 'change targets' as a result of West Ham's growing injury crisis in defence. Some £3 million was handed over to Tottenham to bring centre-half Davenport back to the club where he had enjoyed a loan period two years earlier, with the 24 year old insisting he'd have left White Hart Lane for nobody else but the Hammers. It appeared a short-term solution, and the fact that Davenport would play in five of the first six games after his arrival and then not start again all season added weight to the theory.

The biggest headlines were generated by the signings of defenders Lucas Neill from Blackburn and Matthew Upson from Birmingham. Neill's contract at Ewood Park was set to expire at the end of the season, and he appeared to be heading to Liverpool, with whom he'd been linked since the previous summer. When the Australia international snubbed Liverpool's challenge for a Champions League place to join West Ham's battle against the drop, he was accused of having a mercenary attitude, with it being reported that he was earning as much as £70,000 a week at Upton Park. The 28 year old responded with an 'I wish!' when the figure was mentioned and defended his decision to jump aboard the West Ham ship by insisting that he had no desire to be a mere squad player at Anfield. 'This isn't a backwards step. It's a great leap forwards,' he claimed after his £1.5 million move, although a cynical media remained unconvinced.

The biggest expenditure involved the £6 million capture of former Arsenal defender Upson, who also had no intention of signing a new deal at St Andrew's. With Birmingham chasing promotion to the Premiership, they were desperate to keep the 27 year old but finally relented when the player rang co-owner David Sullivan, who was on holiday in Barbados, to plead for his release. Birmingham managing director Karren Brady complained of 'player power', bitched about West Ham not being 'a major club' and promised to 'give Upson a wave' if the two clubs passed in opposite directions in May.

The signing of Upson took West Ham's transfer-window spending to a dazzling £17 million – more than any other club in Britain – while Seville striker Kepa Blanco arrived on loan. The club was certainly in a desperate position, and Curbishley knew he had paid a little over the odds for a couple of the players. He had tried and failed to raid his old club Charlton for striker Darren Bent, full-back Luke Young and defender Hermann Hreidarsson, while former Russia skipper Alexei Smertin and Arsenal full-back Lauren had also appeared on his shopping list. But chairman Magnússon had been true to his word in terms of investing in the playing squad, and Curbishley could not complain about the financial support he had been given – nor would he try.

One significant departure in January was that of Javier

Mascherano to Liverpool. Both he and Tévez had been urged by Argentina coach Alfio Basile to quit West Ham to save their international careers as a result of their intermittent appearances for the club. 'I hope both of them leave that club as soon as possible,' he said. But Hammers supporters were left scratching their heads at how a world-class Argentina international such as Mascherano could be neglected by two Boleyn bosses and then discarded. The feeling was if he was good enough for Liverpool, surely he was good enough for West Ham. The midfielder had made the last of his seven Hammers appearances in the defeat at Everton at the start of December and had seemingly been ignored by the new management. 'The situation was irretrievable by the time we arrived,' explained Day. 'His head was down, and he was so low it was untrue. We were given information he wanted to go in the transfer window, and that was it.'

Day and Curbishley shared the view of former coach Peter Grant that Mascherano was incompatible with the team's usual style of play. Day saw him as 'a continuity player that doesn't get around the pitch too well' and added, 'West Ham played at a very high tempo, winning the ball back and counter-attacking very quickly, and I don't think he complemented the players we have here.' The initial problem with offloading the midfielder, however, was that FIFA rules prevented any player from appearing for three different clubs in the period between 1 July and 30 June the following year. As Mascherano had played for Corinthians and West Ham since the summer, he was effectively stranded at Upton Park with little hope of clawing his way back into contention. His frustration was understandable – even journeyman Quashie was above him in the pecking order. 'God knows when I would have played again had I stayed at West Ham,' he later said. 'It's obvious I was not the right kind of player for that team. I've asked myself a thousand times why I agreed to go there.'

Liverpool appealed to FIFA for special dispensation to sign Mascherano on the basis that the 'two club only' ruling was planned around the scheduling of the European season, which overlapped with that of South America's. World football's governing body duly acquiesced, although the Argentinian was still not free to complete his transfer to Anfield because of the Premier League's concerns about the nature of the player's third-party ownership. In particular, the Premier League wanted to be satisfied that there was no outside influence on Liverpool's policies as a result of the contract, and after a three-week delay Mascherano was finally granted permission to begin the next stage of his career. A statement issued on 20 February said, 'The Premier League is satisfied that the contractual arrangements proposed by Liverpool FC are consistent with its rules; particularly that the relationship is not subject to third-party influence.' If West Ham supporters were intrigued by the inquest into Mascherano's ownership and the possible implications in terms of Tévez, they would not have to wait long for matters to come to a head.

For the time being, however, the focus was very much on what impact West Ham's six new signings would have on their fortunes as the team looked to climb out of the relegation zone. If anybody was hoping the new arrivals would bring about an immediate change of luck, they were left sadly disappointed when Neill and Upson both suffered injuries on their debuts. An ankle problem saw Neill survive just 48 minutes of the home FA Cup fourth-round defeat by Watford on 27 January – and there was a feeling of déjà vu a fortnight later when a damaged knee prevented him from even making the half-time break as the same opposition claimed a second 1–0 success. Upson suffered similar misfortune when a calf injury struck half an hour into the 1–0 defeat at Aston Villa and the same problem reappeared just 11 minutes into the home game against Tottenham a month later. At least Neill was able to return for the final ten games of the season, although Upson would remain incapacitated – representing a huge blow to Curbishley's survival hopes.

Even more damaging was the news that Dean Ashton's recovery from a broken ankle was not going according to plan. The striker had been expected to return around the Christmas period, but it was obvious to Curbishley upon his arrival that the club's record signing would not be seen in first-team action until February at the very earliest. 'It's not always like it says on the tin,' said Day as he reflected on the saga of Ashton's anticipated recovery. Visitors to the training ground midway through the season were not encouraged as they saw Ashton suffering discomfort and performing the same exercise on the very same step week after week – as if not having moved from the spot. A problem with scar tissue would eventually require surgery and rule him out for the rest of the campaign. As the striker was injured while on England duty, it was understood that the FA paid an initial £300,000 towards his salary costs but a further £950,000 in compensation would reportedly be outstanding by the end of the season, allegedly causing West Ham some frustration as they waited for underwriters to make a decision on their claim.

The embarrassing defeats by bottom-of-the-table Watford – which book-ended losses against Villa and Liverpool – provided continuing evidence of an attitude problem, with the West Ham players failing to show the appetite that had secured victories against top teams such as Arsenal and Manchester United when it came to less glamorous opposition. Harewood was guilty of a costly error when missing a penalty in the league defeat by the Hornets, and Curbishley failed to impress reporters when explaining that he'd been 'told that the player was the team's penalty taker'. It was assumed that the club's manager would have decided who should take spot-kicks rather than be dictated to. But Curbishley made a number of brave and perhaps too-honest admissions as he reflected on his first dozen games in charge of West Ham. 'Let's not get away from it, I haven't delivered results,' he said before confessing that 'because of the inconsistent team selection, the players haven't really seen what Mervyn and I are about'.

Curbishley had repeatedly complained about the difficulties of taking over midway through the season and 'having to learn about players in vital games'. This was surprising given that most managerial opportunities become available in the autumn, and he always knew he would have to impose his ideas quickly. The first ten Premiership games of the new manager's reign had produced only six points, and the overwhelming conclusion was that, despite all the bad luck he had suffered, Curbishley was more a long-term strategist than a short-term saviour. He'd had 15 years to build his success at Charlton, and he was clearly more comfortable with evolution than revolution. If that was the case, then some people thought that he was perhaps the wrong choice for West Ham in their present predicament.

Behind the scenes, certain things were not going well, and the results arguably reflected that. Curbishley's management style was very different to that of his predecessor. Whereas Pardew seemingly had a close rapport with his players – at least when things were going well – his successor was believed to be more distant, and that encouraged suspicion on the part of some players, whose trust was needed if they were to start performing to their potential. Unlike some managers, who had spent half their careers taking charge of different teams and learning how to quickly win the confidence of new squads of players, Curbishley had yet to experience taking control of a club as an outsider. He'd been a player–coach at Charlton and then shared management duties with Steve Gritt for a four-year period before assuming sole responsibility. He had already known the players he was working with or had recruited them himself. So, it was a brand-new experience for him when he was asked to take the reins at West Ham and shake some life into a group of men whom, with a few exceptions, he was unfamiliar with as people.

There had been a natural dilemma for Curbishley in terms of deciding whether to quickly enforce change or keep certain practices in place. Seeing as the team claimed a shock 1–0 win against Manchester United and a highly satisfactory 0–0 draw at Fulham, the inclination was to try and keep things relatively stable. 'We were thinking: let's keep things nice and steady and not do anything too dissimilar. We're not dictatorial, and we like to get to know people anyway,' said Day. Before they knew it, the new management team had presided over the Christmas period, during which the routine of train, play and rest, train, play and rest swallowed up four games in nine days. 'It was a whirlwind,' admitted Curbishley.

Day found it difficult to win the trust of the players in the early weeks after arriving as Curbishley's right-hand man. 'The players thought if they said anything to me it would go straight back to the manager. That wasn't the way I worked and not the way Alan wanted me to work, but the players didn't realise that,' he said. Both men became conscious of a very different mentality at West Ham to what they had experienced at Charlton, which may have been a Premiership club but rarely had big-name stars – such as former England international and Manchester United striker Teddy Sheringham, for example. Day admitted that they were anxious not to 'rock the boat too much' because of the types of characters at the club. 'Because of certain people's personalities and egos, it has been difficult,' he said.

It was believed that there were clashes with several members of the first-team squad. Tévez complained about the manager barely talking to him – not much of a surprise considering the Argentinian had made little effort to learn English and

Curbishley's Spanish extended to ordering a paella and a few drinks on holiday. Benayoun had been charged with the responsibility of communicating with Tévez, having learned the language during his three-year period with Racing Santander, but it was reported that many of Curbishley's instructions ahead of games were simply scribbled on a blackboard.

Goalkeeper Robert Green – one of the more down-to-earth players in the camp – was unhappy with being dropped after the game at Reading, believing he was being made a scapegoat for the humiliating 6–0 defeat. 'I was disappointed to be left out,' he admitted. 'I don't think anybody played well that day, and my form had generally been good.' The former Norwich man hadn't improved his relationship with Curbishley by apparently questioning his comments on Pardew's 'flop' signings, which he had taken personally. Indeed, it was suspected that was the real reason he was excluded from the side for half a dozen games. Green was diplomatic in assessing how Curbishley's style of man-management was different to that of his predecessor. 'They're different among the players, in terms of their mannerisms and the way they are,' he said, shrugging. 'Only time will tell whether one is better than the other.'

Paul Konchesky was considered a likely candidate to experience problems under the new manager. The former Charlton full-back had been sold by Curbishley 18 months earlier, following disagreements about being deployed in midfield. 'There was never any problem between us other than I wanted to play left-back,' he said as he tried to downplay suggestions of a clash of personalities. Simply playing at all was a problem, however, with Curbishley quickly making it clear that he preferred George McCartney in the left-back role, and Konchesky was eventually frozen out of the first-team picture.

Another outcast was Sheringham, who made four substitute outings and one start in Curbishley's first nine games before being totally ignored. The veteran striker turned 41 in April, and the only headlines he made in the second half of the season related to his brief relationship with former Miss Great Britain and *Celebrity Big Brother* participant Danielle Lloyd, 18 years his junior. He was regularly pictured as a playboy out on the town, and his relationship with Curbishley allegedly broke down to the extent that the two men barely spoke. One story was that Sheringham was busy badmouthing his manager in the training ground canteen one day while Curbishley stood right behind him before simply walking off without a word. Sheringham would later complain that his manager didn't 'like or respect the way I play football'. He also referred to Curbishley's 'Baby Bentley' jibe by adding, 'I don't think what car you drive has any bearing on how you perform.' What aggrieved Sheringham as much as not playing was the fact that he was denied a move to Charlton during the January transfer window, although Curbishley quite logically insisted that it would have been foolhardy to strengthen any of the club's relegation rivals.

There were also clashes with midfielder Benayoun and defender Christian Dailly. The former was left out of the side for a handful of games towards the end of the campaign for playing twice for Israel while still shaking off injury. 'The manager did not talk to me, and I really wanted to get away from West Ham,' he confided. He would eventually be granted his wish. Dailly, meanwhile, fell out with Curbishley after dropping out of contention, and the usually affable Scotland international even barred himself from producing his weekly local newspaper column because of a reluctance to tell things as he really saw them.

Defender Ferdinand's nose had also been put out of joint after he was – quite fairly, some would say – criticised for needlessly conceding a penalty in the home league defeat by Watford, and while Reo-Coker had supposedly 'warmed' to his new manager the relationship could never be described as 'hot'. Indeed, Reo-Coker and the other members of his clique in the camp thought that it was wrong for Curbishley to rebuke Ferdinand so openly in the dressing-room. They also didn't enjoy the manager's claim that several players would be moved on at the end of the season.

Aside from the personal issues, some of the more established players were allegedly unhappy with the reports that new recruits had been brought in on huge salaries that dwarfed their own. One agent said, 'If established players see new ones coming in on a lot more money and not doing very much, it's obviously going to cause problems.' And then there were the likes of Matthew Etherington, Jonathan Spector and Hayden Mullins who knew their first-team chances were heavily diminished as a result of the fresh arrivals. Mullins had seen off the threat of a world-class talent such as Mascherano only to then lose his place to Quashie.

If these situations weren't enough to ensure dissent in the camp – the mood was reportedly described as 'awful' by one insider – there was opposition to the new, more intensive training schedules put into place by Curbishley as he sought to implement his ideas. 'We were firefighting for the first two months,' said Day. 'We found it tough getting some of the players to do some of the exercises we wanted because they had been used to doing their own little thing. They didn't want to go the extra yard, in training especially. So we had a little bit of resistance.'

News of that resistance quickly made its way into the pages of the newspapers, leading the management to believe that there was some kind of 'mole' in the camp. The *Daily Mirror* ran a back-page lead story on 13 February claiming that Curbishley 'risked mutiny' by ordering his players into extra training sessions in the afternoons. Day thought it was almost comical that they should be slammed for demanding more from their players: 'I'm sure our fans all thought, "We've just lost four games on the spin. We want our players to work harder!" It came out as if they were saying, "We can't do that. We're Premiership footballers." It was nonsense.'

The negative press coverage played a big part in making Day and Curbishley realise how different managing West Ham was compared to Charlton. They were both Premiership clubs based in London, but the gulf between them was far greater than the six miles that separated them in distance. Curbishley started to admit that both the club and the job were bigger than he anticipated. 'The publicity is something I've not been used to,' he said. 'If we had sticky times at Charlton, they weren't that sticky. It was a settled situation there, and we didn't make too many headlines.' Given his playing career at Upton Park, his experience as a Premiership manager and the close proximity of the two clubs, it was strange to hear him express surprise at the stature of West Ham, although his honesty was refreshing.

Curbishley was also genuinely knocked sideways by the team's poor results in the first three months of his stewardship. And he spoke of how problematic it was trying to switch off from the pressures of the job, living in Essex and being surrounded by West Ham fans, including his own family. 'I've found it difficult,' he said. 'It's just been so intense. When I was at Charlton, I didn't take my work home with me, and I think I had an easy run in terms of my family life. But my boy is a West Ham fan and so are my wife's family, so it's hard to escape. It's a big difference for me, but I weighed it all up before accepting the job, because I knew my life would change. And I think a lot of pundits thought I was putting my reputation on the line by coming to West Ham in this position.'

Many journalists thought Curbishley's job could also be

on the line – in the long term if not necessarily in the short term – if results didn't quickly improve. There was speculation chairman Magnússon was losing faith in his manager's ability to turn things around, especially as he had funded him so heavily in the transfer market. Injuries had prevented Upson and Neill from making an impact, but Quashie and Boa Morte – at a cost of £6.5 million between them – had done little to impress. The latter had been so disappointing he had quickly lost his place to Etherington and would spend most of the next few months on the bench.

Yet Magnússon continued to give Curbishley and Day his full support. He recognised the problems the management had been forced to deal with and had also identified that too many members of the first-team squad had allowed the success of the previous season to go to their heads. 'You have to fight for every goal and every point, and if you think you're a better player than you are – or think the team is better than it really is – then things become very difficult,' he said. From the outset, he had told Curbishley, 'We're in a precarious position. And if it does go wrong, I'm going to back you because we want to come back to the Premiership at the first attempt.'

Publicly, Magnússon always insisted that West Ham could still survive, even though the defeat by Watford had left the club five points adrift of fourth-bottom Wigan Athletic – who had a game in hand – with just eleven matches remaining. Behind the scenes, he maintained a positive attitude, but he had to accept that relegation was a serious possibility. The chairman celebrated his 60th birthday with a party at the Boleyn Ground on 20 February, and he used the occasion to reassure the club's entire staff of their positions. 'There will be no redundancies if we do go down,' he said. 'If you want to stay, you will still have your jobs.' It was an incredible gesture, given that relegation inevitably involves a horde of cost-cutting measures to compensate for the dramatic loss of revenue. 'For a chairman who had only just come into the club to make a statement like that showed he believed in his vision for the future,' Day said. 'It also engendered loyalty. It's not a case of cutting everything to the bone and trying to get back up on the cheap. It's about doing things properly and making sure people are looked after.'

Just four days later, West Ham faced what was considered to be a make-or-break trip to fellow strugglers Charlton, who had drawn level on 20 points from 27 games with a slightly inferior goal difference. Curbishley admitted that it wasn't the 'ideal circumstances' to be making his first return to The Valley, knowing the losers would almost certainly be consigned to relegation. The build-up to the game was predictably intense, with Curbishley's head-to-head against former Hammers boss Pardew encouraging analysis of their contrasting management styles and fortunes in recent weeks.

Charlton had appeared to be a lost cause in December, but Pardew had injected genuine belief into his players with his super-positive thinking, and the rewards had come in the shape of eight points from his first six games before losing to title-chasing Chelsea and Manchester United. Curbishley, meanwhile, had collected just two points from his side's last eight outings. The West Ham manager was hurt when his negative body language was discussed in the media – 'You can't expect me to be happy when I've won one game in ten,' he snapped – but there were those who argued his apparent lack of dynamism was a reason for his disappointing impact at Upton Park. Curbishley's post-match comments became increasingly predictable – 'We need a three-pointer', 'We're waiting for lift-off', 'I'm still getting to know my players', 'Does confidence breed results or do results breed confidence?' and 'We need to catch the fourth-bottom team' were typical examples – and had some people thinking that if his team talks were equally prosaic, it was little wonder his players failed to provide the necessary response.

It was in this climate of increasing negativity towards Curbishley that West Ham ventured across the River Thames knowing they simply couldn't afford to lose. Typically, however, the manager was deprived of important players (including both first-choice full-backs in Neill and McCartney plus Boa Morte and Zamora) to injury while Reo-Coker and Spector were both suspended. The Addicks, meanwhile, were boosted by the return of top scorer Bent following a two-month absence as well as full-back Young. But that was no excuse for West Ham's dreadful display, which saw them crumple to an embarrassing 4–0 defeat. Darren Ambrose, Jerome Thomas and Bent made the game safe for Charlton in a ridiculously one-sided first half before Thomas sealed the drubbing with his second goal ten minutes from time. The home side also hit the woodwork twice as they dominated from start to finish.

Just to complete Curbishley's embarrassment, the West Ham supporters joined the home fans in singing the name of their former boss Pardew. 'That was obviously very hurtful for Alan,' said Day as he reflected on what he described as 'the low point' of their return to West Ham. 'We literally cobbled a team together that day and were very, very poor. That was maybe the point when I started to think we might not make it.' Nobody could blame Curbishley for looking dejected and bereft of hope on the touchline in the final minutes. Even some of his biggest critics felt some sympathy for him as he trudged back along the touchline after the final whistle looking as if the stuffing had been well and truly knocked out of him.

Despite Magnússon's show of support, Curbishley insisted that he was not 'immune' to the sack and said he was 'devastated' by the result and display. 'Are we going down with just a whimper or are we going down with a fight?' he asked, seemingly admitting West

Ham's fate was sealed, before adding, almost as an afterthought, 'Or are we going to get ourselves out of it?' 'Whimper' appeared to be the answer to the manager's question, given the lack of commitment by his players. Curbishley's apparent failure to motivate and organise the team in what he had described as a 'must win' game did not reflect well on his managerial abilities. He was understandably philosophical about Hammers fans turning against him to vocally support their former manager. 'I have to take it with a pinch of salt,' he shrugged. 'It's not nice, but we're not in the nicest of businesses when we're not winning games.' Yet despite the abuse, he insisted his sympathies remained with the supporters. 'Perhaps we should go home thinking about them tonight instead of feeling sorry for ourselves.'

Pardew was anxious not to gloat about seeing his new club leapfrog West Ham in the table and denied accusations that the victory had represented some form of revenge after having been sacked by Magnússon. Indeed, he tried to diffuse the 'battle of the bosses' angle by insisting, 'It's not about me and Alan Curbishley.' In fact, he had felt most uncomfortable when the visiting support had started to chant his name. 'We went through some tough times together so we have a kind of kinship,' he declared. 'I have a genuine love for the club, and that will never die, but I'm manager of Charlton now.'

It was little surprise that there were many West Ham fans who wished that Pardew had been allowed to remain at Upton Park, because, for them, it was inconceivable the club's position could have been any worse. One tabloid newspaper canvassed opinion on the day of the Charlton game, and views ranged from 'I've not been impressed with Curbishley and think West Ham will be too big for him' to 'You can't argue with Curbishley's success at Charlton, but the signings of Boa Morte and Quashie will not keep us up'. Even former Hammers defender Tony Gale, usually so positive about the club, was forced to admit, 'I just can't see them getting out of trouble.' Yet while the defeat at Charlton left supporters feeling punch drunk and reeling on the ropes, they could not anticipate what kind of painful knockout blow was laying in wait for them eight days later.

Successive defeats against the only two clubs below them in the Premiership table – Watford and Charlton – was hardly the best of preparations for the visit of Tottenham, who were pushing for a UEFA Cup place via a top-seven finish. But Curbishley worked hard at trying to lift spirits before the game and was boosted by the return of new signings Neill and Upson, although the latter would not last long before hobbling off for a second time. The Hammers shrugged off that setback, however, to surge into a 2–0 half-time lead, with midfielder Noble opening the scoring on his first league start of the season and Tévez brilliantly curling home a free-kick off the underside of the bar to finally open his goal account at the twentieth time of asking. The 1,141 minutes of pain was over as the Argentinian tore off his shirt and jumped into the lower tier of the Dr Martens Stand to celebrate with his ecstatic supporters.

The one thing West Ham knew they could not afford was to allow Spurs to gain self-belief with an early goal in the second period. But Lee Bowyer, making his first start since injuring a shoulder in the 6–0 defeat at Reading two months earlier, recklessly brought down Aaron Lennon six minutes after the break to concede a penalty that former Hammer Jermain Defoe gratefully converted. That was enough to give Tottenham the momentum they needed, and they were level just past the hour mark when Teemu Tainio volleyed home to make it 2–2. At that stage, an away victory seemed inevitable, but substitute Zamora made an instant impact by heading West Ham into a shock 3–2 lead with just five minutes remaining. Could the Hammers hold out to claim a dramatic first win in 11 league games and give their supporters hope that survival could yet be achieved?

As the game headed into the 89th minute, it appeared they might before Ferdinand carelessly brought down late substitute Adel Taarabt just outside the area. Spurs striker Dimitar Berbatov duly curled the resulting free-kick into the top left-hand corner to leave West Ham kicking themselves at the likely loss of two valuable points. The hosts needed victory and kept pushing forward, but, with 94 minutes on the clock, Zamora lost possession, Defoe raced away to force Green into a weak save and substitute Paul Stalteri was on hand to force the loose ball into the empty net and give Spurs a somewhat fortunate 4–3 win.

It was the cruellest of blows, and Noble was left in floods of tears as the rest of West Ham's players staggered around clutching their heads in disbelief at what had taken place. They had shown conviction and courage, overcome adversity and played enterprising football, only to be denied at the death in devastating fashion. But they had also contributed to their own downfall and the defeat simply confirmed the view that their every mistake was being ruthlessly punished. The result dumped West Ham to the bottom of the table for the very first time that season, some ten points adrift of fourth-bottom Man City – who had two games in hand – and eleven points behind fifth-bottom Sheffield United.

Curbishley accused his players of being 'naive' and lacking 'the confidence and mental toughness to see the game out'. Meanwhile, Spurs boss Martin Jol spoke of 'revenge' after seeing his tummy-troubled side's Champions League hopes disappear at Upton Park the previous season. 'I feel sorry for them, but I shouldn't because they didn't for us last year,' he said. Quite clearly, it was West Ham's turn to feel sick this time around.

# 10

---

# 'THESE KINDS OF THINGS HAPPEN AT EVERY FOOTBALL CLUB'

AS IF West Ham's embarrassment on the pitch during the 2006–07 campaign wasn't enough, a number of statements and apologies had to be issued in respect of the players' off-field behaviour as anarchy appeared to reign. The first serious incident came to light during pre-season when it was announced that winger Shaun Newton had failed a random drugs test towards the end of the previous term and been handed a seven-month suspension from football.

It transpired that Newton had tested positive for cocaine immediately after West Ham's 1–0 FA Cup semi-final success against Middlesbrough on 23 April 2006. The matter remained confidential until an FA disciplinary commission hearing took place on 18 July, after which both the FA and West Ham issued statements confirming the ban commenced from 20 May, the date that saw Newton charged and secretly suspended pending the inquiry. Not surprisingly, there was widespread criticism that the punishment was too lenient given that nearly half the suspension would be negated by the close-season period and the player would be back in action before Christmas.

Many observers thought that West Ham should have followed the example set by Chelsea in previous years when they terminated the contracts of goalkeeper Mark Bosnich and £16 million striker Adrian Mutu for cocaine use. And some found it hard to comprehend that Newton's penalty for taking drugs was less severe than the eight-month ban imposed on Manchester United defender Rio Ferdinand for missing a test in 2003. UK Sport insisted it was time football fell in line with other sports by implementing a mandatory two-year suspension for drug offences, while former Manchester United manager Tommy Docherty went even further by claiming a life ban should have been imposed.

Newton was apologetic and insisted it was 'an isolated incident' that came about as a result of 'going through a difficult time personally'. He added, 'I have let down the gaffer, who as well as being the boss is also a friend of mine.' Many people suspected that had Newton's relationship with Alan Pardew not been so strong – the two played together at Charlton in the mid-1990s – the outcome might have been different. Pardew complained that the episode had 'put a stain on our achievements' but added, 'We will stand by Shaun at this difficult time. West Ham has always had a reputation as a family club, and our belief here is that when a member of your family is in trouble, you look after them.'

West Ham's head of technical support Niall Clark insisted that the club could not 'condone the taking of performance-enhancing drugs or stimulants', but one observer joked that if cocaine was performance enhancing then Newton should have asked for a refund because it clearly hadn't been working. Indeed, many people were surprised that the club had not exploited the episode by removing the 30 year old – who most thought should have known better by his age – from the wage bill. The £125,000 signing from Wolves in 2005 was very much a peripheral figure and some resented the idea of him continuing to collect his reported £12,000 a week for sitting on his backside. Indeed, Newton made just five appearances – four as substitute – upon his return halfway through the season and was then loaned to Leicester City, who he eventually joined on a permanent basis. Cynics suggested that West Ham were extremely careful not to establish a dangerous precedent just in case more valuable commodities on the playing staff ever found themselves in such a position. Former Hammers striker Jimmy Greaves said, 'I know West Ham are a very family-influenced club . . . but it begs the question of how many other players enjoy a sniff and a puff.'

Just a month before Newton was set to become eligible again in December, more unfortunate headlines were made after goalkeeper Roy Carroll was admitted to London's £4,000-a-week Capio Nightingale Hospital as he sought to gain control of his drinking and gambling excesses. Rather amusingly, the Irishman checked in under the name of Jonathan Walker – or should that have been Johnnie Walker in acknowledgement of the famous Scotch whisky? Carroll had played in the first ten games of the season but was always likely to play second fiddle to Robert Green, with the exception of the period at the start of 2007 when the recent signing was dropped. Once again, Pardew was sympathetic to his player when his troubles emerged. 'We fully support Roy – he has gone about tackling his issues in the right way,' he said.

The Carroll issue was a genuine cause of concern for Pardew, not least because it made him aware of another growing danger that threatened to destabilise his squad of players. The root of Carroll's problems was reportedly his gambling, with increasingly high amounts of money being exchanged in the card schools between the West Ham players. Indeed, it was alleged that Carroll owed a high-profile teammate some £30,000 – merely a week's wages for the goalkeeper but a ridiculous amount of money for the man in the street to consider losing.

Pardew's concern was not whether players could afford to pay their debts but whether handing over large sums of money – or simply owing the cash – was creating a disharmony in the camp. 'What has come out of Roy's problem is that there is gambling going on within the group, and I have to sort it out before it becomes a bigger issue,' he said. 'It's a difficult situation for a manager to police, because it is not as if you see piles of money change hands. What you can do is try to educate the players about the problems of gambling and explain that it is not healthy for the person or for team spirit.'

Within a fortnight of Pardew expressing his determination to get to grips with the problem, he was ousted from his position at West Ham, and the gambling continued unabated as his successor Alan Curbishley inherited the task of trying to turn the club around. Indeed, the stakes continued to grow as the players participated in what appeared at first glance to be relatively innocent card games on journeys to games. Not everybody was involved, of course, and one player admitted his concern over his teammates' activities by being reported as saying, 'How can they be in a good frame of mind for a match after that? Players are losing up to £50,000 sometimes, and it's terrible for morale. The atmosphere is dreadful and people don't talk to one another – it's one big mess here.'

Curbishley quickly became aware of the problem and imposed a card-school ban while the players were on club duty. A West Ham spokesman confirmed, 'The club is aware of the fact that gambling is an area of concern, and the manager has made it clear that it must stop. Steps have been taken to eradicate this in the team environment.' But there was nothing he could do to dictate their leisure activities in the afternoons after training, and the betting continued – much to the manager's annoyance. It was reported that he fell out with one senior player who won nearly £40,000 in one afternoon and didn't speak to him for a prolonged period. At a time when divisions between various cliques and groups in the dressing-room were becoming wider, it was perhaps little wonder there was so much underachievement on the pitch.

In February, it was reported that a second West Ham player – Matthew Etherington – was undergoing treatment in an effort to solve his excessive gambling. Etherington had struggled to reproduce his strong form of the previous season, and, shortly after Luís Boa Morte had been signed as competition, the winger admitted he was being counselled at the Sporting Chance Clinic, the Hampshire-based organisation founded by former Arsenal and England captain Tony Adams to help sports people deal with their addictions. Etherington said, 'I've made a personal decision to take steps to tackle a gambling problem that has developed in recent times. As anyone who has suffered an addiction illness will know, this is not a problem that will disappear overnight, and Sporting Chance is playing a key role in my recovery.' The player was subsequently praised for having the courage to confront his problems and publicly admit to the measures he was taking. But Etherington's name would again appear in the news later in the season when it was reported that he had been fined £2,000 and banned from driving for one year by Harlow magistrates after being stopped by police while marginally over the alcohol limit.

The gambling culture at West Ham was a huge headache for Curbishley, but he fought hard to play down the stories that suggested an undisciplined camp, insisting that the club was simply the focus of media attention because of its position at the bottom end of the table. 'Some of the stuff that has come out is clearly sensationalised,' he complained. 'These kinds of things happen at every football club without making the newspapers. It just seems that negative stuff is following us around at the moment, and it's not helping. We're a big club in the bottom three, and so we're considered fair game.'

Anton Ferdinand had brought the issue of player discipline – or the perceived lack of it – firmly into the spotlight when it was revealed that he had broken a club curfew to fly to the United States to celebrate his 22nd birthday in February. To make matters worse, he allegedly told West Ham officials that he had simply gone to the Isle of Wight to visit his sick grandmother. The reality was that he had taken a 9,000-mile round trip to a South Carolina nightclub called Knock Knock to party with a former youth-team colleague who now lived in the USA. The defender might just have got away with his unauthorised jaunt had he not been recognised by a Hammers fan who just happened to be in the club and later broke the story to the *News of the World*.

Ferdinand admitted, 'I've made a stupid mistake. I would never do anything to deliberately shame West Ham, and I ask people to remember I am still relatively young and learning all the time. I can understand this trip looked like I was turning my back on the club's predicament, but nothing could be further from the truth. I haven't lost my sense of duty, and all I can ask is that people judge me on my performances and not this one isolated incident.'

With the Ferdinand story breaking within a few days of the renewed gambling revelations, it was the last thing Curbishley needed as he tried to prepare his players for the home game against Tottenham. It was interpreted as a display of arrogance on the part of the defender, who was accused by the *News of the World* of personifying the attitude problems prevalent at Upton Park at the time. 'Ferdinand's US trip was precisely the opposite of what a professional athlete should have been doing mid-season,' they said, with the Hammers having crashed to a 4–0 defeat at Charlton in his first outing upon his return.

Some observers were surprised that the players had actually been allowed a four-day break – which took place over the blank FA Cup fifth-round weekend – given that Curbishley had repeatedly complained about not having enough training time with his squad. The manager allowing his players to disappear – albeit with restrictions – rather than get to know them better seemed like a wasted opportunity. 'They were all told they couldn't leave the country, so Anton will clearly be disciplined,' said Curbishley, whose embarrassment wasn't eased by admitting that he'd not become aware of the problem until the day before the Spurs game – 'when the press officer spoke to me' – several days after the *News of the World* obtained the story and made club officials aware. 'There's a lot of hearsay, and if you acted on everything people told you, you'd be all over the place,' he said. 'But I knew something was afoot because the big boys came down to the pre-match press conference this week. I asked Anton yesterday if it was true and he apologised, but it wasn't life-threatening and our results have been far more damaging for us.'

In denying that there was a lack of discipline at the club, however, Curbishley gave an indication that the problems behind the scenes were bigger than some anticipated. 'Stories that players are never disciplined are totally off the mark,' he said. 'In fact, I thought there was going to be a story saying they had been disciplined *too much* – that might have been true. We've changed the discipline structure here, and the fines are heavier than they were before.'

Ferdinand, who was fined two weeks' wages for his short holiday, had become no stranger to controversy – with nightclubs a common denominator. As a high-profile Premiership footballer, it wasn't difficult for the defender to attract the wrong kind of attention when trying to enjoy a night out socially, whether it be from girls attempting to win his interest or guys hoping to cause trouble to make a name for themselves. In September 2005, he was out with teammate Nigel Reo-Coker when around £37,000 worth of jewellery, watches and mobile phones was stolen from his vehicle following an alleged dispute over a girl's telephone number outside a south London club called Escapades. A 23-year-old semi-professional footballer playing for Croydon Athletic was subsequently jailed for two years.

The possible threat of a custodial sentence for Ferdinand himself became public knowledge after he was arrested and charged with assault occasioning actual bodily harm and violent disorder following an alleged disturbance outside Faces nightclub in Ilford in October 2006. The 22 year old denied the charges – as did one other man who faced similar allegations – and the trial was scheduled for 12 November 2007.

Ferdinand's name continued to appear at the front end of the tabloids, with the *News of the World* alleging that both he and teammate Carlton Cole had been dating the same 19-year-old girl, who had announced that she was pregnant. Some less-than-flattering photographs of the player appeared in the same newspaper on another occasion after he had dropped a valuable ring on a busy nightclub floor. He eventually found the piece of jewellery but only after much pushing and shoving by those around him. And he was the victim of vandalism when a window of his car was smashed outside his home. 'There was no indication that West Ham fans were responsible,' he reportedly said.

Striker Cole was in danger of becoming a forgotten figure at Upton Park towards the end of the 2006–07 season, but Transport for London chiefs still had note of his name when they sent bailiffs to the club's Chadwell Heath training ground in a bid to recover £800 in relation to a dispute over congestion charges. Senior coach Keith Peacock was duly despatched to the front gates to tell the officials where to go in the best language he knew. 'We've had the bailiffs round, and it's just one thing after another at the moment,' said Curbishley wearily.

Motoring matters remained on the agenda even after the

season had ended with *The Sun*'s front-page story on 18 June 2007 revealing that Teddy Sheringham, Bobby Zamora and the Midlands-bound Newton had been arrested for allegedly swapping speeding points to avoid driving bans. It was particularly embarrassing for Sheringham – whose contract at West Ham was about to expire – as he had only recently been awarded an MBE for his services to football. All three players were bailed, and a month later it was reported that Sheringham and Zamora were cautioned by police for attempting to pervert the course of justice. Cole's name was also back in the news in July when it was reported that he'd had four luxury vehicles – worth a total of £265,000 and including a Bentley Continental GTC – repossessed after he allegedly failed to keep up with payments.

After a season in which Curbishley's 'Baby Bentley' reference was used to explain why West Ham's wheels had fallen off, it was perhaps no surprise that the road ahead would continue to be littered with controversy.

# 11

## 'WE'VE HAD A BIT OF LUCK, BUT I'M NOT COMPLAINING'

'DEVINE' INTERVENTION finally arrived for West Ham in the game at Blackburn Rovers on 17 March 2007 when events suggested that a higher power might just be taking pity on the club's distressing plight after all. Except the intervention came in the form of Jim Devine, the assistant referee who adjudged that a Bobby Zamora strike would count despite the ball being cleared by teammate Carlos Tévez on the goal line. It allowed the Hammers to claim a shock 2–1 success that gave them the belief they could yet pull off a miraculous escape.

From a distance, it seemed as if the West Ham management faced a mountainous task to lift their players after seeing them concede two late goals in the dramatic 4–3 home defeat by Tottenham the previous weekend. The result left the supporters floored and betting slips suggesting some faint hope of the team retaining their Premiership status were surely swept away with the rest of the Upton Park litter. Indeed, at that stage West Ham were listed as 66–1 *on* to be relegated. Boss Alan Curbishley had been obliged to put a brave face on things by insisting there were still 'plenty of points to play for' and that he 'had no intention of giving up'. And while assistant Mervyn Day considered the result 'a kick in the teeth', he believed the overall performance against Spurs to have represented a huge step in the right direction.

Showing an improvement on the 4–0 thrashing at Charlton in the previous game would not have taken much, of course. But the Hammers deserved to beat Tottenham, and the fact they didn't proved difficult for many supporters to stomach. If the team couldn't win when playing well and leading in the 89th minute, then what hope was there? However, there was a definite change of mood within the West Ham camp after the pain of the Tottenham defeat had ebbed away, with Day reflecting, 'All the players recognised how well they had done, so we drew on the positives.'

Skipper Nigel Reo-Coker's return from a two-match suspension was made easier to accommodate at Blackburn with Nigel Quashie being sidelined by an ankle injury that, unluckily for him, would rule the midfielder out for the rest of the season. Some observers believed that Lucas Neill was unfortunate not to retain the captain's armband at Ewood Park, but Curbishley was clearly reluctant to make such a significant change during the season. As events proved, Neill had more than enough to contend with on the day, being given a torrid time by Rovers fans who ignored the defender's six years of loyal service to barrack him for joining West Ham two months earlier. The Australian would later declare that he was 'disgusted' by the treatment he received during the game.

Neill had the last laugh, however, as West Ham claimed a priceless three points with their first away triumph of the season. A home win seemed inevitable when Christopher Samba headed Rovers ahead from a corner just two minutes into the second half. But the game turned when referee Howard Webb awarded the Hammers a 71st-minute penalty after Tévez was caught by Brett Emerton. Replays confirmed there had indeed been contact, but some officials might have accused the Argentinian striker of falling too willingly.

Tévez duly picked himself up to despatch the spot-kick past

goalkeeper Brad Friedel. If Rovers felt hard done by, they had to wait just another four minutes for their sense of injustice to shoot off the radar as West Ham grabbed the lead in bizarre fashion. Midfielder Lee Bowyer appeared to handle in the goalmouth scramble that led to substitute Zamora's shot, while there was little Tévez could do to get out of the way as the ball struck him on the line before being cleared to safety. Webb looked across at his assistant and the goal was awarded, much to the consternation of Blackburn manager Mark Hughes, who as well as realising the ball had not crossed the line believed Tévez to have been standing in an offside position.

If Tévez had been standing behind the line – as the officials clearly believed – then he could not be ruled offside. But that was almost irrelevant, because it was where the ball went that mattered, and it was no surprise that Hughes was still seething after the final whistle – especially with Rovers striker David Bentley being given his marching orders in the last minute. Curbishley was naturally unsympathetic. 'We've had a bit of luck, but I'm not complaining,' he said. 'We've had very little so far this year, so I'm delighted with the three points.' In reality, the victory – the club's first in twelve games – was worth so much more than just three points because another defeat would certainly have sealed West Ham's fate.

If there was any disappointment for the coaching staff, it was that the chance of quickly building some momentum was lost with the following weekend being committed to international games. Reo-Coker and Anton Ferdinand – neither of whom had performed at their best at club level over the previous six months – enjoyed a special day in their careers as the England Under-21 side played the first proper match – a 3–3 friendly draw against Italy – at the brand-new Wembley Stadium.

When the Hammers returned to action at home to Middlesbrough on 31 March, it was vital that they built on their fortuitous victory at Blackburn, and the visitors put up little resistance as first-half goals by Zamora and Tévez proved enough to win the match. Zamora was back in the starting line-up after scoring two goals against Tottenham and Blackburn as a substitute. Tévez, meanwhile, had scored in three successive games and was thoroughly rejuvenated after enjoying a run of four starts. His command of English was still poor, as suggested by his response of 'no' when asked on camera at Blackburn if he was happy with the win. But Curbishley had finally succeeded in conveying to the striker what he wanted from him – even if it had taken longer than expected to understand how to get the best from the Argentinian.

Tévez might not have been happy playing in different positions upon his arrival at West Ham, but there were times when he didn't necessarily appear to be an out-and-out striker, seeming just as content to pick the ball up in deep or wide positions and run at defenders to create a shooting chance or thread through a pass. Curbishley and Day had prematurely judged him on his lack of goals, his disappointing mileage in games – something that would surprise the supporters – and lack of intensity on the training field. But with results going from bad to worse and fans calling for Tévez to be given more of a first-team run, the management eventually relented. 'He hadn't scored, but the crowd kept singing his name, and that put a bit of pressure on us,' Curbishley admitted. 'Perhaps we struggled a little bit to work out how to use Carlos best.'

Day was equally intrigued by the Tévez situation. 'His ProZone stats were awful, and he's not the best trainer. We were wondering why the crowd loved him so much,' he reflected. 'But the turning point was when we pushed him right up against the last defender and told him to stay there. And we found that he was one of those players who comes alive with the ball at his feet. Most forwards tend to run about ten kilometres a match but Carlos only runs about eight to nine. But then we calculated the figures just with the ball, and it was like, "Oh yeah!" So we made the decision to push Carlos right up alongside Zamora and let him use his backside to hold people off. All of a sudden, we saw what the crowd saw.'

What the 'crowd saw' was a wonderfully skilful player with a huge heart, and manager Curbishley was forced to acknowledge by the end of March that the team 'needed his enthusiasm'. The victory against Middlesbrough – only the second time West Ham had recorded back-to-back wins that season – closed the gap on fourth-bottom Sheffield United to five points with seven games left. Suddenly, the situation didn't look quite so bleak after all, although the problem – on paper at least – was that West Ham's fixtures appeared much more difficult than those of the Blades. The Hammers still had to face five of the top seven sides at that stage, while Sheffield were playing five of the bottom seven. Curbishley was unperturbed, however, insisting it was a good thing that West Ham were meeting teams who still had something to play for, because it would encourage more open games.

Nobody could doubt that West Ham's game at Arsenal on 7 April was an 'open' one. For the Hammers, it was far too free-flowing, however, as the Gunners tore into the visitors from the kick-off and created chance after chance without putting one away. The tone of the encounter was set when Robert Green was forced to save from Spanish midfielder Cesc Fàbregas in the opening minutes, and the Hammers goalkeeper remained in brilliant form throughout. Indeed, the 27 year old played the game of his life as he blocked everything that was thrown at him. Arsenal, who were without their injured top scorer Thierry Henry, were also guilty of missing the target on far too many occasions – with 14 of their 25 goal efforts going high or wide.

Hammers fans were not happy when two minutes were added

to the first half, but the extra time worked in their side's favour, with Zamora ignoring offside calls to reach Neill's long punt and lob the ball over goalkeeper Jens Lehmann just seconds before the whistle. West Ham had been the last away team to win at Highbury before Arsenal switched grounds at the start of the season, and it would therefore be appropriate if they could become the first visitors to claim three points at the impressive sixty-thousand-seater Emirates Stadium. Yet few people believed that the Hammers would keep the Gunners at bay, especially as they had recorded just one clean sheet on their travels during the season.

But Green performed marvels to deny Gilberto and Emmanuel Adebayor, and when both Fàbregas and Gilberto struck the woodwork late on it was obvious that the heavens were smiling on West Ham once again. When the final whistle blew, Green threw his gloves into the delirious visiting crowd, knowing they were probably threadbare after being put to so much use that afternoon and good for not much else. And when he reached the dressing-room, his teammates acknowledged his incredible efforts by applauding him back in.

The 1–0 victory not only saw West Ham complete an unlikely league double over Arsenal for the season but made it three wins in succession to move them within two points of fourth-bottom Charlton, who had edged above Sheffield United on goal difference. Curbishley was forced to admit that his men had ridden their luck somewhat after surviving such an intense onslaught but credited the change in fortune to the players finally displaying 'the right work ethic'. He added, 'The penny has now dropped about how hard we have to work.' While it was reassuring to see the team displaying the commitment that had been lacking for much of the season, it was surprising to hear the manager admit that his players had only just started giving 100 per cent for him. Whether that reflected on the players' attitudes or the manager's powers of motivation was a matter of opinion.

Perhaps some of the credit for the new display of desire and determination should have gone to Roberto Forzoni, the sports psychologist who was invited in by Curbishley to talk to the first-team squad towards the end of February. Forzoni was faced with the major task of trying to instil belief and hope into a set of players who were downcast at that time. 'When I came in, the staff were on a low, and they thought they were down,' he admitted. 'The players had lost their way, and there was a lot of adverse publicity.' Initially, the key was to get the players to focus on short-term objectives rather than the long-term situation. 'Who thinks we can stay up?' he asked as he got the squad together for the first time. Only a few hands were raised. 'OK, who thinks we can win on Saturday?' he enquired and thankfully more hands found the air. 'Right, let's forget about relegation and just focus on each game and see how we can maximise our chances of winning,' he told them.

Unfortunately, the players then went and performed abysmally in the 4–0 defeat at Charlton. But it gave Forzoni more ammunition to fire, replaying quotes from commentator Jonathan Pearce and TV pundit Alan Hansen that accused the West Ham players of showing little effort. 'We had to make sure that, whatever happened, we could never again be accused of lacking fight – and the work rate went through the roof,' he said.

It was a brave move by Curbishley, who recognised that an outside influence might serve some benefit, and he admitted after the win at Arsenal that the new spirit 'started with the Spurs game', which followed the Charlton match. 'If you look at the stats, I'm sure we're coming out on top in terms of mileage and intensity,' he said at the Emirates. 'Football is also about confidence, and once the results start coming a lot of things start to fall into place.'

West Ham had certainly pulled off a major shock at Arsenal, but the feeling was that it would be entirely in vain if they then travelled to fellow strugglers Sheffield United the following Saturday and failed to collect at least a point. Victory would see them leapfrog the Blades, but the priority was not to lose a game that was considered a classic example of a six-pointer. The key concern for Curbishley in the build-up was whether Zamora would be fit enough to play after scoring in his last four outings. The striker was nursing a knee injury that had restricted his training to one full session a week in recent times, but he was a naturally fit player, and the manager was happy to name him as long as he wasn't aggravating the problem.

Sheffield United manager Neil Warnock provided evidence that he was starting to feel the heat of West Ham's comeback on his neck as he complained about the lucky breaks the Hammers had been getting. 'I will be very bitter if West Ham stay up by a point,' he said, clearly aggrieved by the decisions at Blackburn that helped throw the Londoners a vital lifeline. Curbishley, meanwhile, predicted 'a long 90 minutes' at Bramall Lane and anticipated 'one hell of an atmosphere' for the game.

The West Ham boss was right on both counts, because it was certainly an endurance test for the travelling supporters who saw their team totally cut to pieces by the Blades, roared on by their ecstatic fans. Michael Tonge opened the scoring for the hosts shortly before half-time with a fierce free-kick before Phil Jagielka headed in from a corner and Jon Stead curled home from distance to wrap up a convincing 3–0 win. Tévez somehow fired over the bar after cleverly creating space for himself when the Hammers were just one goal down, and a leveller would undoubtedly have changed the game. But overall it was an unforgivably lacklustre display by West Ham, and Curbishley lashed into his players after the game, telling them that they had been totally outmuscled when it came to the physical confrontation.

After all West Ham's recent efforts, the defeat in Sheffield felt as if they were back at square one again. 'You've got to pick up points against the teams around you, and we just haven't done that,' admitted Curbishley. 'We've had massive games against teams in the bottom six, but we haven't done enough in those, and that's been our big problem.'

Indeed it was, with the Hammers languishing at the bottom of a table compiled purely from results between the teams in the bottom six at that time, which also included Charlton, fast-falling Wigan and Fulham, and long-doomed Watford. Just as worrying was the fact that Sheffield United topped such a table and still had Charlton, Watford and Wigan to play. Maybe it was just as well that the majority of West Ham's remaining opponents were at the top end of the table, given their obvious inability to scrap it out with the lesser lights. The task of trying to stay up was already tough enough without handing points on a plate to their relegation rivals.

West Ham had discovered to their cost in 2003 that it was not necessarily the number of points collected that mattered but which teams they were taken from. The Hammers completed a headline-making league double over Chelsea that term but were relegated with 42 points – the most any club had dropped out of the Premiership with. The pivotal moment came on 19 April when they lost 1–0 to Bolton, who survived by virtue of that result.

The demoralising defeat at Bramall Lane saw Curbishley admit that he'd failed to make the expected impact following his arrival before Christmas. 'I've had nearly 20 games to turn it around, and I take full responsibility for where we are,' he said, before emphasising, 'We still need to win the majority of our games.' Aside from the obvious lack of commitment, there had been little in the way of creativity against Sheffield United, and that made the omission of Yossi Benayoun all the more difficult for supporters to understand.

Curbishley insisted that there had been no bust-up between the pair after the Israeli playmaker appeared to risk aggravating an injury by featuring for his country. But although recent results had allowed the manager to claim he was reluctant to change a winning side, it seemed obvious to many observers that there had been a clash over where the midfielder's priorities lay. Curbishley was keen to show that an immediate first-team return could not be taken for granted, and he said, 'Yossi is disappointed, but individual situations have gone out of the window now.'

It was inevitable that Benayoun would start against Chelsea a few days later, however, with the manager aware that he needed his best players on the field as the second-from-bottom side entertained the second-from-top. It was a must-win game for both clubs, with Chelsea looking to close the gap on Premiership leaders Manchester United to just three points. And although it seemed ridiculous to suggest that West Ham needed any added incentive given their worrying position, they knew that if they helped ruin Chelsea's title hopes it could potentially make their trip to Manchester United on the final day of the season less daunting.

West Ham attacked the game with the belief they could cause yet another shock against a top-of-the-table team but, in the end, quality told. And it was Shaun Wright-Phillips who once again proved to be a thorn in the Hammers' side. The Chelsea winger had been involved in the collision that saw striker Dean Ashton break an ankle on England duty at the start of the campaign. The 25 year old then spurned the opportunity of moving to Upton Park during the January transfer window. And it appeared he had virtually condemned West Ham to the drop when scoring twice – his only league goals of the season – as Chelsea cruised to an emphatic 4–1 success.

Wright-Phillips put the Blues ahead just past the half-hour mark with a great strike into the far corner. But Tévez, who had been criticised by his manager following a disappointing display in Sheffield, responded in fine fashion with a curling shot from distance that saw the Hammers quickly draw level. Visiting goalkeeper Petr Čech had not been beaten in a league game for nearly 14 hours of play, and it needed a piece of magic from the Argentinian to break his run. Had West Ham been able to consolidate their position for a few minutes, then the outcome could have been different. But they fell behind within 30 seconds of the restart, with Wright-Phillips once again producing a finish of high quality to leave Upton Park stunned.

West Ham's resistance died in the second half as Salomon Kalou and Didier Drogba put the Blues out of sight and left the hosts fearing the worst. Curbishley believed the timing of Chelsea's second goal was crucial and slammed his players during the half-time break for their lack of concentration. 'We score a goal and everybody runs to the corner flag to celebrate when we should be making things nice and secure and solid,' he complained.

The result undoubtedly left West Ham at the point of no return. They remained three points behind Charlton and five behind fourth-bottom Sheffield United – who had a far superior goal difference – with just four games left to play. Even former Hammers manager Harry Redknapp, never a man to refuse a punt, insisted, 'West Ham are dead and buried now.'

Unlike Redknapp, Curbishley was never thought to be much of a gambler. But he started to roll the dice as West Ham entered their final sequence of games by excluding a goalkeeper from his list of five substitutes against Everton on 21 April. It appeared to be a dangerous – and possibly foolish – move at a time when the Hammers could not afford any slip-ups. It allowed an extra outfield player to sit on the bench, but it was questionable whether the benefit of that outweighed the risk of having to use a normal player in goal if Green suffered an injury.

That looked a distinct possibility when the goalkeeper dislocated a finger in the first half of the game against Everton on 21 April. Having experienced the problem before, however, he knew exactly what to do and whipped off his glove to pop the finger back into place. Day insisted that it was necessary to 'give ourselves options' by naming five outfielders on the subs' bench when games had to be won, but to some observers it suggested a lack of confidence in the original team selection.

But everything came good against Everton, with Zamora firing home from twenty-five yards to claim his eleventh goal of the season – and fifth in seven games – to secure a 1–0 win. The Toffees were fifth in the table as they chased a UEFA Cup place, were unbeaten in seven games and hadn't failed to score in their previous nine but could not match the Hammers on the day as the likes of midfielder Mark Noble and defender James Collins once again proved that they were worth their places.

Youth-product Noble had made an important impact with his effervescence and energy over the previous seven games while filling the gap left by the injured Quashie. Along with Tévez, he also played a key role in stoking up the Upton Park crowd in the final two months. 'Mark was there because he was competitive and enthusiastic,' said Day, 'but it wasn't a case of putting him in because we knew the crowd would respond to him. He was in the team on merit.'

On the weekend when bottom-of-the-table Watford were officially relegated, the win against Everton kept West Ham's survival hopes alive, and they moved to within three points of fourth-bottom Sheffield United, who drew 1–1 at third-bottom Charlton. It was an intriguing situation at the foot of the table, with everybody calculating what points would be needed from the remaining fixtures to secure safety. Yet the fear on West Ham's part was that their fate would not be decided on the football pitch at all.

# 12

## 'I'M SORRY, BUT I HAVE NO CONTROL OVER TÉVEZ'

WEST HAM United issued a short statement on 2 February 2007, which confirmed that they were 'fully cooperating with the FA Premier League in response to their recent letter to all Premier League clubs on player registration'. It added, 'The club is in the process of providing the relevant documentation as requested and is confident this matter will be settled in the very near future.' The inference was that the club was simply acknowledging a general enquiry, but it had already become known to some that the Premier League were taking a specific interest in West Ham and the unconventional deals that had brought Carlos Tévez and Javier Mascherano to Upton Park at the start of the season.

The third-party ownership of the two Argentinians had been widely reported upon their arrival, and there was considerable confusion in the media as to how this might contravene Premier League rules. But with the transfers being approved in August, it was believed that the players' contracts, while unusual, must have conformed to regulations. The Premier League's renewed interest in the situation coincided with Mascherano's proposed move to Liverpool when the next transfer window opened. West Ham proved that they were eager to relinquish their contractual hold on the unhappy midfielder by releasing his registration before the transfer deadline of 31 January. But it would take until late February before the Premier League finally confirmed that they were satisfied with the terms of his arrangement at Anfield. And by that time, it was heavily speculated that West Ham could be hit with a potentially fatal points deduction if found guilty of breaking the rules.

On 27 February, West Ham's former chairman Terence Brown resigned from his position as a non-executive director of the club, with no official explanation given. Just three days later, the Premier League confirmed that they were indeed charging the Hammers with two rule breaches in relation to the signings of Tévez and Mascherano. A statement said:

> It is the board's complaint that there were agreements in relation to both these transfers that enabled third parties to acquire the ability materially to influence the club's policies and/or the performance of its teams in League matches and/or the competitions set out in Rule E10. The board's view is that this constitutes a breach of rule U18.
>
> Furthermore, at the time of the transfer agreements for both Carlos Tévez and Javier Mascherano, and until 24 January 2007, West Ham failed to disclose the third-party agreements to the Premier League and/or deliberately withheld these agreements from the Premier League. The board's view is that this constitutes a breach of rule B13, which states, 'In all matters and transactions relating to the League, each club shall behave towards each other club and the League with the utmost good faith.'

The initial response from West Ham, who were allowed 14 days to formally reply to the charges, was that they would 'vigorously defend' themselves, indicating they would perhaps deny the allegations, possibly on the basis that a former hierarchy had been responsible for the transactions. The Premier League subsequently confirmed on 16 March that they had 'received

West Ham's response', and on 4 April an independent three-man panel was appointed to preside over the inquiry that was scheduled for a two-day hearing in London on 26 and 27 April.

Following all the problems that West Ham had already suffered during the season, an investigation that could result in a possible points deduction was the very last thing they needed. With the announcement being made in the week after the crushing 4–0 defeat at Charlton, it appeared that the team was more than capable of getting relegated by itself without any help from the Premier League. But the news was still likely to destroy what little morale there was in the playing camp, while there were also questions as to whether the continued selection of Tévez would possibly bring about greater penalties.

Alan Curbishley discussed the situation with his seniors at Upton Park and was told that he could carry on playing the striker if he wanted. 'It wasn't going to make the situation any worse,' said the manager, and Tévez instantly repaid his faith by scoring his first West Ham goal in the following game against Tottenham. To have dropped Tévez in the wake of the charges could have implied a sense of guilt on West Ham's part and, as time eventually proved, would have done their survival chances no favours whatsoever.

The irony is that the team's results improved dramatically in the two months leading up to the inquiry hearing, and Mervyn Day was of the view that the controversy helped bring the playing squad together. 'What it did was create a kind of siege mentality. It felt like the whole world was against us, and in some ways it drew the players together,' he reflected. 'That's not to say it wasn't slightly unsettling, because at the back of our minds there was the thought that all our efforts could be for nothing. But the players came together for a number of reasons, and that was undoubtedly one of them.'

Meanwhile, West Ham's bosses remained confident that the club's Premiership status would not be directly threatened by the result of the inquiry. Chairman Eggert Magnússon discussed the situation in the club's trophy room in mid-March and dismissed the suggestion that points would be deducted. 'I don't see that happening,' he said. 'There are no problems with the registration of the players, and I believe the Premier League has no case against West Ham.' The use of the word 'registration' was particularly relevant, as the majority of observers had incorrectly jumped to the conclusion that the charges related to the eligibility of Tévez and Mascherano. The general perception, even in the media, was that the Hammers had been fielding illegal players, and because there had been so many precedents set a points deduction was considered mandatory in the event of a guilty verdict. The reality, however, was that West Ham had been accused of entering into an agreement that allowed a third party to exert a material influence, the exact form of which was not truly grasped by many until the full details of the case were published at the end of April.

Interestingly, Magnússon made little effort to pretend that influence did not exist when questioned in March as to whether Tévez would remain at Upton Park in the long term. 'I'm sorry, but I have no control over Tévez,' he said. 'It's no secret that it's not West Ham that owns the player.' What the chairman was admitting was that the terms of the third-party ownership meant the club had no control over the player's movement – the very agreement the Premier League was so unhappy about. Third-party ownership in itself was perfectly legal, as long as clubs retained the authority to determine a player's future.

However, West Ham were being hit with two charges, the second accusing the club of deceiving the Premier League over the existence of the third-party agreements. Magnússon could at least solidly argue that he and much of the new Hammers board were not at the club when the signings were made. Meanwhile, he refused to discuss the reasons for former chairman Brown's sudden exit from the club at the end of February.

As the inquiry drew near, Wigan chairman Dave Whelan led the calls for West Ham to be deducted points in the knowledge that it would help his own struggling outfit save their Premiership skins. At a time when supporters were nervous of the outcome, it seemed strange to see Hammers manager Curbishley potentially undermine his club's defence by admitting he'd also have called for a points penalty if he was a rival boss. 'If the boot was on the other foot, I'm sure we would have done the same,' he said. But word eventually started to emerge that a financial penalty was far more likely to be imposed by the commission's panel – set to be chaired by leading QC Simon Bourne-Arton and including Lord Herman Ouseley, the chairman of Let's Kick Racism Out of Football, and David Dent, a former secretary of the Football League.

However, the whispers failed to prepare anybody for what was finally announced at around midday on 27 April in response to West Ham's guilty plea. The resulting 25-page Premier League report made for fascinating reading when published, not least because the exact terms of the contracts that brought Tévez and Mascherano to West Ham were finally revealed in full detail. In respect of Tévez, it was confirmed that the striker had signed a four-year contract with West Ham that allowed for the owners of his economic rights – namely MSI and Just Sports Inc. – to terminate the agreement during the January 2007 transfer window upon payment of £2 million to the club. That figure would reduce to a mere £100,000 if the player was transferred during any other transfer window during the period of his contract. A similar arrangement had been agreed in respect of Mascherano – who was jointly owned by Global Soccer Agencies Ltd and Mystere Services Ltd – with West Ham receiving £150,000 in the event of any transfer during his five-year contract at Upton Park.

In both cases, neither player – nor West Ham, for that matter – had the power to dictate or object to any transfers, and it was argued by Jim Sturman, the QC representing the Hammers at the hearing, that such agreements were legally invalid as they represented a restraint of trade. This was fully acknowledged by the commission, but the key point was that it was believed that the club had entered into the agreements in good faith. 'We proceed on the premise that West Ham believed they were entering into valid, enforceable contracts and were of that belief at all relevant times,' said the report. It was also recognised by the commission that 'there is no suggestion or evidence that there was such influence, nor any attempt to exert such influence'. However, rule U18 prohibits clubs from entering into contracts that empower a third party to have an influence, whether it is actually exploited or not.

The bottom line was that West Ham had entered into agreements that potentially allowed the players to be moved on without the club's permission – a third-party influence in the eyes of the Premier League. If Alan Pardew and Peter Grant – West Ham's management team at the time of the signings – believed that there were no 'get-out clauses', it would appear they had been seriously misinformed.

The issue of whether the Premier League had been misled by West Ham when signing Tévez and Mascherano was at the heart of the second charge the club had faced. Scott Duxbury, West Ham's legal and commercial director at the time, had telephoned the Premier League towards the end of August to advise them of the likely recruitment of two South American players and ask whether a break-clause involving third parties would be acceptable. The Premier League insisted that he was warned about U18, while Duxbury's claim was that he'd been told there could be a problem without any specific mention of the rule being made. Duxbury subsequently spoke to Paul Aldridge, West Ham's managing director, who – according to the report – said he would place the fact of the third-party ownership into 'what he called side agreements'. Without checking rule U18, Duxbury believed that non-disclosure of the third-party agreements was permissible.

With the subsequent explosion of publicity over the signings, the Premier League contacted Duxbury to ask if West Ham had entered into any third-party agreements. According to the report, there was a conflict about whether he offered an unequivocal 'no' or not, with Duxbury claiming that he ducked the question by insisting that all the necessary documents required for registration had been provided. Richard Scudamore, the Premier League's chief executive, was unconvinced and arranged a meeting with Aldridge on 8 September, when he was allegedly given 'a categorical assurance' that there were no documents of any sort in relation to the transfers that had not already been submitted. When asked how West Ham had managed to secure the services of two Argentina superstars with no fee being paid, Aldridge allegedly claimed the players had been brought to Upton Park as part of MSI front-man Kia Joorabchian's efforts to buy the club and that a gentleman's agreement would allow them to move for a small fee if the takeover bid was unsuccessful. Of course, it's unlikely any of this would have come to light had Joorabchian taken charge of West Ham, because he would not have been considered a third party any more, and the original rule breaches would probably have been overlooked.

The Premier League remained satisfied that everything appeared to be in order until 24 January 2007, when they wrote to West Ham in relation to a 'proposed report' into third-party ownership. Mascherano's move to Liverpool – which was on a fixed-term loan basis from his third-party owners and hence breached no regulations – may well have triggered the Premier League's interest in the subject, but there were also unsubstantiated rumours that they could have been alerted by other means. If that were not the case, some would question why West Ham risked opening up a viper's nest by allowing Mascherano to move to Liverpool, given that certain parties at the club knew of the side-agreements with MSI. But Mascherano was desperately unhappy, and there was no way the Hammers could have retained him for a prolonged period in his state of mind.

Nick Igoe, West Ham's finance director, dealt with the Premier League's request for all documentation relating to players under third-party ownership and sought the permission of both Magnússon and Duxbury before forwarding the paperwork, which, of course, disclosed the full details of the agreements. The fact that the club freely handed over the documents counted heavily in their favour.

In summarising, the Premier League's report expressed surprise that Duxbury had been unfamiliar with rule U18 but concluded that they were 'happy to accept he was under considerable pressure, not only by reason of the constraints of time but also from his superiors'. The report was particularly critical of Aldridge, who was accused of telling 'Mr Scudamore a direct lie', while the club was branded as being 'responsible for dishonesty and deceit'. At the same time, the commission acknowledged a number of factors that fell in West Ham's favour – the club had pleaded guilty, were under new ownership and had disclosed the information themselves. It was therefore declared that 'a deduction of points would not be proportionate punishment', especially as that penalty would have 'consigned the club to certain relegation'.

There were some observers who believed the consequences

of a points deduction were irrelevant, holding the view that if an offence merited the loss of, say, six points then that penalty should have been applied whether the club involved was Manchester United at the top of the table or West Ham United at the bottom. Others, meanwhile, insisted that it was right for the Premier League to take into account the repercussions of any penalty to ensure the punishment did not become disproportionate to the crime.

However, the Premier League's independent commission was keen to stress how seriously they viewed the breaches and declared that any financial penalty would reflect the fact that a points deduction could, in different circumstances, have been imposed. The report subsequently announced that West Ham would be fined a total of £5.5 million, with £2.5 million being in respect of the breach of rule U18 and a further £3 million for the breach of B13. It also stated that the fine would have been £8 million – if no points were deducted – had West Ham denied the charges and the matter gone to trial.

Regardless, the total figure – the equivalent of losing ten places in the Premiership table in terms of prize money – represented a record fine for a British club, way in excess of the £1.5 million imposed on Tottenham Hotspur for financial irregularities in 1994. West Ham responded to the verdict by issuing a statement:

> West Ham received a fair hearing. The club's submission that the contracts gave no actual influence to any third party was accepted by the commission. The club regrets the fact they fell foul of the FA Premier League regulations, but the new owners of the club now want to focus on matters on the pitch and remaining in the Premier League. The threat of a points deduction has now been removed and the club's fate remains in its own hands.
>
> The club believes that promotion and relegation issues should be decided on the pitch and we are

> pleased that the commission agree with that view. The
> club will reflect on the financial penalty that has been
> imposed and will take advice before commenting on
> the possibility of an appeal or any further steps that
> might be taken.

Gordon Taylor, chief executive of the PFA, was not alone in his
view when he said, 'If West Ham were in a comfortable mid-
table position, I think there would have been a points deduction
as a deterrent for the future.'

While relieved to have avoided a points penalty, many of the
West Ham staff were shocked by the size of the fine. Day had
read a story in the *Daily Express* that suggested the fine could
be as little as £300,000 prior to the announcement. 'So when
I heard the figure was £5.5 million, it was like, "Jesus!"' he said,
while admitting to concerns that the fine could have an impact on
manager Curbishley's spending plans in the summer – especially if
the club was relegated. 'The chairman had promised to back us, but
you have to be realistic – that's a ridiculous amount of money.'

The impact of the verdict and punishment sent shockwaves
through the football world and prompted a bitter reaction from
some parties – for differing reasons. Former managing director
Aldridge was upset at being censured by the Premier League
report without having had an opportunity to defend himself
and refutes the criticism aimed at him. 'I'm very comfortable
I acted in accordance with the legal advice we received at the
time,' he said. 'Naturally, my sympathies lie with the club in
respect of what seems a very harsh sanction. However, my own
personal and professional reputations have been besmirched.
The findings accuse me of acting dishonestly and lying. This is
hardly natural justice in my view, and I have placed the matter
in the hands of my lawyer.'

The Premier League report did indeed acknowledge that
Aldridge had not been invited as a witness to the hearing. 'He

has not made a statement, and we do not know what he may have said as to this,' it said. According to the BBC, former chairman Brown was also considering taking legal action after West Ham allegedly sent him a letter terminating the benefits of the personal contract agreed with the new owners at the time of the club's sale. Brown also instructed his lawyers to confirm to one newspaper group that he had exerted no influence on how the transactions involving Tévez and Mascherano were structured. At the time of the verdict, it was reported that West Ham were considering their options in terms of what action, if any, they might take against members of the club's former hierarchy.

And in what appeared to be a profitable time for the legal profession, struggling clubs such as Wigan, Sheffield United, Fulham and Charlton sent a letter to the Premier League advising them that they were taking professional advice on whether to contest the decision not to punish West Ham with a points deduction. Clearly, they all knew their own survival chances would be considerably boosted if the Hammers were deprived of points they had already earned.

Interestingly, BBC sports editor Mihir Bose expressed the view that the inquiry panel had been concerned about the issues at the top of the Premiership table as well as the bottom. West Ham were due to visit Manchester United on the final day of the league season, and Chelsea, who were in second place at the time of the verdict, obviously hoped that their fellow Londoners would still have a chance of survival going into their final game.

Bose wrote, 'The Premier League commission feared a possible backlash from Chelsea had West Ham entered the final fixture at Old Trafford already relegated because of a points deduction. There were fears that last season's champions may have claimed the commission had interfered with the destination of the Premiership.' At a time when the media focus was heavily centred on how the inquiry's decision would impact on the relegation picture, it was an intriguing theory.

Another was that the commission was conscious of a possible appeal from West Ham that could throw the Premiership relegation situation into chaos, with nobody knowing how things really stood at the bottom of the table until a points deduction was endorsed at a later date. And with the club expected to be relegated anyway, it's possible the panel was keen not to influence events just in case West Ham presented some kind of legal challenge.

The Hammers eventually confirmed that they would not be exercising their right of appeal against the £5.5 million fine in the form of a club statement. Chairman Magnússon said, 'It's time to draw a line under this matter. The fine imposed was very significant, but we accept that mistakes were made, and it is now time to move on.'

Unfortunately for West Ham, the matter would remain in the public eye for a considerable length of time. Aside from the club's relegation rivals investigating what measures could be taken to overturn the commission's verdict, there was huge opposition from the same parties that Tévez was allowed to continue playing for the Hammers for the rest of the season. The Premier League had not opposed the striker's continued participation in games after the charges were initially brought on 2 March, but the commission's report did state that 'the FAPL had the power to have then terminated his registration'. The commission explained that they chose not to take this course of action because, but for the inquiry's investigation, it might have been possible for West Ham and the Premier League to 'reach a similar situation pertaining to Liverpool and Mascherano' in respect of Tévez. The report also confirmed, however, that the Premier League could now terminate the registration of the player if they so wished.

It was initially reported that Tévez would not be able to play in the following day's vital relegation clash at Wigan unless he was 're-signed' – causing much confusion, as the transfer window was closed. The reality was that West Ham simply destroyed the third-party agreement that contained the offending clauses, and the Premier League, satisfied that this had been done, allowed the player's registration to remain in place. The letter sent by West Ham to the Premier League stated, 'We hereby notify you that the private agreement (as so amended, varied, modified or replaced) is hereby terminated with immediate effect and shall cease to have any further force or effect.'

The club also issued a statement that said, 'Following discussions with the FA Premier League, we can confirm that Carlos Tévez is available for selection for the rest of the season, including the game against Wigan Athletic. The actual registration of Carlos Tévez has not been called into question, and he remains a West Ham United player approved by the Premier League.'

Such assurances failed to convince certain parties who would voice their concerns with considerable force in the days, weeks and months to come. In the meantime, Tévez – who appeared to have little control over events involving and surrounding him – simply continued to try and focus on his football. He certainly didn't feel responsible for the situation that had cost West Ham £5.5 million. 'This is not my problem. It's between the club and the Premier League,' he said. 'I don't feel guilty because I have always acted in good faith. The fans know that, and that is why they love me. Ever since I have been at West Ham, I have only ever worried about playing as well as I can and giving my best for the team.' That he would continue to do so was not in any doubt as the Hammers embarked on the three games that would determine their Premiership fate.

# 13

## 'THE FINISH WAS SPECTACULAR AND DESERVES A PLACE IN HISTORY'

WEST HAM chairman Eggert Magnússon and his Wigan counterpart Dave Whelan exchanged pleasantries as they took their seats shortly before kick-off at the JJB Stadium on 28 April 2007. But one of the men had considerably more reason to smile than the other, with the Hammers having been given the massive psychological boost of knowing that the threat of a points deduction – which had been hanging over their heads for at least two months – was now removed. Magnússon had not exactly been dancing for joy 24 hours earlier when learning of the £5.5 million fine imposed by the Premier League for the club's 'dishonesty and deceit' in relation to the signings of Carlos Tévez and Javier Mascherano prior to his taking over. But he knew that was a price worth paying if West Ham could continue to show the spirit that had seen them win four of their previous six games and somehow achieve a miraculous escape from relegation.

Manager Alan Curbishley was certainly aware that his players could not afford a repeat of their pitiful performance at fellow strugglers Sheffield United a fortnight earlier. He knew victory against Wigan – who had not won for six games – would lift the Hammers to within goal difference of their opponents, and in the dressing-room beforehand he challenged the 'right team' to show up on the pitch. He was not to be disappointed, with Luís Boa Morte, Yossi Benayoun and Marlon Harewood all putting the ball in the net to give West Ham a stunning 3-0 victory.

Winger Boa Morte marked his best outing following his £5 million move from Fulham by lobbing home on the half-hour mark to open his Hammers account. He then ran clear to unselfishly tee up substitute Harewood late in the game after Benayoun had doubled the advantage after the break with a shot into the far corner. Tévez, meanwhile, was simply magnificent: he had a hand in two of the goals, hit the woodwork and generally gave the hosts a torrid time.

Whelan shook Magnússon's hand after the game but reserved his true feelings for the media in the aftermath of a match that had a significant impact on the relegation picture. The Wigan chairman was particularly unhappy that the Premier League inquiry's verdict was announced on the eve of a crucial fixture, believing that the visitors had arrived very much on a high. 'We were never going to win that match,' he complained. 'West Ham were on fire, and why not? They had just got away with murder.' Indeed, he later claimed that Premier League chief executive Richard Scudamore apologised in person for the unfortunate timing of the decision.

Whelan was also unhappy with many of the explanations given by the independent commission for failing to dock West Ham points for their indiscretions. In seeking to justify its decision, the panel claimed in their report that they took into account the feelings of the club's players and, in particular, the supporters who had shown 'loyalty' during a difficult few months. It gave Whelan reason to believe that West Ham had been given preferential treatment because of their status in the game and the size of their support. 'If you take into account fan loyalty, a club like Liverpool could do whatever they wanted and they would never even get fined,' he moaned. 'Had it been Wigan, Watford or a smaller club, it would have been a ten-point deduction, no question.'

It was a view shared by Wigan manager Paul Jewell, who made little effort to disguise his anger after his side's heavy defeat. 'One of the reasons for not taking off points was because of the fans. So, they don't get punished because they've got a big fan base?' he said, missing the fact that the report had not mentioned the *size* of West Ham's support at all. Jewell also displayed his chairman's sense of paranoia by adding, 'If it had been us, they would have taken points off – but they bottled it.' The Wigan boss revealed his belief that 'they decided not to take points off West Ham because if they had, they might have to look at one or two other London clubs higher up the league'. Yet somewhat contrarily, he suggested the Premier League was unhappy with the independent commission's verdict by professing that they wanted Wigan to 'right an injustice'. He claimed, 'We know the Premier League were desperate for us to beat West Ham because an insider told one of our men that.'

None of this concerned Curbishley, who insisted the decisions of the previous day had made little difference to his players' outlook. 'I don't think any of us have been taking too much notice of it,' he shrugged. 'We've just got on with things and have now given ourselves a chance, but we still need to pick up the majority of the points available to us.' And fittingly, given that West Ham's fan base seemed to be one of the topics of the day, the manager paid tribute to the 5,500 visiting supporters by insisting that they would have 'come here anyway' regardless of the club's offer of free coach travel – an initiative apparently instigated by the players as a gesture of gratitude.

Charlton had a similar idea in terms of swelling their ranks at Blackburn on the same day, but 'Operation Ewood' resulted in a disastrous 4–1 defeat that saw the Hammers move two points ahead of them in the table. Sheffield United gave their survival hopes a major boost with a fortuitous 1–0 home win against relegated Watford, whose chances were undermined by the absence of striker Steve Kabba for the first time since his January move from Bramall Lane. The issue of the missing forward attracted little media attention at the time but that would not remain the case.

If West Ham thought that they had heard the last of Wigan's whining, they were sadly mistaken, as later that week it emerged that Whelan had helped arrange a meeting between the so-called 'Gang of Four' – Wigan, Charlton, Sheffield United and Fulham – at the Harrods offices owned by the Cottagers' chairman Mohamed Al-Fayed, whose side had slipped back into trouble. Whelan spoke of 'suing the Premier League or West Ham' in a bid to seek 'justice' following the commission's failure to impose a points penalty on the Hammers. The meeting, on Friday, 4 May, lasted four hours, and an announcement that a letter of warning had been sent to the Premier League came later that evening. The correspondence reminded the Premier League of its 'duty to act in good faith and with reasonable diligence' and sought confirmation that the body would 'act as set out above'.

The four clubs might also have been hoping to unsettle West Ham ahead of their vital home game against Bolton, but, if anything, it seemed to have the opposite effect, as the hosts sailed into a three-goal lead within the opening thirty minutes. Tévez had been presented with the Hammer of the Year trophy before the game – collecting 84.5 per cent of the vote in a poll the fans had initially called to be scrapped in protest at the poor season – and he delivered an appropriately magical display in what was likely to be his final home outing for the club. The Argentinian produced two clinical finishes to sweep West Ham into a 2–0 lead before showing great vision to pick out midfielder Mark Noble with a wonderful cross for the third goal. At that stage, the supporters were dreaming of the team clocking up a cricket score that would overturn the goal-difference advantages held by most of the relegation rivals. However, Bolton pulled one goal back through veteran midfielder Gary Speed midway through the second period to at least give the scoreline some respectability.

The only thing that really mattered, though, was that West Ham held out for three points, and the 3–1 success lifted them out of the relegation zone for the first time in five long months. That was thanks to Wigan suffering a surprise 1–0 home defeat by Middlesbrough in their final home game, which left them three points adrift of safety and seemingly heading for the drop. Hammers boss Curbishley was unhappy that Fulham had been able to guarantee their safety that weekend with a 1–0 home victory against a Liverpool side that was heavily understrength due to their imminent Champions League final appearance. And he was left with mixed feelings on the Monday evening when second-bottom Charlton fell to a 2–0 home defeat by Tottenham that condemned them – and Alan Pardew – to relegation. While he would have been disappointed to see his old club drop out of the Premiership following a seven-year stay, he could at least console himself with the knowledge that West Ham's safety was under less threat as a result.

Quite aside from the Premier League inquiry, good fortune had remained on West Ham's side during the season's run-in. Bolton's hopes at Upton Park were undermined by the departure of long-time manager Sam Allardyce, and even though Sammy Lee was quickly appointed – as 'Big Sam' was replaced by 'Little Sam' – they obviously lacked their usual resilience. Like any team involved in a dogfight, the Hammers needed other results to go in their favour, and a crucial one was Sheffield United's 3–0 defeat at Aston Villa later the same day. A point would have been enough to secure the Blades' survival, but their collapse left them knowing that a one-goal defeat in their final game at home to fellow strugglers Wigan would send them down by the smallest margin of goal difference – if West Ham avoided losing at Manchester United, that was.

Almost as significantly for West Ham, Chelsea's 1–1 draw at Arsenal on Sunday was not enough to keep their title hopes alive, and Manchester United were duly crowned Premiership champions. This was the ideal scenario for the Hammers, who had feared the possibility of heading to Old Trafford to face a team still needing a point to win the league. At least only one side would now have anything seriously to play for, although that guaranteed nothing against one of the biggest clubs in the world. But the build-up to the final round of games was overshadowed by the continuing row over Tévez with Wigan – feeling even more vulnerable than they had the previous week now that they knew only a last-day victory would save them – making even more demands.

One Sunday newspaper referred to the imaginary sound of Whelan 'choking on his Bovril' the previous day as the Wigan chairman learned of Tévez's double against Bolton while his own side was dropping into the bottom three. And with every foot the West Ham striker put right, the more determined Whelan was to contest his continuing eligibility. The Premier League had responded to the Gang of Four's letter of 4 May with a circular to all member clubs that any legal action against them would be 'bound to fail'. But Whelan again wrote to the Premier League to demand evidence of how Tévez could still be allowed to play for West Ham on the basis that third-party agreements with MSI/Just Sports Inc. had been disposed of. 'Surely the contract can only be terminated by both parties?' he enquired. 'Could we see concrete evidence of this, and was the termination complete before 28 April when Tévez faced Wigan?'

Furthermore, he questioned the new West Ham hierarchy's integrity when referring to Scudamore's visit to Wigan the previous week: 'At that meeting [which also included Wigan manager Jewell and chief executive Brenda Spencer], you clearly stated that West Ham told you blatant lies regarding the contracts of the Argentinian players. Are you being told lies again?' The Hammers responded to the growing clamour by insisting that they had complied with the Premier League's demands. 'West Ham acted in accordance with the conclusions of the inquiry, and all the relevant documents were passed to the Premier League,' said a spokesman. And Scudamore confirmed, 'Having been through nine months of this, don't just think we've got a verbal agreement. We have a copy of the letter of termination sent to the third party, proof of receipt and proof it was served on Carlos Tévez.'

Sheffield United plc chairman Kevin McCabe – whose club had written to other chairmen to seek support – questioned how Tévez could still be registered as a West Ham player if the third-party agreement was destroyed. 'If that contract has been terminated, Tévez must have got a new contract,' he said. 'But how can you get a new contract outside the transfer window?' There was clearly plenty of confusion about the matter with *The Sun* claiming Tévez was still 'partly owned' by MSI and therefore 'on loan' to West Ham for the rest of the season. The *Telegraph* had its finger closer to the pulse by warning on 11 May that 'by tearing up this [third-party] agreement, West Ham have left themselves open to legal action by Kia Joorabchian, the president of MSI'.

Scudamore was riled by McCabe's outburst that dissenting clubs were being treated 'like lepers'. The Premier League chief executive defended the disciplinary process, denied that West Ham had received favourable treatment because of their size and sought to expose the true motives of the Gang of Four.

'Our rules don't allow either a kangaroo court or other clubs to decide these issues,' he said. 'If it's something we think is serious, an independent commission hears the evidence, which is what happened in this case. I'm not escaping the fact that not everybody thought the sanction was right, but it's what our rules provide for. The commission was convened correctly.'

He added, 'The suggestion that we wanted to keep West Ham in the Premiership at the expense of the so-called smaller clubs is one of the most offensive things I've ever heard. The idea we'd manipulate who is in the [Premier] League and who isn't is ridiculous. But this is an emotive time, and with the league being as lucrative as it is people are desperate to stay in it. People are hanging on by any means they can – that's what all this is about.' Sheffield United, meanwhile, insisted that they were acting on a point of principle rather than any self-interest. 'We don't expect to get relegated, but we will support the club that does,' vowed McCabe.

The conspiracy theories began to surface in the days immediately before West Ham's game at Manchester United. A single point would be enough for the Hammers to survive irrespective of the outcome between Sheffield United and Wigan. They would still be safe if they lost – as long as Sheffield United were not beaten at home by Wigan. If that were the case, West Ham would only stay up if Wigan won by three more goals than Manchester United – not particularly likely. The big fear for the Hammers was that if they were losing heavily at Old Trafford, Sheffield United – who sat above West Ham on goal difference only – would then know that they could afford to lose by a couple of goals and both they and Wigan would then survive. Given the two northern clubs felt a strong sense of injustice after seeing West Ham avoid a points deduction, it was suspected that might be the ideal scenario for them.

Hammers boss Curbishley warned Sheffield United that they

could not afford to think along such lines by reminding them of their dramatic relegation in 1994 when they conceded two late goals at Chelsea while Everton staged a remarkable – and somewhat controversial – comeback against Wimbledon. 'I don't think Sheffield will forget what happened to them several years back,' he said. 'You can't legislate for what might happen on the day, and I don't think these conspiracy theories have entered anybody's minds, because it's so dangerous. I don't see any other outcome this weekend than everybody trying their hardest to win.'

Mervyn Day later admitted, however, that he was concerned that Sheffield United might take their foot off the gas if they seemed to be safe. 'The only fear we had was that if we were 4–0 down at half-time, they might psychologically relax, because they wouldn't feel under any pressure. So, it wasn't about conspiracy theories – it was all about trying not to give Sheffield United an edge,' he said. 'We never thought it would be a case of their goalkeeper Paddy Kenny throwing one in over his shoulder.'

Manchester United's team selection for their final league game of the season was also hotly debated. The fact that they had already won the Premiership suggested that they might not be as desperate for victory as usual. But just as significant for West Ham was the fact that the Red Devils were playing in the FA Cup final the following weekend when they would be looking to achieve the highly revered league and cup Double. Such an opportunity doesn't come along often, even for a club as successful as Manchester United, and most observers believed that there was little chance of Sir Alex Ferguson risking injury to his top stars – in what was now a meaningless game for them – ahead of their big clash with Chelsea at the new Wembley Stadium. But West Ham couldn't allow themselves to acknowledge that they might enjoy any benefit of playing an understrength side, and boss Curbishley insisted,

'Alex has already said he has got to respect the league and will be putting a strong side out. Whatever team he selects will be going out to win, and I'm sure it's going to be packed with familiar names.'

Curbishley once again imposed a media ban on the West Ham players to try and keep them focused on the big game ahead. But Tévez admitted that he was really enjoying the task of trying to help save the club and revealed how much he was looking forward to playing at Old Trafford. 'Fighting against relegation is completely new to me, but I'm treating it as a challenge, and I like it,' he said. 'If you're competing for a championship, you know you can always win it another time. But fighting relegation is very different, because it is so dangerous. Playing against Manchester United in their stadium is one of those special matches and even more so when there's something so important at stake. For Manchester, the match will be a celebration of their title win, but for West Ham it is life itself. Our objective is victory.'

Tévez had been likened to Paolo Di Canio by many Hammers supporters, and the memory of the Italian striker's FA Cup fourth-round winner at Old Trafford in 2001 was still fresh in their minds. It would be fitting if the Argentinian could achieve a similar feat in a game that was far more crucial to the club's future.

The main factor from West Ham's point of view was that their fate was in their own hands going into their final match. Just eight games earlier, after the devastating 4–3 home defeat by Tottenham on 4 March, that situation had almost appeared to be an impossibility. Wigan boss Jewell bizarrely tried to claim all the pressure was on West Ham, because if they lost they needed Sheffield United to avoid defeat. But he seemed to forget that the Hammers needed just one point to guarantee safety, whereas his own side needed all three. Blades manager

Neil Warnock – nicknamed Colin by his friends – meanwhile insisted that his side was just 'ninety minutes away from the greatest achievement of my career', even though they had appeared to be safe before losing six of the last ten matches. Amid all the psychological games, Curbishley tried to keep his focus on what really mattered. 'There's been a lot said about us in the last month or so, but we've just been keeping our heads down and concentrating on the football,' he said. 'Maybe others should be doing the same.'

However events panned out on Sunday, 13 May 2007, it was going to prove a significant day in the history of West Ham United. Typically, it was drizzling with rain in Manchester, but naturally there was a celebratory mood within Old Trafford as the pre-match formalities took place. The West Ham players formed a guard of honour for the new Premiership champions, who had waited four years to reclaim the trophy, denying Chelsea a third-successive title in the process. Ferguson was presented with the Barclays Premiership Manager of the Year award while Portuguese winger Cristiano Ronaldo – whose place in British football was questioned after being blamed for England striker and club teammate Wayne Rooney's costly dismissal at the World Cup finals the previous summer – was handed the Barclays Player of the Year trophy.

Up in the stands, meanwhile, a somewhat furtive-looking Joorabchian took his seat in the same row as the West Ham hierarchy – including chairman Magnússon, funder Björgólfur Gudmundsson and deputy CEO Scott Duxbury – and immediately behind Premier League chief executive Scudamore. Duxbury's position at Upton Park had appeared to be in question after the Premier League inquiry's report on the rule breaches that resulted in the £5.5 million fine. But Magnússon appeared to accept the explanations of the former Manchester United lawyer – who joined West Ham in 2001 and moved onto the board three years later – and he remained at the chairman's side.

Most eyes were on the field, however, and there were perhaps mixed feelings as Manchester United's players lined up for action. It was certainly a much stronger team than the one that had started the meaningless midweek league game at Chelsea – in which eight players were rested – with goalkeeper Edwin van der Sar, former Hammers midfielder Michael Carrick and Wayne Rooney all returning. But West Ham fans could take some comfort from the fact that Ronaldo, ex-Hammers defender Rio Ferdinand and midfielders Ryan Giggs and Paul Scholes were all absent from the home side's starting XI. West Ham, meanwhile, lined up as expected, although left-back George McCartney suffered a knee injury half an hour into the game and was replaced by Jonathan Spector.

By that time, those associated with West Ham had reason to bite their nails, as Wigan had gone ahead at Bramall Lane with a 14th-minute strike from Paul Scharner. At that moment, Sheffield United were back in the bottom three, but it would only take one goal from Manchester United to put West Ham down there instead. If there was any consolation, it was that the Premiership champions seemed content to operate in second gear, with Rooney shrugging off a couple of missed chances with uncharacteristic good humour. Midfielder Yossi Benayoun needed to come to the Hammers' rescue, however, when he cleared off the line from Alan Smith and then blocked Kieran Richardson's follow up before the ball was hacked clear. 'Send them down, send them down' was the chant from the home crowd; 'Staying up, staying up' came the reply from the visiting end when news of Sheffield United's equaliser by Jon Stead came through ten minutes before the break to return the Premiership table to its earlier order.

West Ham felt aggrieved when home defender Wes Brown

clearly appeared to have blocked a Tévez shot with his hand, but that was quickly forgotten when the Argentina hit man shot the visitors into a shock lead in first-half stoppage time. Tévez played the ball to Bobby Zamora on his right and bulldozed his way through the defence to collect the return as it dropped and slot past van der Sar from a tight angle. Old Trafford was stunned as West Ham celebrated Tévez's seventh goal in ten games and what was surely the most important.

Curbishley and Day were brought back down to earth, however, when they returned to the dressing-room just moments later to discover that Wigan had scored for a second time through a David Unsworth penalty. 'We were up and down like a yo-yo in that first half,' reflected Day. 'I was still worried, because I knew that Manchester United were the type of team who if they got one goal could easily score two, three or four. We started the second half really well, but then I saw United bringing on the three musketeers. I looked across at Alex and thought, "Why are you doing this to us? You're supposed to be a mate of Curbs'."'

Those 'musketeers' were substitutes Giggs, Ronaldo and Scholes, who were all thrown into the arena with more than half an hour to play. The hosts duly stepped up a gear, and Hammers goalkeeper Robert Green, who had denied John O'Shea in the first period, was forced to save well from both Ronaldo and Scholes in the final 15 minutes. Even the fact that Wigan had been reduced to ten men for the last quarter of an hour, after Lee McCulloch received a second yellow card, failed to ease the nerves of the West Ham fans, who refused to believe that their side was safe until the final whistle actually blew. Day admitted he 'could have killed' the fourth official when the board displayed three minutes of added time, but, after what seemed an eternity, referee Martin Atkinson eventually signalled an end to the proceedings. West Ham had beaten Manchester United 1–0 away and, against all the odds, pulled off arguably the greatest escape act of all time.

Curbishley and Day jumped into each other's arms as the party began. Meanwhile, 50 miles away in South Yorkshire, Sheffield United's players were on their knees as their failure to even draw with a ten-man Wigan side saw them drop back into the Championship after just one season at the salvation of their opponents. Whereas the contrast of emotions could not have been greater at Bramall Lane, back at Old Trafford there was the unusual scene of two sets of supporters trying to out-celebrate each other with every one of the 75,927 spectators – possibly minus the corporate 'prawn-sandwich brigade', as they were famously dubbed by former skipper Roy Keane – having reason to express joyful emotion. For the second year running on 13 May, West Ham looked on as their opponents collected silverware, except on this occasion they went home with a prize that was far more valuable than either of the trophies presented. But while they had won many friends as FA Cup final losers the previous season, it quickly became apparent that they had only made enemies as Premiership survivors next time around.

Assistant boss Day felt 'relief rather than elation' after the win in Manchester, which he described as 'the longest game of my life'. Manager Curbishley, meanwhile, hailed his side's 'amazing achievement' of winning seven games out of nine, during which they beat Arsenal and Manchester United for a second time without conceding a single goal. The victory at Old Trafford saw West Ham take their tally to forty-one points and finish 15th in the Premiership table – one place above Fulham – and claim prize money of £2.919 million.

The fact that Wigan's victory meant West Ham needed a positive result against Manchester United made survival even more satisfying for Curbishley. 'Seven wins out of nine is unbelievable when you look at the opposition we've played,' he said as he sat down after the game. The manager recognised Tévez's outstanding contribution to the team's revival in the final ten games but was keen to acknowledge that it would have counted for nothing had many other players not come good during the run-in. 'Tévez has been tremendous, but there have been some magnificent performances throughout the side over the last two months,' he declared. 'Green has made some great saves, Anton Ferdinand and James Collins have been strong at the back, and people such as Lucas Neill, Mark Noble and Bobby Zamora have all played their part in what has been a fantastic team effort.'

Down in the dressing-room, the jubilant West Ham players embraced each other in recognition of the magnificent endeavours that had seen them come back from the dead. Publicly, they had always maintained that survival was possible, but many of them had feared, in their heart of hearts, that the club had already passed the point of no return in the early part of the year when absolutely nothing was going right. But just as there was no single reason why the Hammers were struggling earlier in the campaign, there was no one factor responsible for their recovery. There's little doubt that a siege mentality had developed as criticism of the club intensified – particularly around the time of the Premier League inquiry – and that collective bonding proved invaluable as players started to pull in the same direction late on in the season.

Curbishley's management style and methods, while initially resisted in some quarters, had begun to gradually take effect as the players eventually absorbed his philosophies – not least that nothing was earned without hard work. As the manager was quick to admit, it was incredible how fortune turned in the team's favour once they started to deserve it. Curbishley had frequently asked if confidence bred results or vice versa, but the answer was that they both did – as the Hammers proved. With his seven goals, Tévez was inevitably the focal point of West Ham's recovery, but, as Curbishley acknowledged, one man alone could not have made the difference. Without Green's heroic display at Arsenal, the Hammers would have been relegated. Without Zamora's brilliant winners against the Gunners and Everton, it would have been all over. Without Neill's leadership qualities, Noble's infusion of energy and enthusiasm and Benayoun's intelligent play, the white flag would have been raised. Without Collins and Ferdinand's bravery and courage in defence, the floodgates would have opened with fatal consequences.

West Ham's survival wasn't to suggest that all the problems that had undermined the club in the earlier part of the campaign had disappeared – far from it. But the manager could at least address those in the close-season knowing they hadn't cost the club its Premiership status – although defeat at Manchester United would certainly have done so. Not surprisingly, relegated Sheffield United manager Warnock was quick to complain he'd been 'sold a dummy' by United boss Ferguson in terms of how strong his team selection would be for the visit of West Ham. Warnock failed to acknowledge that if his own team had even drawn against Wigan, the result at Old Trafford was irrelevant. But Ferguson – who complained that his side should have won a penalty after O'Shea went down under the combined challenge of Boa Morte and Green in the second half – hit back at the criticism. 'We had twenty-five strikes at goal, four shots off the line and a penalty turned down,' he insisted. 'I think I played the right team – players who would relish the challenge and who needed a game.'

There was certainly no shortage of commitment from the less-established Manchester United players such as O'Shea, Richardson and Darren Fletcher, who were pushing for FA Cup final places and could hardly be considered novices after making 113 appearances between them during the season.

'I feel for Sheffield United, but we did our best, and West Ham have been in championship-winning form,' added Ferguson. Hammers chairman Magnússon also expressed compassion for the Blades but insisted it was right for the relegation issue to be settled by results of games and nothing else. 'Of course I feel sympathy for the clubs that are no longer in the Premiership, but it was right that football matters were decided on the pitch,' he said. 'Who can say that West Ham did not achieve this on merit? The finish was spectacular and deserves a place in history.'

Goalkeeper Green believed it was unlikely the team would get the credit they deserved, however. 'We won't get the plaudits for winning seven of our last nine games, but none of us gives a monkey's about that,' he grinned. 'We have achieved the impossible, and nobody can deny us our right to stay in the Premiership after that.' Little did he realise to what lengths some people would go to question that right in the months to follow.

# 14

## 'WE WILL NOT BE DRAWN INTO THIS FORM OF PUBLIC MUDSLINGING'

ALAN CURBISHLEY was entitled to have a spring in his step on Monday, 14 May 2007, but if he was hoping West Ham's victory at Manchester United and Premiership survival would finally bring about the 'positive press' he was looking for, he was left disappointed. Indeed, even the manager's trademark sense of realism failed to prepare him for the vicious media assault that took place in the immediate aftermath of the season's thrilling climax. 'Cheats Do Prosper' and 'The Sickening Swindle' were just two of the horrific headlines that appeared, as it was deemed that West Ham's success and Sheffield United's failure represented a huge miscarriage of justice.

It was perhaps inevitable that Carlos Tévez scoring the winner at Old Trafford would provoke a maelstrom of fury, the popular view being that the Premier League had been negligent in allowing West Ham to save themselves at all. Had the Hammers been docked points for the rule breaches relating to the signings of Tévez and Argentina teammate Javier Mascherano, then Sheffield United would not have been relegated. Whether the Blades deserved to remain in the Premiership on that basis was ignored. The fact that West Ham had been fined a record £5.5 million was downplayed and only mentioned in the context of the estimated £40 million the club would earn by staying up – making the breaking of Premier League rules a profitable business in the eyes of the critics, many of whom were still under the misconception that Tévez had been ineligible for most of the season.

The myths and misunderstandings angered West Ham's assistant boss Mervyn Day, who was unhappy that the hysteria had been allowed to overshadow the team's accomplishments. 'Some of the things written about us have been absolutely scandalous,' he said. 'There's no doubt it has taken the gloss off the players' achievements. They have been decried because people haven't understood the situation and accused us of using ineligible players when that was never the case. The Premier League report was published for everybody to read, yet people failed to pick up on the essential point that the registration of the players was valid all the way through.'

Dave Whelan was one of those people, and the Wigan chairman was the first to call for 'justice', despite his team being responsible for sending Sheffield United down with their 2–1 victory in the final game. In fact, as he consoled his Blades counterpart Kevin McCabe at Bramall Lane, he told him, 'You get stuck into West Ham. We're right behind you.' The very next day, Whelan called for a new Premier League hearing in the belief that Tévez had been 'registered illegally again'. It was also claimed that relegated Charlton and survivors Fulham, who finished below West Ham, would remain actively involved in trying to force some new form of action. Middlesbrough also expressed their support on the basis that they had been relegated ten years earlier when docked three points for failing to fulfil a league fixture against Blackburn because of a lack of players.

Unnervingly for West Ham supporters, FIFA threatened to intervene with president Sepp Blatter saying, 'We will look at this, and if we feel something was wrong, we will have to open our file.' At a time when fans should still have been on a high following their team's miraculous escape act, the constant speculation that West Ham's Premiership status could potentially be questioned helped bring many of them back down to earth. The Premier League insisted that they had 'implemented the rule book and correct processes to the letter' and claimed that they were 'more than happy to give FIFA any assurances they need'.

They also moved to clarify the facts of the matter in the wake of a mass of inaccurate reporting. 'This has never been a case of West Ham fielding an ineligible player,' confirmed a Premier League spokesman. 'From the day West Ham signed Tévez, they owned his registration. The only problem we had was the existence of a clause in the agreement that would allow Kia Joorabchian and MSI to sell the player. In the eyes of the inquiry, that was a breach of rule U18, which forbids any third party from influencing the policy of any team. West Ham were fined and presented with three options – to tear up the contract with MSI, remove the offending clause or release Tévez. On the day of the inquiry's judgment, West Ham chose to terminate the third-party agreement with Joorabchian.'

Sheffield United plc chairman McCabe appeared to be paying little attention, however, with it being confirmed on 16 May that the relegated club had submitted a formal challenge to the Premier League inquiry's decision to fine West Ham instead of imposing a points sanction. 'We will argue the commission's decision failed to meet the same general obligations of those required of public bodies, namely to act lawfully, fairly and reasonably,' a statement said. 'Sheffield United will also argue that the League should have cancelled Tévez's registration.'

The Premier League acknowledged receipt of the claim for the matter to be referred to 'arbitration' and confirmed that the request was under consideration. On the same day, the Blades parted company with Neil Warnock after a seven-and-a-half year association – shortly after Paul Jewell's resignation at Wigan – as the manager claimed relegation had hurt him as much as the death of his mother. Equally as head-scratching was McCabe's bizarre suggestion that the Premiership could be expanded to 21 teams to accommodate Sheffield United. 'It's a very simple solution,' he claimed, yet he failed to explain why the Blades should be reinstated if the Hammers remained in the top flight as well.

Meanwhile, Whelan remained on the warpath by accusing Premier League chief executive Richard Scudamore and chairman Dave Richards of being guilty of a 'dereliction of duties' and calling for their resignations. He also demanded documentary evidence of Tévez being allowed to play for West Ham, although it appeared to pass him by that the Premier League did not report to Wigan Athletic and was precluded from providing confidential information to any club. Scudamore responded to the email – which was circulated to all the other Premiership outfits – by explaining to Whelan that the termination of Tévez's contract was merely one of several options available and by no means mandatory if other conditions were met.

It was also requested that Whelan – whose Rugby League team, ironically, would soon be docked four points for breaching their salary cap for a second year running – communicate his complaints directly to the Premier League in a formal manner rather than trying to whip up media hysteria. At the same time, the Premier League wrote to all the Premiership outfits advising them that any legal action 'would fly in the face of the disciplinary structure that the clubs themselves created' and be doomed to failure. West Ham's only response at this time came when Eggert Magnússon complained that 'there have been all sorts of misinterpretations'. He added, 'Some of the things that have been said about this club are unjustified. There should be no dispute – everyone agrees on this including FIFA and the Premier League.'

However, on 22 May the Premier League revealed that Sheffield United's claim would indeed be referred to an arbitration tribunal. This, apparently, was the club's right, although it was reported that the Premier League was in no hurry to schedule the hearing, in order to give the Blades time to withdraw their request and save themselves unnecessary cost. A few days later, Brighton wrote to the FA to ask if they had grounds to contest their FA Cup third-round elimination by West Ham in January as a result of Tévez's participation. Their argument was that Bury had been expelled from the competition for having fielded an ineligible player, but their appeal proved to be in vain, as the precedent didn't apply.

The two-day arbitration hearing was subsequently scheduled for 18 and 19 June, and Sheffield United's publicity machine went into overdrive as the club sought to win support for their self-dubbed 'Campaign for Fairness'. McCabe continued to trot out the well-worn line that 'the club that played by the rules has been relegated at the expense of one who fielded ineligible players'. It might have been fair to claim that MSI would not have allowed Tévez and Mascherano to sign for West Ham had the contentious third-party agreements not been agreed to – but that did not make the two players ineligible as far as Premier League rules were concerned. Such misleading propaganda helped create a groundswell of support for the Blades, who also made little acknowledgment of their failings on the football field. It had nothing to do with West Ham that Sheffield accumulated only thirty-eight points, won just two of their final eleven games and that midfielder Phil Jagielka handled the ball to gift victory to Wigan.

Meanwhile, the argument about the Blades playing 'by the

rules' was brought into question when reports revealed that the Premier League were investigating claims that Watford striker Steve Kabba had been prevented from appearing against his former club on 28 April because of an alleged agreement – as indicated on both club websites. No action was taken on the basis that there was no contractual evidence of any such deal having been struck when he switched clubs in January – although that did not rule out the possibility of a verbal agreement having been made.

McCabe continued his media campaign in the weeks ahead of the arbitration hearing. 'I firmly believe Sheffield United will win and the previous decision will be overturned for reasons of an irrational decision that was made by the first panel,' he said. Many people assumed that the arbitration panel had the power to change the decision to fine West Ham, but that was never the case, the objective being simply to establish whether the original independent commission had acted in accordance with Premier League rules. Chief executive Scudamore insisted that had been the case, although former West Ham managing director Paul Aldridge's complaint that he had not been asked to give evidence raised the question as to whether the first inquiry had indeed been flawed in some way.

Actor and Sheffield United director Sean Bean – who allegedly called manager Warnock 'a f**king w**ker' after the fatal home defeat by Wigan – then jumped aboard the bandwagon by leading a delegation of supporters to London's Houses of Parliament on 13 June. The star of *When Saturday Comes*, in which he played a Blades striker, delivered a passionate speech in one of the House of Commons' committee rooms to Sheffield Attercliffe MP Clive Betts and Alan Keen MP, chair of the All Party Parliamentary Football Group, in which he spoke of 'justice' and 'balancing the weak against the powerful'. 'We cannot let the God of money rule over the power of football,' he added, without acknowledging that the Blades' motives were primarily finance driven.

Yorkshire and Humber MEP Richard Corbett reiterated the theme by saying, 'West Ham's punishment just goes to show how much the Premier League is geared up to favouring the richer clubs. United have not been treated fairly, presumably because they are not a fashionable club from the capital.' Later that week, Sheffield United took a small delegation to Brussels to meet with European Commission officials to explain their campaign, with McCabe adding, 'We believe we have maybe got a human-rights issue because of the loss of jobs at the club.'

The arbitration process began on 18 June with a three-man panel made up of chairman Sir Philip Otton, a retired judge of the Court of Appeal, David Pannick QC and Nicholas Randall convening in central London. Sheffield United and Fulham both had legal representation – with the so-called Gang of Four now a slimline Gang of Two – as did the Premier League. Liverpool CEO and former Premier League chief executive Rick Parry gave evidence after being called up by Sheffield United, but suggestions that MSI front-man Joorabchian would throw the cat among the pigeons by appearing and discussing West Ham's controversial unilateral termination of his third-party contract proved unfounded.

McCabe emerged at the end of the hearing the following day to reveal that no decision was imminent, but it would be announced by the Premier League before the end of the month. It seemed a strange outcome, given that the original inquiry – in which a mountain of evidence was examined – only took two days to produce a decision, while a relatively straightforward process – one that simply investigated whether the original hearing and verdict had been conducted within Premier League regulations – would take up to another fortnight to conclude.

This prolonged the agony for West Ham supporters, some

of whom feared the club's Premiership place could still be in jeopardy, although some comfort could be taken from the fact that the following season's fixtures had already been published. The Hammers, all being well, would kick off at home to Manchester City, while Sheffield United could look forward to entertaining Colchester United in their first match. It was considered highly unlikely that the Hammers and Blades could simply swap fixtures if the original commission's process was proved to be unsound.

In fact, the general view was that the later the decision was announced, the less likely it would be in Sheffield United's favour, given that the matter would then have to be returned to the Premier League, who would need to organise a brand-new inquiry to reconsider the original evidence. By that time, the new season would have arrived, while any subsequent points deduction that threatened West Ham's status would inevitably have been appealed against. There was always the possibility that a points sanction could have been applied to the 2007–08 season, but that would not help Sheffield United, of course.

The delayed verdict did nothing to help West Ham while manager Curbishley was trying to recruit new players. Newcastle midfielder Scott Parker had been signed for a £7 million fee at the start of June, but there was little activity for the rest of the month, and, although the Hammers insisted it was a case of business as usual, the uncertainty could potentially have undermined their efforts to bring players to the club.

Finally, on 3 July, the arbitration report was published with the panel ruling against Sheffield United's claim for the matter to go to a retrial. However, in the same way as the original commission had given the Blades reason to appeal by suggesting that West Ham would have lost points had the case been heard earlier in the year, the arbitration panel also made statements that allowed the relegated club to feel justified in battling on.

The report said, 'We have much sympathy for Sheffield United's grievances. We go so far to say that this tribunal would, in all probability, have reached a different conclusion and deducted points from West Ham.'

As far as West Ham and the Premier League were concerned, this was completely irrelevant. The arbitration panel had never been given the authority to retry the case and should not, therefore, have hypothesised about what they might have done had they presided over the original hearing. This was at least acknowledged when the report stated:

> However, the fact that we disagree with the decision, or that others may have genuine passionate criticisms of it, is insufficient to warrant intervention. The tribunal has to test the decision on the basis of whether it was irrational or perverse when it was reached. This is a very strict test and is very difficult to satisfy on a question very much of judgment and discretion.
>
> The tribunal can well understand that in the light of subsequent events [West Ham winning their final three games to avoid relegation], the outcome of the decision turned out to be unfortunate in the extreme. However, we have to judge it at the time when it was taken and we are satisfied the decision at that time fell within the parameters of the options open to the commission. It is thus impossible to find that the decision was irrational or perverse.

In effect, the panel did not concur with the original decision but had absolutely no grounds to overturn it. This was the inevitable outcome, given that there was never any evidence to suggest that the Premier League's inquiry had not fully complied with their rule book. Sheffield United may not have approved of a verdict that failed to throw them a Premiership lifeline, but that did not mean it was wrong. Not surprisingly, however, the Blades took encouragement from the expressions of sympathy and insisted that they would continue their fight. For some, it was reminiscent of the scene from the *Monty Python and the Holy Grail* movie in which the Black Knight gradually loses both his arms and legs in a swordfight with King Arthur before stubbornly declaring, 'All right then, we'll call it a draw.' The analogy was perhaps appropriate, given that Michael Palin of Monty Python fame had lent his name to Sheffield United's campaign.

West Ham consciously maintained a low profile in relation to the arbitration process in the belief that the matter actually had little to do with the club. This was a dispute between Sheffield United and the Premier League, as far as they were concerned. But Magnússon finally acknowledged the events when he said, 'We are happy this matter is finally closed and all parties can now move on.' Ten days later, the Blades had 'moved on' to the High Court in London as they chased compensation of £50 million by claiming that the arbitration panel had made an 'error in law' by deciding against them. They had finally accepted that they were a Championship club once again but insisted that they were owed damages for their enforced relegation. Their appeal was rejected, although the club's lawyers issued a statement insisting that 'Sheffield United are not precluded from taking further action against the Premier League or West Ham'. The reality, however, was that the Blades had few viable options left and were running up a sizeable legal bill.

West Ham's preparations for the 2007–08 season effectively began on the morning of Wednesday, 16 May when Curbishley met Magnússon and deputy chief executive Scott Duxbury at Upton Park to discuss the summer's transfer budget. The manager and assistant Day had provisionally drawn up two lists of potential targets based on survival and relegation. 'The difference between the pair of them was massive,' admitted Day, who anticipated a high turnover of players and something of a clear-out. Striker Teddy Sheringham and goalkeeper Roy Carroll were released at the end of their contracts and subsequently joined Championship outfit Colchester United and SPL giants Rangers respectively. Full-back Paul Konchesky and striker Marlon Harewood were both told that they would be allowed to leave the club subject to acceptable offers being received, while it was considered a certainty that want-away midfielder Nigel Reo-Coker would be moved on.

Reo-Coker had wasted little time in suggesting that his future lay away from Upton Park when he admitted in a television interview at Manchester United that 'to play at my best I need to be happy'. He added, 'I made a promise to West Ham that I would keep the club in the Premier League, and I've done that.' Interestingly, when both Curbishley and Day paid tribute to the players who had made a major contribution towards the club's recovery in the final ten games, their captain's name was conspicuous by its absence. Within a few weeks, Reo-Coker had submitted a transfer request, complaining that he had not been sufficiently 'supported'. He added, 'There's been a lot of negative press that was very hurtful, and it's heartbreaking to see I'm not wanted.'

Whether he wanted more backing from the club's directors, management or fans was never made clear, but none of the parties were too unhappy to see the player eventually move on to Aston Villa for a fee of £8.5 million once he'd completed his England Under-21 commitments. West Ham did remarkably well to receive such a generous figure for the 23 year old, who'd had a disappointing season, had burned his bridges by demanding a transfer and had no other clubs seriously interested in him. The silence from the top teams he had envisaged being on his tail was deafening, while Tottenham even contacted one newspaper to disassociate themselves from reports suggesting that they were set to make a bid. Predictably, Reo-Coker complained about being 'hung out to dry' and being made a 'scapegoat' by

West Ham once he'd sealed his switch to Villa Park. He added, 'If people want to see me as obnoxious, arrogant or bitter, then that's their prerogative.' Meanwhile, Magnússon said, 'We need grown-up men at this club.'

The midfielder had led England to the semi-finals of the European Championship in Holland, but it was a heartbreaking experience for all three West Ham players involved in the tournament. Midfielder Mark Noble was left in tears as the youngsters were held to a late 1–1 draw by the hosts and then beaten 13–12 in an incredible penalty shoot-out in which Reo-Coker and, finally, Anton Ferdinand wasted kicks. It was the second time in a year that the defender was left devastated by spot-kick woe following his failure at the FA Cup final.

Reo-Coker returned to England to seal his switch to Villa and was soon joined by former club teammate Harewood as the Midlands outfit handed over a fee believed to be around £4 million for yet another West Ham player who had not enjoyed the best of seasons. Wigan had been close to signing the twenty-seven-year-old striker, who had scored just four goals in thirty-five outings in his fourth and final season at Upton Park, but the Hammers could not have been blamed if they were reluctant to do business with them. Former Charlton man Konchesky, meanwhile, said goodbye to manager Curbishley for the second time in his career when he completed a £3.25 million move to Fulham in the middle of July. But his old boss accused him of having 'no class' after the full-back followed up his departure by claiming that 'there are still a lot of unhappy players at the club who don't like him'. And right-back Tyrone Mears was allowed to make a £1 million switch to newly promoted Derby County, whom he had joined on loan back in January.

The most significant departure at that time, however, was that of Yossi Benayoun to Liverpool. West Ham jumped the gun somewhat by allowing their official website to declare towards the end of May that the midfielder had agreed a new five-year contract. 'The chairman is very ambitious, and West Ham have the best supporters in England,' said the Israeli as he explained his motives for extending his stay at Upton Park. However, the 27 year old then left the country on international duty to play games in Macedonia and Andorra without having put pen to paper. In a repeat of the situation the previous year, the actual contract remained unsigned, while Liverpool's name again became linked. With Benayoun only too aware of their interest (Curbishley later complained that his 'head had been turned'), it was inevitable he would want to go to Anfield, and, despite his sudden U-turn, few supporters begrudged him his eventual £5 million move, although his creativity would obviously be missed.

Less than a week after Benayoun's move, West Ham lost yet another midfielder in rather different circumstances when new recruit Julien Faubert sustained a serious injury that would rule him out for an estimated six months. The France international had only recently been signed from Bordeaux in a £6.1 million deal. But the 23 year old suffered dreadful luck when rupturing an Achilles tendon during West Ham's 1–0 defeat against Czech side Sigma Olomouc in a pre-season friendly in Austria on 17 July. A year earlier, it had been Dean Ashton who was crocked before the season had started; next time around it was Faubert as fortune again frowned on the Hammers before the big kick-off.

But Ashton gave supporters a boost when he finally returned from his ankle problems in the friendly win at League Two newcomers Dagenham and Redbridge. The striker admitted that he had feared for his career during his prolonged absence, but he suggested that he hadn't lost his goalscoring touch with a fine long-distance effort in the 1–1 draw at Leyton Orient on 24 July. And he would score his first goal at Upton Park for 17 months when claiming the winner in the 2–1 friendly success against Italian giants Roma less than a fortnight later.

West Ham had broken their transfer record when signing Ashton from Norwich for an initial £7 million in January 2006. But it was a sign of the club's huge ambition under new chairman Magnússon that they were prepared to more than double that expenditure in a bid to sign Darren Bent from Charlton. Former Addicks boss Curbishley had signed the striker from Ipswich Town for a £2.5 million fee in 2005, and his sale two years later was considered a necessity following the south London club's relegation. Bent had scored 37 goals in 79 outings for Charlton, but it was still a shock when it was confirmed that the Hammers had agreed a deal worth £17 million – with midfielder Hayden Mullins to be used as a £1.5 million makeweight – to bring the 23 year old to Upton Park. Magnússon met the player on Thursday, 14 June and was under the impression that he would sign after the discussions were concluded.

However, Charlton immediately released a statement in which chief executive Peter Varney revealed that Bent had decided against the move. 'West Ham were the only club to meet our valuation, but he has decided not to join them,' he said. 'We therefore look forward to him starting the new Championship season with us, which is a massive boost to our chance of returning to the Premier League.' West Ham quickly responded by claiming that they had been 'unable to agree personal terms' with the player and had therefore ended their interest in him. Yet Magnússon appeared to contradict that statement by revealing his frustration the following day: 'We were so close to signing Darren and thought everything was in place to conclude what would have been the biggest transfer in West Ham's history. Throughout all the negotiations, all the signs were positive. Therefore, I was surprised when I learned Darren had decided not to join us, and I feel let down and disappointed.'

It was claimed in some reports that Bent had not wished to reacquaint himself with former boss Curbishley, but if that were true he would not have entered into talks with the Hammers. The reality was that he much preferred a move to Tottenham, who could immediately offer him UEFA Cup football and potentially push for a Champions League spot after finishing fifth in the Premiership the previous two seasons. Spurs had been reluctant to match the figure demanded by Charlton, but it appeared that Bent rejected West Ham after immediately learning that a move to White Hart Lane was still a realistic proposition.

Charlton played their cards perfectly by insisting that they were happy to keep the striker, and Tottenham were eventually forced to agree a club record figure of £16.5 million to acquire his services later in the month. Many Hammers followers believed Bent was overpriced and were not particularly unhappy to see the deal collapse. Magnússon acknowledged this when he said, 'I have been encouraged by the reaction of our supporters. Some of the feedback suggests that they are less disappointed than I thought they might be. The view seems to be that perhaps this wasn't the best deal we could do at this stage. Lessons have been learned.'

One of those lessons may well have been that having 'an open wallet' – as Magnússon would later describe it – was no guarantee that players could necessarily be lured to the club. Everton were angered when England striker Andy Johnson was said to be attracting West Ham's interest, and Magnússon was forced to appease them with a statement denying any bid. Middlesbrough's out-of-contract hit-man Mark Viduka resisted Curbishley's overtures and remained in the north-east, moving to Newcastle. Former Hammer Jermain Defoe insisted he wanted to stay at Tottenham. And Manchester City confirmed that West Ham had met the £5.5 million figure required to trigger Joey Barton's release, but the midfielder's heart was so set on a move to Newcastle that he didn't even bother travelling to London for talks. Again, the majority of Hammers supporters were only too pleased to see Barton – who was set to be charged following an alleged training-ground assault on City teammate Ousmane Dabo – head elsewhere.

The *Daily Star* used the lack of new faces following Parker's arrival from Newcastle to suggest on 27 June that 'there was a growing feeling within the club that Alan Curbishley might not be the man to turn the Hammers into top-six contenders'. The story added, 'The owners are understood to be concerned that the former Charlton boss seems to be unable to attract top players to the club.' The manager certainly hadn't done badly in persuading Lucas Neill, Matthew Upson and Luís Boa Morte to join a relegation battle in January and star names would indeed follow. Nevertheless, a rumour that senior players had spoken to Magnússon about management concerns also did the rounds in the summer, and it was suggested that Blackburn boss Mark Hughes was being considered as a possible replacement.

If there had been opposition to Barton's possible arrival, there was considerably less resistance to West Ham signing fiery Welsh dragon Craig Bellamy from Liverpool for a club-record £7.5 million. The 27-year-old striker was no stranger to controversy off the field – having faced two court hearings following alleged incidents in Cardiff nightclubs and been involved in an altercation with Liverpool teammate John Arne Riise while reportedly brandishing a golf club – but it was still considered to be a major coup to persuade him to quit Anfield for Upton Park. 'I wanted to make sure that if I left Liverpool it would be for a club that is going to be pushing for Europe,' said Bellamy. 'The opportunity to be a senior figure at an ambitious club like West Ham is very attractive.'

Further evidence of that ambition came with the signing of attacking midfielder Freddie Ljungberg from Arsenal. The thirty-year-old Sweden captain had enjoyed nine years with the Gunners, and although injuries had undermined his contribution in the final two seasons the Hammers were still getting a quality player for the £3 million invested. Goalkeeper Richard Wright arrived on a free transfer from Everton, while long-running efforts to sign Newcastle midfielder Kieron Dyer eventually came to fruition when he completed a £7 million move in August.

Throughout the summer period, various reports emerged claiming that West Ham were prepared to offer salaries in excess of £80,000 a week to entice players to the club. The Hammers were accused of inflating the transfer market and forcing up salaries as targets played one club off against another. After the Bent deal collapsed, Magnússon insisted that such figures were inaccurate and even went so far as to reveal the club's maximum wage. 'The club will be run on sensible business lines to build a secure, long-term future,' he said. 'That includes our policy on players' wages, which are set at a ceiling of £55,000 a week. Despite the figures being circulated, no player at West Ham earns more than that at present.'

Magnússon had targeted a Champions League place for West Ham within five years of his arrival, while he also announced plans to relocate the club to a brand-new 60,000-seater stadium within the same period. 'I would hope for it to be ready before the 2012 Olympics are held,' he said. It was widely believed that the Icelander was considering a site close to West Ham underground station after a move to London's planned Olympic Stadium was formally rejected in early 2007. Magnússon also indicated the club's training headquarters could be moved to a new location in the near future to accommodate state-of-the-art facilities.

Personnel changes at Chadwell Heath in the close-season saw veteran Keith Peacock step down with Glyn Snodin – formerly Curbishley's reserve-team manager at Charlton – recruited from Southampton as first-team coach and Kevin Keen reverting to his previous role of reserve-team boss. Five other former members of the Addicks backroom team were reunited with Curbishley, while physio Steve Allen and head of technical support Niall Clark linked up with their old boss Alan Pardew at Charlton. 'Obviously there is an irony in the fact that some of our new staff members have joined us from Charlton while others have headed in the opposite direction,' said the Hammers boss. 'But from my point of view, the only criteria our new additions have been selected on is their ability to do the job.'

Curbishley had tried to ignore the furore surrounding Sheffield United's vain attempts to win Premiership reinstatement at West Ham's expense, but his planning for the new season wasn't particularly helped by the constant speculation regarding the future of Tévez. The striker had already suggested before the win at Manchester United that he could be on his way during the summer. 'I've stopped learning English, as I don't know where I am going to be next season,' he said. Day admitted in a conversation a few days after Old Trafford that it would be 'unlikely' that Tévez would remain at West Ham 'unless Eggert pulls out an inordinate amount of money'. This suggested that some kind of agreement was in place with Joorabchian to either buy the player outright – in terms of his economic rights – or let him go.

Magnússon himself had admitted he 'would like to see Tévez at West Ham for the next few seasons' – a change from his original stance a few months earlier – but that 'a lot of things have to be resolved before that happens'. BBC sports editor Mihir Bose, who used Winston Churchill's description of Russia as 'a riddle, wrapped in a mystery, inside an enigma' to sum up the confusing situation in the light of the apparent termination of the third-party agreement, anticipated problems by asking, 'If MSI sues West Ham for breach of contract, which is not altogether unlikely, then what happens?'

On 19 May, Tévez was reported as saying he wanted to join

'one of Europe's big clubs' and revealed his delight that Real Madrid were apparently interested in his services. Indeed, over the next six weeks he was also linked with Inter Milan, Liverpool, Arsenal and Manchester United, all of whom he seemed happy to join at one stage or another. Yet he was also quoted as saying that 'the priority is what suits West Ham'.

On 5 July, it became public knowledge that Manchester United not only led the race for Tévez but that the player had agreed to sign for them once he returned from playing for Argentina in the Copa America later in the month. The Red Devils had been discussing the terms of a deal with Joorabchian for a number of weeks. Less than 24 hours later, Hammers chairman Magnússon issued a statement in which he said, 'Carlos Tévez is a registered West Ham United player, contracted to the club until June 2010. There is no agreement with West Ham United for Carlos to leave the club, and we expect him to return for next season's preparations. No decision can be reached without the agreement of West Ham United.'

Magnússon was obliged to respond in this manner, because the only contract recognised by the Premier League was the one registering Tévez with the Hammers for a remaining three years. For Joorabchian and MSI to circumnavigate West Ham by directly negotiating a transfer to Manchester United would suggest the third-party influence on the club's policies still existed. As far as the Hammers were concerned, this wasn't possible because the offending contract had been ripped up.

A Premier League spokesman confirmed, 'Any deal would have to be struck with West Ham.' However, Joorabchian's lawyers claimed that the player's personal terms had already been agreed with Manchester United. Manager Sir Alex Ferguson followed up on 8 July by confirming 'the essential parts are agreed' but that he assumed 'the Premier League must be holding up the deal'. That 'deal', it was understood, was for the Premiership champions to take the striker on a two-year loan from MSI and partner Just Sports Inc. followed by an option to buy.

The next development came when it was announced that Tévez had been booked in for a medical at Manchester United's Carrington training complex on Wednesday, 18 July – a few days after Argentina's meeting with Brazil in the Copa America final. Indeed, Joorabchian confirmed the news when interviewed by Sky Sports on his way into a Labour government fundraising dinner at Wembley Stadium. He also claimed that it had been 'mutually agreed' with West Ham that the striker would stay until the summer of 2007 before being allowed to move on to a bigger club. Joorabchian added, 'Carlos is a bit sad, as he felt very attached to West Ham last season, but he feels confident he is a Manchester United player now.'

Tévez played in Argentina's 3–0 defeat by Brazil in Venezuela on 14 July and flew into Britain two days later ready to complete the formalities of his transfer. The 23 year old appeared happy as he carried his young daughter Florencia out of Manchester Airport, but it wasn't long before West Ham announced that they had denied Manchester United permission to conduct any medical with the player. Once again, the Hammers insisted that no deal had yet been agreed with them for the player's registration to be transferred, and Tévez eventually jetted off on a family holiday while the 'administrative bits and pieces' – as Joorabchian termed it – continued to be disputed. It would later be reported that Tévez had indeed undergone a provisional medical before leaving the country.

West Ham had three potential motives for digging their heels in. One was that they genuinely wanted Tévez to stay at the club, knowing how important he had been at the end of the previous campaign – and they did indeed try to persuade him to stay. A second was that they saw the player's three-year contract as a perfect means to recover the £5.5 million fine they had recently been forced to pay. The third – and by far the most crucial – was that they had to be seen to be complying with the Premier League's stance that the holders of the striker's registration had the principal right to negotiate and profit financially from his sale. To allow anything else to happen would potentially expose them to further Premier League charges if it was suspected the original offending agreements with MSI still existed in one form or another. In the context of the Sheffield United challenge to West Ham's Premiership status and the eligibility of Tévez to have continued playing, the club had to hold hands with the Premier League every step of the way.

Intriguingly, it had recently been reported that a Brazilian federal judge had issued arrest warrants for both Joorabchian and Russian tycoon Boris Berezovsky in relation to MSI being suspected of using Corinthians football club – who Tévez and Mascherano played for prior to joining West Ham – for money-laundering activities. This was not the first time such an allegation had been made. Joorabchian immediately denied any wrongdoing, while Berezovsky claimed that the story was 'an extension of the Kremlin's politicised campaign against me' and that he was 'not involved in any dealings connected with Carlos Tévez'. Rather amusingly, he added, 'I'm an Arsenal fan.'

The Russian authorities had been attempting to try the London-based 61 year old – a sworn enemy of president Vladimir Putin – in absentia for embezzlement, and on 18 July it emerged that he had only been spared his life when MI5 and MI6 discovered a plot to have him murdered and despatched his would-be assassin on a flight back to Moscow. 'I am preparing to be killed,' he admitted as he resigned himself to suffering the same fate as former fellow exile Alexander Litvinenko.

With Russian hit men and Interpol on his case, it wasn't the best of weeks for Berezovsky – who had denied funding Joorabchian's attempts to purchase West Ham the previous autumn – but at least there was no immediate arrest made. Neither was there for Joorabchian, although how Interpol failed to locate somebody that Sky Sports had tracked down remained something of a mystery. Towards the end of July, Corinthians announced that they were severing their co-ownership agreement with MSI less than halfway through their ten-year agreement.

Joorabchian's primary concern at that time was West Ham, however, and he issued a statement through MSI to lambast the club for blocking his efforts to move Tévez on to Manchester United:

> West Ham consistently provided private assurances while at the same time making contradictory statements to the public at large. We see no alternative but to bring the true circumstances to the attention of a higher authority to aid a rapid conclusion to this issue.

The Hammers responded with their own statement:

> West Ham totally rejects the latest outburst and threats issued in the name of Kia Joorabchian. We will not be drawn into this form of public mudslinging, but these latest statements cannot go unanswered. It is absolutely clear that the only contract relating to Carlos Tévez recognised by West Ham United and the Premier League is the player's four-year contract, which runs until June 2010. All other arrangements were terminated by West Ham on 27 April 2007 and no legal challenge to that termination has occurred. West Ham United can also confirm that all documentation regarding Carlos Tévez has already been submitted to the Premier League and fully scrutinised by them. However, a transfer cannot occur without agreement between two clubs and the Premier League. Without such an agreement, we believe that it is in the interest of all parties to resolve this issue as quickly as possible through the procedures laid down by FIFA. Public

> threats and accusations are irrelevant; let FIFA decide
> and West Ham United will accept that judgement
> whatever the outcome.

Allowing FIFA to rule on the matter effectively absolved West
Ham of any responsibility whichever way the decision went,
but the governing body – reluctant to rule over a situation
involving not just football regulations but the law itself – issued
a statement on 24 July in which they recommended that the case
be referred to the Court of Arbitration for Sport in Lausanne,
Switzerland. 'We believe this to be the fastest way to solve this
impasse,' they said. This was unacceptable to Joorabchian, who
responded by issuing High Court proceedings against West
Ham. 'The companies seek the court's intervention to release the
registration in accordance with contracts entered into between
the parties,' said a statement issued on behalf of MSI and Just
Sports Inc.

It was inevitable that Joorabchian would look to take legal
action as soon as his attempts to move Tévez on to Manchester
United came into serious jeopardy. He questioned West Ham's
right to unilaterally terminate their contract with him, and, as
the owner of the striker's economic rights, he was never going to
sit back and allow a valuable commodity to slip from his control
because of what Premier League rules dictated. Furthermore,
he was convinced that he had a binding agreement with West
Ham for Tévez to be released in the summer – irrespective of
the original third-party agreement. News of what was described
as a 'secret' document emerged after a provisional High Court
hearing in London on 31 July when Joorabchian's legal team
produced papers to support their claim that Tévez should be
allowed to join Manchester United.

Mr Justice Blackburne was presented with one document
that was reportedly signed by Hammers director Duxbury on 1
December 2006 – after Magnússon's takeover was completed –

that allegedly agreed to Tévez's release the following July. However, West Ham's lawyers questioned the validity of this contract by casting doubt over the authenticity of the striker's signature, as the club had not witnessed the countersigning themselves. Additionally, it was subsequently reported that the Hammers had 'terminated' this agreement along with the offending third-party arrangement with MSI on 27 April. Whether they were entitled to do so was expected to be established between 22 and 24 August when the full three-day court hearing was scheduled. In truth, however, neither Joorabchian nor West Ham – nor the Premier League, for that matter – really wanted the dispute to be decided by the courts.

West Ham had ripped up third-party agreements in the belief they were never legally enforceable, but the media were quick to pounce on news of the 1 December agreement by claiming its existence questioned West Ham's credibility, and the club certainly wanted to avoid the risk of further unwanted publicity. Joorabchian, meanwhile, knew his third-party contracts would be examined from a legal point of view and that there was a genuine risk that Tévez might not be able to complete his move to Manchester United before the transfer window closed at the end of August. It was therefore a great relief to everybody when it was announced on 3 August that an out-of-court settlement had been reached. West Ham would receive £2 million to release the registration of Tévez, who would join Manchester United on a two-year loan agreement with MSI. The Premiership champions would pay MSI £10 million for the loan and have the option of paying around £25 million to secure the striker's signing on a permanent basis in 2009.

It was a good deal for West Ham in the sense that they received £2 million for a player whom the club had originally agreed to release for £100,000 – the amount that Joorabchian had been offering – although it failed to compensate them for the Premier League fine. The Hammers issued a statement in which Magnússon said, 'I am obviously pleased that we have finally reached the end of this saga through agreement and common sense. All parties can now move on and truly focus on the new season.' With Sheffield United keeping a close watch on the matter, the Premier League quickly ratified the deal. They said, 'The decision of the board, having received leading counsel's opinion, is that the agreement reached is compliant with the rules of the Premier League and consistent with the undertakings given by West Ham United to the Premier League board at various times since 27 April 2007. This will lead to the cancellation of Tévez's registration, thereby releasing him to join another club in due course.'

West Ham embarked on an excellent public-relations exercise by announcing that they were generously donating £500,000 of the Tévez fee to the Football Foundation in order to boost playing facilities for local youngsters. But the gesture failed to mark the end of the Tévez controversy with Sheffield United announcing on 16 August that they intended to sue West Ham to secure compensation for their relegation. The Blades issued a statement in which they claimed the existence of the 1 December document, presented at the High Court on 31 July, undermined West Ham's defence that a previous hierarchy was solely responsible for agreements with MSI. 'West Ham failed to disclose a critically important, additional third-party agreement,' they declared.

However, the Hammers insisted that the Blades had no case and responded with a statement that said, 'Not only does Sheffield United's claim lack legal merit, but it's based on their incorrect belief that West Ham withheld an agreement from the Premier League and the April disciplinary commission. West Ham made the Premier League fully aware of the existence and status of the agreement in question. Sheffield United's latest assertions clearly demonstrate a fundamental misunderstanding of the situation, and any proceedings brought by them will be vigorously defended. The club will not permit these repeated slurs to go unchallenged and are in discussion with legal advisers in relation to the action they might take.'

The whole affair resulted in the Premier League amending their regulations to get to grips with third-party ownership, with chief executive Scudamore saying, 'We will have to be more circumspect when dealing with clubs from now on. We've changed the rules so that the clubs are in no doubt that they must send any documentation surrounding any deal whether they think it's relevant or not.' West Ham boss Curbishley, meanwhile, was disappointed that Tévez had resisted the club's efforts to keep him. 'He knew that we were keen for him to stay, but he decided his future was elsewhere,' he said. 'Obviously, he had a big say in events for us last season, and I'm sure he'll get a rapturous reception when he comes back with Manchester United.'

The West Ham supporters were naturally disappointed to see Tévez leave Upton Park but not the least bit surprised. In fact, they were generally philosophical about the whole matter. They knew that they had been lucky to see such a world-class superstar in their team's colours for one season and bore him no resentment for moving on, well aware that he was merely a pawn in a much bigger game. There was certainly no better way for the Argentinian to say goodbye than by scoring a last-day winner at Manchester United to help keep West Ham in the Premiership. It was meant for the script to be written that way. Indeed, the entire 2006–07 campaign – undoubtedly personified by Tévez – could easily have been viewed as a work of fiction, except many people would not have believed its incredible storyline.

The same could also have been said of the two-year period following the club's promotion back to the Premiership in 2005 as West Ham attempted to adapt to the changing demands of football and compete at the highest level. It would prove to be a time of triumph and trauma, but Tévez's departure appeared to signal the end of one era and the beginning of another.

Ambitious chairman Magnússon promised to fulfil his 'vision for West Ham to challenge for the highest honours' over the coming years. And whatever remained in store beyond the summer of 2007, it was safe to say that the events were unlikely to mirror the agony and the ecstasy of the previous two seasons. 'We've all learned a lot in recent times,' admitted Curbishley. 'Let's hope it stands us in good stead for what's to come.'